ARTS PATRONAGE IN INDIA

The stage but echoes back the public voice
The drama's laws the drama's patrons give
For we that live to please must please to live.

Samuel Johnson, at the opening of
the Drury Lane Theatre, London

# Arts Patronage in India

## Methods, Motives and Markets

*Edited by*
JOAN L. ERDMAN

MANOHAR
2023

We gratefully acknowledge the support of the Committee on Southern Asian Studies at the University of Chicago, and the Publications Committee of the American Institute of Indian Studies for grants towards the publication of this collection.

First published 1992
Reprinted 2021, 2023



ISBN 978-81-85425-82-5

*Published by*
Ajay Kumar Jain *for*
Manohar Publishers & Distributors
4753/23 Ansari Road, Daryaganj
New Delhi 110 002

*Printed at*
Replika Press Pvt. Ltd.

## CONTENTS

Introduction—The Patronage of Cultural Performances in India 1
JOAN L. ERDMAN

Cultural Performance as a Blurred Genre : Remarks to Inaugurate a Conference 19
MILTON SINGER

**PERFORMANCE TRADITIONS AND PATRONAGE**

Context into Text: Performance and Patronage in a Tamil Oral Tradition 31
STUART H. BLACKBURN

The Audience as Patron: Dramatization and Texture of a Hindi Oral Epic Performance 47
KARINE SCHOMER

**CHANGING PATRONS**

A Tradition of Change: The Role of Patrons and Patronage in the *Kathakaḷi* Dance-Drama 91
PHILLIP B. ZARRILLI

Petitions to the Patrons: Changing Culture's Substance in Twentieth Century Jaipur 143
JOAN L. ERDMAN

**MOTIVATIONS, MARKETS, AND LOGISTICS**

Patronage in India's Musical Culture 181
BONNIE C. WADE

Market Structure and State Patronage in Karnataka's Feature Film Industry: Implications for the New Cinema 195
MANJUNATH PENDAKUR

A Performance Model from South India 213
NORMAN CUTLER

Patronage and the Dance in India, or "You Think
Learning to Dance Was Hard!" 225
SHARON LOWEN

Index 239

# ACKNOWLEDGEMENTS

We are grateful to the Committee on Southern Asian Studies of the University of Chicago for their support of the three-day seminar during which most of these papers were originally presented. We would like to thank Bernard Cohn, Nazir Jairazbhoy, Kathleen L. L'Armand, Joseph Miller, V. Narayana Rao, Daniel Neuman, Marta Nicholas, A.K. Ramanujan, Susanne Rudolph and Richard Schechner for their contributions to the conference and comments on the papers, and Lloyd and Susanne Rudolph for their hospitality. The field research for many authors whose papers are included here was supported by the American Institute of Indian Studies, which has been a key patron for South Asian studies for three decades. In addition, some research was supported by grants from various U.S.-India Fulbright fellowships. Finally, we acknowledge and appreciate the cooperation of performing artists and organizations in India, *sine qua non.*

Chicago, July 1991 Joan L. Erdman

# THE CONTRIBUTORS

**Stuart H. Blackburn,** who teaches at University High School in San Francisco, is the author of *Singing of Birth and Death: Texts in Performance*, and a co-editor of *Another Harmony: New Essays on the Folklore of India* and *Oral Epics in India*. He is presently preparing a translation and study of a Ramayana performed as shadow puppet theater in Kerala.

**Norman Cutler** is Associate Professor of Tamil in the Department of South Asian Languages and Civilizations at The University of Chicago. His study of Tamil *bhakti* poetry, *Songs of Experience: The Poetics of Tamil Devotion*, was published in 1987. His current research on *Tirukkural* and its commentaries is the first stage of a long-term project concerning textual interpretation and the role of commentary in Tamil literary culture.

**Joan L. Erdman** is Research Associate in the Committee on Southern Asian Studies at the University of Chicago and Professor of Anthropology in the Department of Liberal Education at Columbia College Chicago. Her study of Jaipur patronage, *Patrons and Performers in Rajasthan, The Subtle Tradition* was published by Chanakya in 1985. She is curtently completing an autobiography of dancer and actress Zohra Segal, and a book on Uday Shankar's Indian dance and its contexts. Her recent publications include "Play with *Laya*: Tempo, Pace and Cadence in Indian Music and Culture" (in *Poetics East and West*, edited by Milena Dolezelova-Velingerova), "Jaipur, City Planning in Eighteenth Century India," (in *Sastric Tradition in the Indian Arts*, edited by A.L. Dallapicolla), and "Performance as Translation: Uday Shankar in the West," (*The Drama Review* 1987).

**Sharon Lowen** is a performing artist, teacher and researcher specializing in the classical Indian dance forms of Odissi, Manipuri and Chhau. She has divided her time between India and the United States since 1973 and has performed in films, television, and on concert stages internationally, receiving numerous awards and honors. She is currently based in New Delhi, India, and is a Visiting Fellow at the University of Hyderabad.

**Manjunath Pendakur** teaches political economy of media and international communications in the Department of Radio-TV- Film at Northwestern University. He is the author of *Canadian Dreams and American Control: The Political Economy of the Canadian Film Industry* (1990), and is currently preparing a book on mass culture and cinema in India based on research supported by the American Institute of Indian Studies.

**Karine Schomer** is Research Associate in the Center for South Asia Studies at the University of California, Berkeley, and Dean of Arts and Sciences at Golden Gate University, San Francisco. Her publications include *Mahadevi Varma and the Chhayavad Age of Modern Hindi Poetry* (University of California Press, 1983), and contributions to *Oral Epics in India* (1983) as well as to the Berkeley Religious Studies volumes *Sikh Studies* (1979), *The Divine Consort* (1982), and *The Sants* (1987).

**Milton Singer** is Professor Emeritus in the Department of Anthropology, and Paul Kapper Professor Emeritus in the College, The University of Chicago, and Fellow Emeritus of the American Academy of Arts and Sciences. In the 1950s and 60s he helped organize teaching and research programs on South Asian civiliza- tions at the University of Chicago. He reports that the cultural performances concept was suggested to him by observations made in Madras on his first trip to India in 1954-55, under Robert Redfield's Comparative Civilizations program. Details of these observations can be found in *Traditional India* (1958), *Krishna: Myths, Rites and Attitudes* (1966, 1968), and *When A Great Tradition Modernizes: An Anthropological Approach to Indian Civilization* (1972, 1980 and 1986). In the 1970s Singer updated Warner's 'Yankee City' studies and added an analysis of symbols based on Charles Peirce's general theory of signs, or Semiotics. Recent publications include *Man's Glassy Essence: Explorations in Semiotic Anthropology* (1984) and an article in *Semiotics, Self, and Society* (1989), edited by Benjamin Lee and Greg Urban.

**Bonnie C. Wade** is Professor of Music in the Department of Music of the University of California at Berkeley. Her ethnomusicological work has focused primarily on India (especially North India). Publications on Indian music include *Khyal: Creativity Within North India's Classical Music Tradition* (1984), *Performing Arts of India: Essays on Music,*

*Dance, and Drama* (editor) in 1987, and a textbook, *Music in India: The Classical Traditions* (1987). Wade's recent research is on paintings of the Mughal period as a source for documentation of the history of music in North India.

**Phillip B. Zarrilli** is Associate Professor of Theatre and Drama, Director of the Asian/Experimental Theatre Program, and a member of the South Asian Studies faculty at the University of Wisconsin-Madison. His books include *The Kathakali Complex: Actor, Performance, Structure* (1984) and, with Farley Richmond and Darius Swann, *Indian Theatre: Traditions of Performance* (1990). His recent research on *kalarippayattu*, the martial art of Kerala, will be published as *Paradigms of Power in a South Indian Martial Art: "Conquering Even the God of Death."*

# Introduction

# The Patronage of Cultural Performances in India

Joan L. Erdman

## From Cultural Performance to Patronage

When Milton Singer suggested in his 1972 book, *When A Great Tradition Modernizes*, that "cultural performances" provided units of observation of a civilization's great tradition, he was moving in tandem with a revolution already underway. The study of other cultures' music and dance, as performance arts and as sophisticated traditional systems had been inaugurated at University of California at Los Angeles by Mantle Hood's Ethnomusicology program, and at Wesleyan University in Connecticut by the World Music Program, as well as in other pockets of academe in the United States. Beyond a comparative stage, these programs sought to understand the other musics *in their own terms*, an anthropological argument for recognizing our ethnocentrism and moving beyond its pale.

Singer suggested that anthropologists look at cultural performance locations and specialists, the recruitment and training of these specialists, performance remunerations, motivations of the various persons concerned, attitudes toward their careers, the relations of performers to audiences and patrons, and to other performers and the communities from which they come and in which they perform[1]. Following Singer's lead, and interest in

Singer 1972:72-4 contains this analysis of cultural performance and its components.

India's performing arts, scholars began to study various types of performances through participant-observation with the specialist artists themselves, in India.

A major text for such studies was (and still is) Norvin Hein's *The Miracle Plays of Mathura*, based on fieldwork in India which had begun in 1949, and published twenty years after its completion. Hein, a professor of comparative religion at Yale University, had sought every form of religious drama in the Mathura region, and became an attentive and increasingly knowledgeable spectator. In discussing the patronage of the Ramlila in the thirteenth through sixteenth centuries during Muslim rule, Hein points out that

> It was a period of hardship and change for all sophisticated Hindu arts in North India. The Hindu upper classes who had patronized them were generally destroyed or impoverished or drawn into the study of Muslim arts and literatures. The Muslim rulers who sometimes took up the maintenance of Hindu dancers were in no position to appreciate and demand the full art of the ancient dance-manuals. The classical Hindu dance was expensive: It required long and costly training of its performers and therefore had to find munificent patrons. It could be an effective means of communication only in the presence of audiences educated in its symbols (Hein 1972:124).

Discussing the patronage of the Raslila at a later date, Hein says that while irregular support for performances continued from the temples, the less prosperous princes had withdrawn their grants, shortening the list of patronage institutions for this dramatic art (Hein 1972:158).

The late Jon Higgins discussed patronage as a determinant of change in South Indian (Karnatak) music, and pointed out that change is not the enemy of tradition, but rather the core—"the soul of a vital art form constantly in the process of becoming" (Higgins 1976:20). He characterized recent changes in Karnatak music as attributable to the "sudden and complete shift in the first half of the century from the court to the public, from prince to populace" (*Ibid*:21). Higgins focuses on changes in the music. From the viewpoint of north Indian performers and particularly for Jaipur musicians before independence, the relationship between patron and performers is a crucial change (Erdman 1985). research in Ahmedabad and Jaipur.

In fieldwork in Gujarat (1971-72) while studying *tabla* performance, and in my 1976-77 research in Rajasthan, I found that performers gave high priority to issues of patronage, especially since they saw their traditional modes of patronage in decline with the demise of previously generous princely patrons. Government patronage, seen as a replacement for the earlier state rulers, was providing neither the personal attention nor the freedom the artists craved. Nor, in the artists' opinions, did government bureaucrats offer knowledgeable critique of their performances and works. I wondered whether this was the case in other parts of India and in other media.

In order to explore the changes in the patronage of the performing arts before and after independence, I focussed on two periods in Rajasthan's cultural performances: the present (the 1970s) and a time 30-80 years earlier, for which both extensive records and living memories were available. As an ethnographer I extended Singer's study of cultural performances to the past, by trying to find records which voiced the concerns of performance specialists in the earlier period. Although a few recordings of their music were eventually found (and fewer of the dance of the period), I had to rely mainly on written records, which meant that issues of patronage took priority over musicological ones. The relations between patrons, performers, audiences, connoisseurs, and critics could be explored even in a period when the performances themselves had not been recorded or videotaped.

The question of arts patronage in other regions and media in India remained unexamined, although research and writing about contemporary performance traditions increased significantly. Music from various parts of India, folk dramas and singing, musical instruments and musicological theory were explored, by literary scholars, anthropologists, historians, musicologists, folklorists and others. While the patronage of these arts was an integral part of each study, the comparison of methods, motivations, changes, and ideologies required reading between the lines to glean references to supporters of the particular form or genre. In 1982, with the support of the Committee on Southern Asian Studies and the South Asia Language and Area Center at the University of Chicago, a group of scholars interested in cultural performance studies gathered to hear and discuss papers addressing patronage issues in various Indian arts. Before turning to those papers, some reflection on patrons and patronage will be rewarding.

## The Study of Patronage of the Arts

Patronage has multiple meanings and intentions. It may refer to support, encouragement and mentoring; a commercial establishment's trade from its customers; a collective clientele; or the power of distributing political favors and positions. To patronize someone may mean supporting or purchasing their services or obversely, acting in a condescending manner towards them. An important combination in India is the patron who is both benefactor and customer. Depending upon who the patron is, and how s/he behaves, the performer will treat the patron accordingly. Joseph Berland calls his delightful account of the Qalandar, nomadic entertainers in Pakistan, *No Five Fingers Are Alike*, signifying the performers' aptitude for selecting appropriate strategies for the pleasure and benefit of their audiences/patrons. Listening to the Qalanders' nightly campfire reminiscences, he heard discussions of specific markets (neighborhoods, streets, etc.) for begging activities, and evaluations of innovative strategies, performances, and routines (Berland 1982:3). The Qalanders turned out to be experts in the investigation and estimation of individual and group behavior. Such is the necessity of all artists who would seek a patron. Knowing the nature of the patron allows the artist to solicit the support and encourage the interest of potential benefactors.

Whether formal and bureaucratic, as with the petitions of the artists in Jaipur's Gunijankhana before independence, or embedded in the performance itself, as with the *Alha* singers in northern India, expertise is the strategic necessity for finding patronage. Individual patrons and large audiences—whether connoisseurs or mass public—must recognize the artists' interest in them, in providing quality entertainment at whatever level is called for, if they are to be reciprocally interested in supporting the arts. There are many ways in which this show of interest can be accomplished, from sending resumes to appropriate power-holders, to providing respite from an otherwise tense daily whirl. It is not surprising that cultural performances have come to be seen as extensions (mainly in the east) of or distraction (mainly in the west) from the mundane world, and thereby related to religious ritual, though not always constructed with parallel requirements for correctness.

While political patronage carries the semantic onus of excess in appointing persons friendly but not qualified for the position to office, artistic patronage inspires honor and respect whether or not the artistic venture succeeds. The mere willingness to provide support for an aspiring artist is sufficient to bring merit to the benefactor. Aesthetic success is, in any case, difficult to judge, since in addition to knowledgeability it depends on taste and opinions, which are matters of individual assessment, albeit in terms of conventional and socially-accepted norms. Investment in a failed artist may be a financial loss, but it is a patron's gain for having tried to promote something wonderful. The artist's only work is to produce art; if s/he fails to find supporters and viewers, then the artist alone suffers—potential audiences/admirers will never know what they have missed. Unfortunately when a political patronage appointee neglects to fulfil the obligations of the position, others will probably suffer from this failing.

There are numerous ways of encouraging patrons to step forward, and India is no different from the west in this necessity. As in New York, so also in New Delhi, concert and theatre programs list categories of supporters, benefactors, patrons and sponsors, and thank them for their support. While ticketed programs are still regarded as less prestigious than invitational programs in India, they are growing and in Bombay largely replacing or being added to traditional open-door or personal invitation events. Access to the artists directly, participation in the planning and organizing of cultural events, special educational lectures and workshop sessions, as well as economic benefits of supporting not-for-profit cultural organizations or popular shows encourage patrons and sponsors[2]. Performers themselves must often find their own patron in India, where programs are sponsored by cultural societies and institutions, villages and states, as well as major donors and sometimes major artists. Since arts management is not yet a profession recognized in India, individual arrangements for productions, tours, programs, and publicity are the norm. Without management

[2] The recent success of English-language theater and musicals is Bombay can be traced to the role of large corporations in underwriting the costs, as good public relations and expansion of their philanthropy. See Sanjoy Hazarika, "Broadway Musicals are Big in Bombay," in *New York Times*, December 31, 1988.

agencies for the perfoming arts, government and government-sponsored institutions and major privately-supported institutions are seen as avenues for artistic advancement.[3]

In Hindi one word for patron is *sanrakshak*, meaning a supporter, protector or guardian. An alternative term is *astiya*, which is dependence or sustenance, a resort or retreat, a harbor or home.[4] In India one idea of patronage stems from the religious merit of sacrifice, the *yagna* (religious sacrifice) of Vedic antiquity. A patron, or *yajman*, who is the sacrificer supporting the *yagna*, makes an offering to the deity through the mediation of religious specialists who are Brahmin priests. The sponsoring of a *yagna*, and appropriate participation in it, is a sign of the patron's devotion and connection to the all-powerful being.[5]

Support beyond financial backing is essential for students to persevere in their performing arts. A decision on the part of a talented artist from a non-traditional-artists' family to become a professional performer in India, as in other parts of the world,

[3] Attempts have been made to develop management agencies, notably by the late Rajender Shankar in Bombay in the 1950s and 60s. But the reluctance of artists to share their fees with management discourages all but the most altruistic from venturing into agency or managing artists. The Indian Council for Cultural Relations, and the Sangeet Natak Akademi also provide some of the services of management in organizing performances and tours sponsored by government, but their administrators are supported by government salaries, rather than the earnings of the programs presented, as would be the case in a management agency. The Birlas, Tatas, Bharat and Charat Rams, and more recently, Indian Tobacco Company and Vazir Sultan Tobacco Company have been major arts patrons, with varying interests and goals.

[4] The Hindi usage is based on research materials from India, and two dictionary definitions, *Bhargava's Standard Illustrated Dictionary of the Hindi Language* (Hindi-English and English-Hindi editions), compiled and edited by Prof. R.C. Pathak (Varanasi: Bhargava Book Depot, 1973 repr.), and *A Practical Hindi-English Dictionary*, edited by Mahendra Chaturvedi and Dr. B.N. Tiwari (Delhi: National, 2nd ed., 1975).

[5] *Jajman*, properly spelled *yajman*, is a host or the sponsor of a sacrifice, who offers money and gifts to the Brahmins who perform it. The connection between patrons and those who sponsor a sacrifice is performative as well as contractual. The patron both affirms the right of the Brahmins to perform the sacrifice and, as the sacrificer, offers gifts to those who sanctify, by their authority, the sacrificial performance. He cannot sacrifice without them, and without him, no sacrifice can be performed, since it requires a host or sponsor. In this scenario, the priest is the artist, and the sacrificer the patron, although exact semantic translation could be misleading.

often entails parental disapproval, difficult training years, limited potential for supported apprenticeship, and a strong will to continue. Folk artists continue to train some of their young to take up their professions[6], but fewer offspring of folk artists are becoming professionals, despite efforts by government agencies in particular to sustain and encourage some endangered folk performing arts.

So in this volume we shift our studies of cultural performance as a way of entering a civilization, as Singer suggested more than a decade ago, to a focus on patrons and patronage of these performances. We replace the idea of an ethnographic object, cultural performances, with an effort to understand an anthropological process, relations between patrons and performers. The performances remain: specialists and their media, linguistic and non-linguistic, the content and particular forms, patterns and styles, genres and traditions are still integral parts of the cultural structure and social organization of Indian civilization. To Singer's study of the Radha-Krishna *bhajana*s (devotional songs) in Madras (Singer 1980) there is an essential extension which becomes clear when the cultural performances are considered as changing and developing traditions in the civilization of India, while the socio-economic infrastructure of culture is itself undergoing great changes.

No study of cultural performance in India today can ignore questions of patronage, the sources and kinds of support rendered by individuals, societies, government offices and officials, industries, and the public as audiences, critics, benefactors and financial underwriters. The expansion of responsibility for patronizing cultural performances has been paralleled by an increase in public cultural activity, especially since Indian independence. While patronage by communities and rulers continues, others have

[6] The patronage of folklorist Komal Kothari in western Rajasthan is encouraging the folk professional Manganiyar and Langa musicians to teach their arts to their children, a process that was languishing without the dual recognition that the folk musicians can continue to earn and thus training the children will result in a capacity to earn their livelihood as adults. By serving as manager, agent, benefactor, critic, scholar, admirer, and supporter of these folk musicians' arts, Padma Shree Komal Kothari is making the next generation of artists possible and increasing the artists' own knowledge of their art and their audiences (see Kothari 1987).

joined the ranks of supporters of the arts, and the demands or requirements of performing artists are measured in cost as well as quality and appropriateness. National performing arts require national productions, tours, and support. Opportunities for young artists as well as encouragement of these culture-bearers to take the arts as their life work demands contests and rewards, paid positions and performance contexts, honors and respect. In folk performances as well, support must be garnered from an interested public, and patronage rewarded with thanks and public congratulations, as well as consideration of state support through tax benefits.

A concern with the quality and quantity of cultural performance in modern times has spurred new nations to found departments of culture[7], and parts of the western world to offer national support for cultural events and productions. The British Arts Council, the French Ministry of Culture, and the National Endowments for the Arts and for the Humanities in the United States are evidence of recognition that modern nation-states must offer monetary support and encouragement to artistic establishments and individuals for their survival. Such support may be through grants and fellowships, awards and prizes, training and apprenticeship, or by creating media opportunities for presentation, or through tax policies which offer advantages to private supporters of the arts and their study. Since "culture" has become a popular term rather than the preserve of the elite, the use of public monies to support cultural performance has been considered appropriate in democratic and socialist nations alike. While there are artists at all levels of the socio-economic scales, and audiences from all sectors of the polity, the search for excellence and rewarding of extraordinary artistic achievement has given honor to both performers and their patrons.

Nowadays an indigenous issue for Indian cultural performances is the development of infrastructure for performing arts, and the ways in which modernization can proceed without excessive westernization diluting Indian cultural essentials. Patronage can be considered part of a cultural policy which has shown energy in spreading Indian culture abroad to provoke recognition of the civilization and the rich arts of this new nation. The policy includes an

[7] See my earlier "Who Should Speak for the Performing Arts? The Case of the Delhi Dancers" for a description of India's post-independence creation of academies for the arts at the national level (Erdman 1984).

effort to reorganize domestically with plans such as cultural zones to encourage artistic participation and excellence. The new patrons in India seem to understand well that any nation which neglects its own cultural performances misses opportunities to display its history and discipline, beauty and characteristics, fundamental values and entertaining delights. A major issue in cultural policy relates to the various media and their support, as well as to the respective responsibilities of private and public sector. A brief review of the literature on patronage as a cultural policy and practice illustrates this point.

## Patronage as an Issue of Culture

Writing about patronage in various societies, whether focused on artists, philanthropists, impresarios, or the media itself, demonstrates that there are universals of framework and topics for discussion. While at one extreme there is the stability and functioning of a theatre-state (Geertz 1980), at the other there is the fluidity of change and ways in which cultural performances incite and reflect it (Bharucha 1983, McKinzie 1973, Peacock 1968, Singer 1980). There are handbooks for sponsors who wish to present performances (Wolf 1983), and biographies of particular patrons who may be individuals (Rao 1983) or nations (Erdman 1984, Harris 1970, Havens 1982, Netzer 1980), or combinations with private philanthropical foundations (Bremner 1960, Haskell 1971, Rosenzweig 1982). Some writings which deal with patronage focus on the media itself (Donahue 1987, Blackburn and Ramanujan 1986, Hogwood 1977, Lord 1974, Lynes 1985, McLuhan 1964, Schechner 1985, Strong 1984, Wade 1984). The artists are the core of other volumes (d'Azevedo 1973, Neuman 1980, Smith 1961) which bring together monographs and papers approaching questions in the production, organization, traditions and support of artworks in different societies. For some scholars history (Lynes 1985) or cognitive psychology (Berland 1982) or anthropology (Cohn 1987) provide disciplinary understanding of the process of performance and its support.

Patronage studies are inherent in efforts to develop theories of performance. Performance theory as a field of study incorporates all kinds of performances from dance marathons to Bharata Natyam, from experimental theatre to the Ramayana reenactment at

Ramgarh. Performances range from re-creations of texts as annual dramas to extemporaneous and unrehearsed events in which what happens is created at the moment. The line from habit and ritual to ad libbing and impromptu is long, and encompasses most performances within cultural traditions, whether enduring or endorsing the always-new. There is the beginning of a literature on performance theory (see Schechner 1988), which Milton Singer calls for in his remarks which follow this introduction, and which is addressed by several papers in this volume.

Whatever the approach to art, artists, artworks, patrons, the cultural traditions and social context of art and artist, there are historical accounts to be incorporated, and distinctions to be made in relationships and periods. The papers in this volume are all devoted to India, and consider a variety of media, regional and supraregional groups, and periods. As a contribution to the growing literature on patronage, the volume suggests that the particular cultural context in which the performance and its patronage occur determines who considers what kind of creation and exchange have taken place. By exploring patronage as a function of cultural performance, the papers recognize the social obligations and responsibilities of non-artists to artists and their works. While philanthropy is differently defined and conducted across cultures (though each has a tendency to be ethnocentric about its own infrastructure as essential to indigenous culture), the fact that arts flourish in all social, economic, political and climatic settings confirms the recognition of art as a resource for human culture. By exploring several of the ways in which Indian culture provides patronage for the arts, this volume contributes to cross-cultural considerations as well as introducing scope for further study. Interdisciplinary subjects, such as the patronage of the arts, provide opportunities for scholars to share their intellectual concerns in a format which appears to be as enlightening as it is challenging. Anthropologists, translators of the literatures of great traditions, linguists, historians, musicologists, communication specialists, and artists have sought an understanding of India's patronage and performances through their specialized means.

## A Forum for Discussing Patronage and Performance

In 1982, a conference which continued a tradition of study of key scholarly issues in Southern Asian Studies at the University of Chicago, convened to discuss "Cultural Performance and Patronage in India." The scholars who met over several days were experts in particular fields of cultural studies, including language and literature, music, anthropology, theatre, area studies, and performing arts. Eight papers were presented, of which six appear in this volume. As organizer of the conference, I confined my participation to remarks and comments, but include my paper on Jaipur patronage and the petitions of the artists with the others for publication. One comment in particular, that of Norman Cutler in response to papers by Bonnie Wade and Manjunath Pendakur, suggested a substantial argument about patronage, and was enlarged for inclusion here as a short paper. We had invited artist Sharon Lowen to participate and perform; her insightful paper is a revised transcript of the talk she gave when Carole Farber was unable to present her paper on Bengali folk theatre at the last minute. Papers by Joseph Smith and Nazir Jairazbhoy were not ready for publication here, and we hope they will appear elsewhere. At the opening dinner, Professor Milton Singer agreed to offer "remarks", which bring us up to date on his thinking about "cultural performance" as a concept in the anthropological study of civilizations. Since the opportunity to consider patronage arises from scholarly focus on cultural performances in India, it seems important to share his remarks on this topic which he proposed many years ago, and which has inspired so much research and writing since.

Finding scholars whose research had explored performing arts in other parts of India and convincing them to turn their attention to patronage issues was not difficult. All had encountered questions of support for performing artists, whether in live performances of single artists or troupes, or in the marketing of the particular media. No art reaches its public without mediators; few artists are their own managers or agent. If they were, they would not be able to spend sufficient time on their art to practice and polish it to a fine quality. Folk and fine artists alike depend on family networks, generation-to-generation patronage arrangements, and village or urban organizers to present their arts. Management has always been seen as integral to an artists' work, and self-management can be a frustrating and undignified job if an artist has no training in how to market his/her artworks.

Yet some kind of management is required, in this post-princely world, for patronage. Artists courting potential patrons, as if they were modern-day princes, are subject to the competition of other artists searching for monied benefactors, who are not necessarily qualified to be arbiters of aesthetic worth. In our contemporary world, critics judge the arts and wealthy benefactors support it—they are not always the same people. Collectors of artworks prefer objects which they can display; performances are not viable commodities for display and inventory. A performance is ephemeral; it happens when it happens, and afterwards is gone. It can be recorded, photographed or painted, videotaped or filmed, but a performance is not a film, and a film happens only when it is shown. No collector can invite you to see a film collection without showing you some footage; seeing reels lining walls is not an aesthetic pleasure, though it may foreshadow a future excitement.

Thus patronage for the performing arts has an ephemeral quality as well. It exists for the performances: audiences, critics, benefactors, donors, supporters, managers, and organizers, not to mention impresarios, are all patrons for a period of time, or investors in artists' potential. Their commitment must be to the *process* of performing, or to a performance artist or troupe which requires constant practice and care. The performance itself lasts only as long as its own duration; all replays are mere restatements of a previous event in an earlier time, not the art itself. Unlike ritual, which takes its legitimacy from reenactment, performance is a genre which represents only itself, and, like life lived, happens in the moment. It is immediate, and performing artists often require prompt compensation and affirmation to continue.

Patronage and performance are intimately related in the modern world. Patrons who must spend their days engaged in essentially non-aesthetic and highly demanding work find their leisure enhanced by the arts, whether performed or exhibited, sophisticated or entertaining or both. The aesthetic provides a relief from decision-making and encourages individual and personal assessment of what is wonderful and beautiful. Nor is patronage confined to those who contribute financial support; in all nations volunteers provide support through organizations and arrangements, donated time, and loving care for artistic endeavors. For all who participate in cultural performance, as performers or patrons, volunteers or paying sponsors, there is a sense of being part of a regional, supraregional, national or international culture, a satisfaction in knowing or hearing or seeing what is pleasing or amusing or provoking or even arousing, and an understanding that the arts provide a complement to personal and social action and emotion which is uniquely their strength and gives succor and satisfaction. It is not surprising that the arts are closely connected to religions, for their performance and goals are often the same. Nor is it possible to deny that leisure can also be enjoyed in the conflict and contention which sports engender and develop, whether in team play or individual achievement. There is, in fact, a "sporting element" to many arts (musical competitions, auditions, martial arts, for example), and an "artistic component" in numerous sports (gymnastics, ice-skating, diving, for example). In fact, leisure studies consider the "play" of both arts and sports as a single topic. But while there is much that can be learned from sports as professional leisure activity, the arts embody culture in a distinctive manner incorporating history and myth, in texts which are more than the rules of the game or the records of achievement. It is in the arts, in cultural performance, that a civilization reconsiders its values, teaches them to its young, restores them to immediacy, and accepts changes in their significance and importance. What is performed (or not performed), what is said (or not said), what is supported (or not supported) in the arts is a nation's heritage. By taking an interest in its continuation, and giving support to its continuity in performance, patrons occupy a special role in society, which gives them status at the same time as they derive it from their actions.

Patronage in India was mainly in the hands of temples, ruling princes and nawabs, wealthy merchants and foreign governors prior to independence. Popular involvement in patronage, through folk festivals and support of touring folk professionals, as well as small institutions for learning particular arts, was extensive. Folk patronage in an earlier era is largely undocumented by scholars; the history of most folk professional performances is traceable by generations of artists rather than records of payments and other support. Contemporary texts, which embody references to patrons, suggest ways in which folk patronage is encouraged today and perhaps in earlier times. Reference to patrons within texts and within performance traditions indicate the encouragement of such support. And stories which artists tell to contemporary patrons and to adept students suggest ways in which patronage was developed and continued for particular performing traditions.

In the early twentieth century, prior to independence in 1947, new riches, nationalistic fervor, and development of theatrical stages provoked changes in patronage even before the demise of the erstwhile princely states. Tagore's Santiniketan and his dramas with dance and song, Vallathol's Kerala Kalamandalam and Rukmini Devi Arundale's Kalakshetra (originally part of the Theosophical Society) provided institutions which patrons could support through contributions and volunteer service. The Indian People's Theatre Association (IPTA), the Uday Shankar Culture Centre at Almora, the music conferences begun by Bhatkhande, and the Madras Music Academy with V. Raghavan's keen interest and support all offered new patronage for performing artists. But it was the mass media of radio, films and phonograph records which drew artists from their local patrons into a wider regional or national network of cultural performance. And after independence the commercial avenue of film, government-supported radio staffing, the proliferation of performing arts schools and teachers, the recording industry, and their interaction created for cultural performance in India a different world from that presented to performing artists in the previous century. The intentions of earlier patrons were replaced by new incentives for modern patrons, though early intentions gave clues to artists for securing modern support. The development of the film industry raised complex issues of distribution, "stars", credits and finance. A renaissance in classical dance offered challenges to dancers in finding legitimacy, approval, opportunities and propriety as well as patronage for their performances, and ways to manage without professional management agencies. Folk performances were not immune to modern media or communications revolution. Competing with films for popular audiences beyond their traditional inherited patronage, folk professionals installed neon lights and microphones to give the glitter the public now expected. Without royal patronage, fetes and festivals had to be dropped or re-created to please a new patronage group whether government, merchant, organization or public. Professional folk artists could hear all kinds of music on radio, and had to decide whether to change their performances to accord with mass media conventions of timing and topic.

Modernization has undoubtedly created new questions for patronage of cultural performance in India, and spurred new cultural policies, as in all parts of the world. By looking closely at some of the issues in India, we can return to American national questions about arts patronage and cultural performance with heightened clarity and a greater awareness of the possibilities. Where once people scoffed at the idea that the developing nations could teach the west something about modernization, the suggestion is not so ridiculous today when communication and travel offer access to dialogues about culture not possible in earlier times. Each civilization has developed its own manner and conventions for promoting and supporting cultural performances, and, as Indian experts researched the west in the 1950s when the national academies of literature, visual arts, and performing arts (Sahitya Akademi, Lalit Kala Akademi, Sangeet Natak Akademi) were being created, so also we can search the praxis and conceptualization of patronage in India today for America's greater understanding and pragmatic directions.

Performers gain their patronage from a variety of sources, and through a multiplicity of methods. Selling tickets is one among many funding methods in contemporary India. Some performances incorporate textual references and appeals designed to bring spontaneous contributions from spectators and audiences. Other performance genres see their operations as a business, with arrangements and fees settled by contract, or by ritual obligations. Yet further performances are structured in a way which confirms the culture of the performers and viewers together, giving them a legitimacy which prompts support for the artistic production. And finally, politics brings patrons to the arts for status and power gained through control of cultural production and producers. In each of these cases, the relationship between patronage and performance is specific and expected. They form, when taken together, a system of linkages between the production of the arts and the consumption of the arts which is characteristic of all cultures, and which legitimizes the arts as an integral part of culture, rather than only a superstructural artifice.

Each paper in this volume addresses a specific issue of patronage and performance. Milton Singer's opening remarks recognize a theory of the performing arts as a branch of the study of culture and suggests that Peircean sign systems can offer an analysis of symbolic representations in cultural performance. The papers by Stuart Blackburn and Karine Schomer consider performer-patron relations in traditional cultural performances of a Tamil and a

Hindi oral tradition, respectively. Schomer suggests that audiences for the epic *Alha* practice "preventive censure", since they are text-sensitive. In his concise analysis of the bow song tradition of Tamil Nadu, Blackburn shows how performers influence patronage by introducing context into the performance text. Two papers focus on changing traditions and the relationship between social forces and the directions of patronage. Phillip Zarrilli traces the development of the Kathakali dance-drama through three periods of its patronage, and charts its crystallization, refinement, and response to new market economy contexts. My study of the performing artists' petitions to their patron-ruler in Jaipur focuses closely on terminology and performative aspects of dialogue, in order to capture the expectations performers had of their patron, and the ruler's responses to them.

Three contributions to the volume deal with the intention and motivation of the patrons (Wade), the marketing of artworks (Pendakur), the logistical and social aspects of managing a dance career (Lowen). Bonnie Wade creates a schematic for patronage of music and musicians based originally on a study of paintings of performance and patronage situations. Manjunath Pendakur provides a convincing discussion of distribution as the key problem for new wave filmmakers in Karnataka. Norman Cutler's elegantly constructed comment on the Wade and Pendakur papers suggests the ways in which two patronage situations which are strikingly different can be brought into dialogue in a performance model. The necessary for self-management of a classical dancer's career, and the process of learning from experience makes Sharon Lowen's paper both an analysis and an account of contemporary patronage issues in India.

Searching for patronage in another culture's performances produces an understanding of the system from outsiders' points of view. The writers in this volume, with one exception, are not Indians, but all are scholars and artists with sincere and learned interest in India's performing arts. They hope that their insights will be equally interesting and engaging for Indian and non-Indian readers. As India searches for appropriate combinations of new patronage for its civilizational arts, such explorations are illuminating constructs of the issues concerned. And they bring to light, gradually, what local and regional connoisseurs and artists have known for a long time. By sharing these subsystems with a wider public, and by bringing them into international comparative view, supporters of the arts can consider alternatives and make choices of ways to ensure the continuity of cultural traditions in the performing arts. There are many audiences in this world, and many potential patrons for the arts in society. I hope that among the readers of this book will be artists, for whom support is so essential, and encouragement in their work so integral to their continuance.

## References


Berland, Joseph C. 1982. *No Five Fingers Are Alike. Cognitive Amplifiers in Social Context*. Cambridge: Harvard University Press.

Bharucha, Rustom. 1983. *Rehearsals of Revolution. The Political Theatre of Bengal*. Calcutta: Seagull Books.

Blackburn, Stuart H. and A.K. Ramanujan, eds. 1986. *Another Harmony. New Essays on the Folklore of India*. Berkeley: University of Califonia Press.

Bremner, Robert H. 1960. *American Philanthropy*. Chicago: University of Chicago Press.

Cohn, Bernard S. 1987. *An Anthropologist Among the Historians and Other Essays*. New York: Oxford University Press.

d'Azevedo, Warren L., ed. 1973. *The Traditional Artist in African Societies*. Bloomington: Indiana University Press.

Donahue, Suzanne Mary. 1987. *American Film Distribution. The Changing Marketplace*. Ann Arbor, Michigan: UMI Research Press.

Erdman, Joan L. 1984. "Who Should Speak for the Performing Arts? The Case of the Delhi Dancers," in *Cultural Policy in India*, edited Lloyd I. Rudolph, pp. 77-104. New Delhi: Chanakya Publications. (also *Pacific Affairs*, Summer 1983).

Erdman, Joan L. 1985. *Patrons and Performers in Rajasthan. The Subtle Tradition*. New Delhi: Chanakya.

Geertz, Clifford. 1980. *Negara. The Theatre State in Nineteenth-Century Bali*. Princeton, New Jersey: Princeton University Press.

Haskell, Francis. 1971. *Patrons and Painters. A Study in the Relations Between Italian Art and Society in the Age of the Baroque*. New York: Harper & Row Icon Editions.

Harris, John S. 1970. *Government Patronage of the Arts in Great Britain*. Chicago: University of Chicago Press.

Havens, Thomas R.H. 1982. *Artist and Patron in Postwar Japan. Dance, Music, Theater, and the Visual Arts, 1955–1980*. Princeton: Princeton University Press.

Hein, Norvin, 1972. *The Miracle Plays of Mathura*. Delhi: Oxford University Press.

Higgins, Jon B. 1976. "From Prince to Populace: Patronage as a Determinant of Change in South Indian (Karnatak) Music," in *Asian Music* VII, 2:20-26.

Hogwood, Christopher. 1977. *Music at Court*. London: The Folio Society.

Kothari, Komal. 1987. "Patronage and Performance." A paper presented at the International Seminar on Rajasthan, Jaipur, December. Unpub.

Lord, Albert. 1974. *The Singer of Tales*. New York: Atheneum.

Lynes, Russell. 1975. *The Lively Audience. A Social History of the Visual and Performing Arts in America, 1890-1950*. New York: Harper & Row.

McKinzie, Richard D. 1973. *The New Deal for Artists*. Princeton: Princeton University Press.

McLuhan, Marshall. 1964. *Understanding Media. The Extensions of Man*. New York: Mentor Book.

Netzer, Dick. 1980. *The Subsidized Muse. Public Support for the Arts in the United States*. Cambridge: Cambridge University Press.

Neuman, Daniel M. 1980. *The Life of Music in North India. The Organization of an Artistic Tradition*. Detroit: Wayne State University Press.

Peacock, James L. 1968. *Rites of Modernization. Symbolic and Social Aspects of Indonesian Proletarian Drama*. Chicago: University of Chicago Press.

Rao, P. Chantsal. 1983. *B.M. Birla. His Deeds and Dreams*. New Delhi: Arnold-Heineman.

Rosenzweig, Robert M. with Barbara Turlington. 1982. *The Research Universities and Their Patrons*. Berkeley: University of California Press.

Schechner, Richard. 1985. *Between Theater and Anthropology*. Philadelphia: University of Pennsylvania Press.

Schechner, Richard. 1988. *Performance Theory*. New York: Routledge.

Singer, Milton. 1980 [1972]. *When A Great Tradition Modernizes*. Chicago: University of Chicago Press.

Smith, Marian W. 1961. *The Artist in Tribal Society*. Proceedings of a Symposium held at the Royal Anthropoligical Institute of Great Britain and Ireland. Occasional Paper No. 15. London: Routledge & Kegan Paul.

Strong, Roy. 1984. *Art and Power. Renaissance Festivals 1450–1650*. Woodbridge, Suffolk: The Boydell Press.

Vasari, Giorgio. 1965 [1568]. *The Lives of the Artists*. A Selection Translated by George Bull. Harmondsworth, Middlesex, England: Penguin Books.

Wade, Bonnie C. 1984. *Khyal. Creativity Within North India's Classical Music Tradition*. Cambridge: Cambridge University Press (Cambridge Studies in Ethnomusicology).

Wolf, Thomas. 1983. *Presenting Performances. A Handbook for Sponsors*. 5th edition. New York: American Council for the Arts.

# Cultural Performance as a Blurred Genre:

## Remarks to Inaugurate a Conference

Milton Singer

When Helen and I were in Madras on our first visit, in 1954-55, we went to some of the concerts and events around December. I noticed that cultural *sabhas* such as the Madras Music Academy had a regular kind of scheduling of their programs. Early in the morning they would have the pundits give extremely learned and philological papers. They sounded just like academic meetings anywhere. In the early afternoon they had competitions, especially for children, in music and dance and story-telling. Not until the evening did they have the outstanding performances, such as Balasaraswati, Subalakshmi and other renowned artists. If I were giving a morning speech, I would have quite a long paper, I assure you, and quite learned. But since I am offering introductory remarks, I will give you a ritual reading of the titles and subtitles of what I would have said in a pundit discussion.

Culture has been an important, perhaps one of the most important concepts of anthropology, at least for the last hundred years. The charter definition that is usually identified is that of Edward Tylor, who defined it in 1871.[1] It's usually called an omnibus definition, because he included just about everything—art and the arts of life and pleasure, and all the habits acquired by man as a member of

"Culture or civilization, taken in its wide ethnographic sense, is that complex whole which includes knowledge, belief, art, morals, law, custom, and any other capabilities and habits acquired by man as a member of society" (Tylor [1871] 1958:I, 1).

society. In the hundred years since Tylor made that definition, many operations have been performed on the culture concept by anthropologists (Boon 1973). I did try to do a schematic summary of some vicissitudes of the culture concept in an article in 1968 in the *International Encyclopedia of the Social Sciences*. I think if I tried to review those, we would never get to the anthropology of performance. If you think of the work in musicology or dance, folksong, drama and novel, poetry, sports, film, you will be impressed by the extent to which anthropologists have been following the advice Robert Redfield gave them in 1950. He said that anthropologists who have been working with the natural scientists on their right, should now turn to the humanists on their left (Redfield [1950] 1962). Alot of this work, which is still going on, and is represented by the participants in this conference has been quite impressive. But it has been rather lacking—I say this not in any spirit of carping because it applies to my own work as well—in a general theory of performance that would begin to establish this field of culture as a performing art as a legitimate branch of anthropology.

That we need such a theory of culture as a performing art, and of performing as a branch of culture theory, is I think much too obvious to need any special argument. I want to quote the words of Victor Turner, who was probably as active in this field of ritual and performance as any anthropologist I know, from a lecture he published in India. In an essay called "The Anthropology of Performance he says

> If man is a sapient animal, a tool-making animal, a self-making animal, a symbol-using animal, he is no less a performing animal, Homo Performans. Homo Performans, not in the sense perhaps that a circus animal may be a performing animal, but in the sense that man is a self-performing animal. His performances are, in a way, reflexive. In performing he reveals himself to himself (Turner 1979).

I think that is a very good starting point for any general theory of performing arts as a branch of culture.

Before I go further, I would like to point out that perhaps ahead of his time the Dutch historian Huizinga, in a book called *Homo Ludens. A Study of the Play Element in Culture*, published in

Dutch in 1938, came pretty much to the same conclusion that Victor Turner did in 1979. Huizinga made several very important observations. He drew on a good deal of the anthropological literature, as well as on cultural history, his own field, and on literary sources. One of the things he pointed out was that the subtitle, "a study of the play element in culture," was not as he had originally phrased it. He preferred "the play element *of* culture," by which he meant he was interested in finding out to what extent culture was play, or to what extent play was culture. Everybody he met, including his publisher, insisted that wasn't a good title, so he changed it to "the play element *in* culture."

A second important observation Huizinga made, after surveying the play element in history and various cultures, was that one of the characteristics of play was agonistic relations—relations of fighting, competition, rivalry—but combined with some notions of unity and friendliness. In 1938 Radcliffe-Brown, in his notion of "structural opposition," had already formulated the idea of friendly antagonists, friendly opponents, as a fundamental type of relationship in all societies. And that kind of opposition, which he called "structural opposition," he combined with the "logical opposition" of cultural categories, as distinctive of Australian totemism as well as of totemic and even non-totemic rituals in other societies (Singer 1984a:37-46). Huizinga, I think, was already on the right path, but he wasn't really taken up until many years later. I won't go into the reasons and the facts about that development, but one of the things that struck me as I thought and read about the question of cultural performances was that you have an interesting sort of dialectic among anthropologists. Anthropologists find that ritual in "primitive" societies very often includes performance. Then when anthropologists study modern society, they try to show that modern performances are really rituals.

One of the most dramatic examples of this dialectic is Lloyd Warner, who studied aboriginal totemism among the Murugin in Australia. He published his book in 1937; the field work was done between 1926 and 1929. One of his controlling models, or, if you prefer literary language, one of his controlling metaphors, was that the totemic rites were like Greek dramas. In Lloyd Warner's study Durkheim's idea that the totem is tha flag of the clan was also elaborated and developed. In fact, Durkheim, a founder in the study of aboriginal religion, used the performing arts model and metaphor to describe and analyze totemic rituals. Dance and song, drama, music, and recreation, as well as the famous "effervescence" when everybody assembles, were all a part of his description of totemic rituals and beliefs. Thus his famous definition of ritual as "a dramatization of origin myths" was not merely a bright idea of Durkheim's, but really an outcome of his performing arts model (Durkheim [1915] 1948).

Just how much interest Durkheim had in the performing arts in the Paris and France of his time, I don't know. Somebody should look into that; it might be a interesting bit of investigation. Lloyd Warner went to Yankee City in 1930, where his staff did field work for five years. When he finally wrote a cultural study of Yankee City in *The Living and the Dead* (1959), he turned the model around, and said Yankee City ceremonies, performances such as the Tercentenary celebration of the founding of Massachusetts Bay, were much like the rituals he had observed in Australia.

That kind of dialectic wasn't peculiar to Warner; I think it runs through all anthropological literature. In 1977, Barbara Meyerhoff and Sally Moore edited a volume called *Secular Ritual*, in which their purpose, as they put it, was "to explore the nature of non-religious ritual, ceremony and formality in social life." In an interesting article in that volume, Max Gluckman argued that drama, games, and athletic contests are not rituals in the same wav in which you have primitive ritual. The difference is that there are elements of individual choice and uncertainty in games, dramas, and athletic contests. That particular argument is aimed, judging from the text, at what he considered to be Victor Turner's attempt to spread ritual over both primitive and modern societies, especially in his book *The Ritual Process* (1969). It's interesting that Turner, in his latest essay, "The Anthropology of Performance," and even in earlier publications beginning perhaps with his book *Dramas, Myths and Metaphors*, had already begun to make the distinction between the "liminal" and the "liminoid." The liminoid was characteristic of modern societies and modern genres of cultural performances, the liminal of the more primitive (cf. MacAloon 1984). I think this is just one example of the continuing dialectic that anthropologists play with as they try to study both primitive and modern societies. They find it difficult to delimit what is primitive ritual and what is modern performance.

I ran into this problem myself in 1954-55, when I was trying to apply Redfield's ideas about the social organization of tradition in Madras, and found that many so-called rituals and performances were constantly merging into one another. It was very difficult to set up any criteria that would allow me to differentiate a ritual from a performance. I finally gave up and decided to call them all "cultural performances" because they were, first of all, performances, that is, enactments of some episode or feature of a myth or legend, or historical story-plot, whether they were songs, dances, dramas, recitations, prayers, festivals or the like. Second, they were for me observable units of a feature of a cultural tradition in these various media. A third, and perhaps most important characteristic of these cultural performances was that they were identified and exhibited by members of the society as encapsulating forms of their culture which they considered suitable to display for themselves and outsiders.[2] In other words, the cultural performances were for them expressions of a cultural self-image. Specific studies of particular cultural performances followed—the most intensively studied were the Radha-Krishna *bhajan*s of Madras City (Singer [1968] 1980). I always felt there was one aspect of the notion of a cultural performance that needed to be analyzed much further, namely, the idea that the encapsulation in a cultural performance of some feature of a society's culture or mythology or history, or even social structure, required symbolic representations of some sort, verbal or non-verbal. They were always present, and it didn't appear very clear how one might analyze these symbolic representations to show that they expressed a society's world view, or its value system, or even a characteristic cultural perception of self and person.

It was only after I found that Peirce's theory of signs and semiotics could be of some use in anthropology that I saw some light. My efforts in this direction are, at least in a preliminary way, formulated in the paper "On the Semiotics of Indian Identity" (Singer [1981] 1984). If you conceive of a self in the terms that Peirce did, as both subject and object of a system of signs, I think

[2] In the preliminary analysis of the cultural performance concept I made in 1955 I noted cultural *specialists* and *performers, audience*, cultural *media* and *stage*, the cultural *policy-makers*, and the *themes* and stories. Although *patrons* were mentioned (Singer 1980:74), they were not given the attention which Joan Erdman's studies have shown they merit.

you can show how such a conception allows you to relate the self and the person to much broader and vaguer ideas such as a world view, and a value system.

Victor Turner in "The Anthropology of Performances," confronts that same problem. After introducing his initial notion of "social drama"—that social conflicts and their resolution take a dramatic form, he found it necessary to introduce a notion of *cultural* performances to take account of aesthetic genres such as theatre, film, music and art. He shows how they express something like the world view and values of a society. Turner acknowledged help from the German philosopher Dilthey, and his notion of *weltanschauung*. Redfield too was influenced by Dilthey in trying to formulate his idea of world view (cf. Singer 1976:202-208).

When I reanalyzed the Madras study of the Radha-Krishna *bhajans*, for example, I found it was quite easy to cast a good deal of it in terms of a Peircean semiotics. The details of that you can read about in the article (Singer [1981] 1984). I also found, to my surprise, that it was no accident that it was so easy to revise the analysis by bringing in a semiotic self acting out in these Radha-Krishna *bhajans* a kind of idealized conception of an Indian self in terms of *bhakti* (devotion and mutual sharing). Peirce himself acknowledged that he may have been influenced by some of the Indian sources when he was growing up in Concord, hearing people at his family's house who had been influenced by Indian and American transcendentalism (Singer 1984:184-85). To some extent, you can say it was a pre-established harmony, and it's hard to say who should get the blame. It is a good example of why I couldn't quite take all of Kim Marriott's very good advice to see if I could frame an ethnotheory, an American indigenous theory of performance, because it's very hard to find any pure theorists who don't influence one another.

I want to conclude by coming back to the initial problem: if you're dealing with cultural performances in different cultures, you have to experience them in their own terms, but if you try to understand them in terms of the language and concepts from your own culture, you've got a problem in intercultural communication. The outcome of that may not always be positive; I hope it will be. I've been reading a paper by Frits Staal, not the 1979 paper, which is called "The Meaninglessness of Ritual," but a more recent paper called "The Search for Meaning: On Mathematics, Music, and

Ritual" (Staal 1984) in which he comes to the same conclusion as in his earlier paper about the meaninglessness of ritual. Argued in a brilliant fashion in terms of what he knows about music, mathematics and ritual, Staal says in effect that if you do a structural analysis of ritual, that's the only meaning it really has, because particular rites can be used to serve different ends. Durkheim pointed this out in connection with an Australian initiation rite involving exactly the same procedures as another Australian rite to increase species.

Staal argues that if one rite can serve different purposes, then there is no generalized meaning that it can have, but what you should concentrate on are just the structural relations of the rite. I'm not quite satisfied with Staal's conclusions, although he's made a very impressive study of some of the ancient Vedic rites in India. I think that there may be a lot more meaning in these rites and in the performances than Frits Staal seems to acknowledge. He thinks the meanings of ritual are similar to the meaning of "program music," as distinct from "absolute music." The distinction between a sonata and a symphony, he believes, can be explained in terms that are wholly musical, and have nothing to do with whether the piece was written in a particular season, or had a particular programmatic story to it. Similarly, there is "absolute ritual" and there is "program ritual"; and if you believe in the "meaning" of program ritual, you're just unsophisticated. Staal's paper is very challenging to anyone trying to arrive at a science of ritual, or at a general theory of cultural performance. I think we have to meet Staal's challenge, but we can only do it by studying the specific performances and rituals and trying to continue the dialectic that anthropologists have been pursuing now for almost a hundred years.

I know that your papers during the conference will have much to say and to contribute towards some of these problems. The quotation I would like to end with is from *The Mirror of Gesture* (Coomaraswamy and Duggirala 1936), an ancient Sanskrit manual on classical dance, because I think it illustrates so well a modern view of the interrelationship of some of these cultural media in a cultural performance.

> The song should be sustained in the throat;
> its meaning must be shown by the hands;

the mood (*bhava*) must be shown by the glances;
time (*kala*) is marked by the feet.
For wherever the hand moves, there the
glances follow. Where the glances go
the mind follows. Where the mind goes
the mood follows. Where the mood goes
there is the flower, the *rasa*.

## References


Boon, J.A. 1973. "Further Operations of Culture in Anthropology: a Synthesis of and for Debate." In C. Schneider and C. Bonjean, eds., *The Idea of Culture in the Social Sciences*. Cambridge: Cambridge University Press.

Coomaraswamy, A. and G.K. Duggirala. 1936. *The Mirror of Gesture*. New Delhi: Munshiram Manoharlal.

Durkheim, E. 1948 [1915]. *The Elementary Forms of Religious Life*. Glencoe: The Free Press.

Geertz, C. 1973. *The Interpretation of Culture*. New York: Basic Books.
[1966] "Religion as a Cultural System".
[1972] "Deep Play: Notes on the Balinese Cockfight".

———. 1983. *Local Knowledge: Further Essays in Interpretive Anthropology*. New York: Basic Books.
[1980] "Blurred Genres: The Refiguration of Social Thought'

Huizinga, J. 1949 [1938]. *Homo Ludens: A Study of the Play Element in Culture*. London: Routledge & Kegan Paul.

MacAloon, J.J., ed. 1984. *Rite, Drama, Festival, Spectacle: Rehearsals Toward a Theory of Cultural Performance*. Philadelphia: ISHI.

Meyeroff, B. and S. Moore, eds. 1977. *Secular Ritual*. Amsterdam: Royal van Gorcum.

Radcliffe-Brown, A.R. 1952 [1951]. *Structure and Function in Primitive Society*. London: Cohen and West.

Redfield, R. 1962. *Human Nature and the Study of Society*. M.P. Redfield, ed. Chicogo: University of Chicago Press.

———. 1950 *Social Science among the Humanities*.

Singer, M. 1968. "The Concept of Culture," in *International Encyclopedia of the Social Sciences* 3:527-543. New York: Macmillan and Free Press.

———. 1976. "Robert Redfield: Development of a Social Anthropology of Civilizations." In J.V. Murra, ed., *American Anthropology: The Early Years*. St. Paul: West Publishing Company.

———. 1980. [1972]. *When A Great Tradition Modernizes*. Chicago: University of Chicago Press.
[1955] "Search for a Great Tradition in Cultural Performances".
[1968] "The Radha-Krishna *Bhajans* of Madras City".

———. 1984 [1981]. "On the Semiotics of Indian Identity." in *Man's Glassy*

*Essence: Explorations in Semiotic Anthropology*. Bloomington: Indian University Press.

————. 1984a. "A Neglected Source of Structuralism: Radcliffe-Brown, Russell and Whitehead." *Semiotica* 48:11-96.

Staal, F. 1984. "The Search for Meaning: Mathematics, Music and Ritual." *American Journal of Semiotics* 2,4:1-57.

Turner, V. 1969. *The Ritual Process: Structure and Anti-Structure*. Chicago: Aldine.

————. 1974. *Dramas, Fields and Metaphors*. Ithaca: Cornell University Press.

————. 1979. "The Anthropology of Performance". In *Process, Performance and Pilgrimage*. New Delhi: Concept Publishing Company.

Tylor, E.B. [1871] 1958. *Primitive Culture: Researches in the Development of Mythology, Philosophy, Religion, Art and Custom*. 2 vols. Gloucester Smith Publisher.

Warner, W.L. 1958 [1937]. *A Black Civilization*. New York: Harper & Row.

————. 1959. *The Living and the Dead: A Study of the Symbolic Life of Americans*. New Haven: Yale University Press.

# PART ONE

## Pertormance Traditions and Patronage

# Context into Text: Performance and Patronage in a Tamil Oral Tradition

Stuart H. Blackburn

One of the useful things about the study of performance is that it encourages a mingling of literary and cultural studies. Its simultaneous focus on text and context leads toward an anthropology of aesthetic forms and a poetics of culture. Though patronage might seem to lean toward the social science side, it too requires attention to both context and text. Obviously it is only with reference to a specific artistic product in a specific cultural setting that a discussion of patronage makes sense. Patronage, in fact, can take us inside the performance event where text and context (from the performers' perspective) are totally fused, or (from our own) totally confused. From this vantage point inside the event, the relations between performance and patronage can be illuminated by a study of text-context relations. What I find, at least within one Tamil tradition, is that singers use these relations to influence patronage—and not by putting the text into context, but by putting the context into the text.

## Patronage and Performers in the Bow Song Tradition

This paper discusses performance and patronage in the bow song (*vil pāṭṭu*) tradition of Tamil Nadu.[1] The bow song is found

[1] My work has centered on the bow song tradition in an area of Kanya Kumari District known as Nāñcil Nātu; for more details about the tradition, see T. Kōmatināyakam, *Tamiḻ Villup Pāṭṭukaḷ* (Madras, 1979), or my article on oral performance in the *Journal of American Folklore* 94 (1981):207-27, or my "Performance makers in the interpretation of an Indian story type," in Blackburn and A.K. Ramanujan (ed.) *Another Harmony: New Essays on the Folklore of India*, Berkeley: University of California Press, 1986.

only in the two southernmost districts of the state (Tinnevelley and Kanya Kumari) and in the contiguous areas of Kerala. But within this small region, converging on the tip of the subcontinent, the bow is played in almost every village. The tradition is oral (though palm-leaf manuscripts and other written forms play important roles); it is narrative (the songs recount the histories of local deities); it is musical (singing is accompanied by a huge bow and four other instruments: hourglass-shaped drum, earthern pot, wooden blocks, hand cymbals); and it is religious (a ritual performance held in local temples during a festival).

Every year, sometime between January and May, in every local temple, the bow is played to invoke the gods and goddesses enshrined within it. These deities are of two types. Some are born from and associated with pan-Indian deities (mostly Śiva and Pārvatī); most, however, are local deified heroes. During the three-day temple festival or *koṭai* ("offering"), the life histories of these gods and goddesses are sung on the bow as part of a larger ritual sequence in which they are fed and honored. Bow song performances, without which the festival could not take place, have the ritual role of invoking the gods and goddesses to come and possess their human mediums, who then dance and later act as intermediaries between local people with their requests and the powerful supernaturals. The bow singers, the dancers, and their audience are from the low- and middle-level castes.[2] And they are mostly men; only the lead singer in a group of five or more performers may be a woman. Despite their role, the singers command no high ritual or social status. Neither landowners nor the most marginal laborers, they fall in the middle range of village incomes. Though some are agricultural workers, most singers are small renters (some do own an acre or two), are engaged in small-scale trade, or do some other non-agricultural work. The bow song tradition, in other words, is village-based and non-élite.

The same is also true of its patronage. Although they sang literally outside the palaces of the Maharajas of Travancore, who were renowned for their support of music and hosted performers from all over India, the bow singers received no courtly recognition[3]. Likewise, the great temple centers at Sucindram and Kanya

[2] Singers are predominantly Nātār or Piḷḷai; some are Kōnār, Tēvār, or Cālaiyār.

[3] Before 1947, Travancore was probably second only to Tanjore in the support of Carnatic music.

Kumari are surrounded by bow song performers, but do not extend their great wealth to support this folk tradition. Instead, the tradition is supported by local audiences in villages and towns, and only by certain castes. Brahmins and other high castes (Nayar, Goldsmith) do not patronize the tradition for reasons of ritual purity (there are animal sacrifices) and social prestige (possession is not considered a mark of sophistication). Untouchables do not host performances for lack of resources. Since a caste will not invite to its temple a singer of lower social status, the Untouchables must be able to support their own singers; and they are not able to.

The patronage system is two-fold. Most of a bow singer's earnings come from a larger amount raised by the local temple community to finance the festival. The size of this community varies from temple to temple, but its membership is uniformly defined through a share (*paṅku*) system. The contributing units or "shareholders" (*paṅkāḷi*) may be either households or all males over a certain age. The community for a goddess temple controlled by a populous and dominant caste in a village, for example, may have a hundred or more shareholders, and several hundred members in all. They can easily raise one or two thousand rupees for their festival. On the other hand, a lineage temple in the same village (or even same caste) might have ten shareholders who could only gather a total of, say, five hundred rupees.[4] Once the festival dates have been set and the contribution per shareholder calculated, the call goes out for money. When a little has been received, verbal contracts are made with a bow singing group (and with other persons whose services are required for the festival) and sealed with a little advance money.

The total amount paid to the bow song group from the temple community fund varies by community and group. A community with average economic resources, however, might pay a good group about three hundred rupees for a three-day festival (at least during the period 1977-1979). From this total, the group must pay its own travel expenses, which may come to fifty rupees. The remaining two hundred and fifty rupees are divided among the

[4] The size of the temple community, however, is not always an indicator of the total funds raised for the festival. One goddess temple controlled by a dominant caste had 114 shareholders, and each contributed 14 rupees, totaling about Rs. 1,600. In a small lineage temple, twenty-two adult males gave 100 rupees each, or a total of Rs. 2,200.

performers according to a share system. Normally the lead singer receives two shares (one and one-half for singing and one-half for the bow); the others get one share each.[5] A group of six members would then divide the money into seven shares, or about seventy rupees for the lead and thirty-five apiece for the others.

The other part of the patronage system is individual donations made during a performance. Donors may be members of the temple community or may simply come to the festival as an interested village resident. Most of the audience outside the temple community are members of other castes which host bow song performances in their own temples; Brahmins are never seen, and Untouchables are not common. The donation made from the audience is small, usually one to five rupees. But its return is not insignificant. The gift makes religious merit and socially valued publicity for the donor; it also, as we shall see, holds the promise of some more pragmatic return. And these small donations accumulate into a considerable sum for the performers. A talented group, in front of an average village audience, can earn an extra fifty or one hundred rupees during a performance. This sum is added to the money paid to them from the temple community fund, and the total is then divided through the share system just described. A popular lead singer can then earn one hundred rupees or more for a festival, the other performers half that. Since a group performs about fifteen times in a season, the total earnings present a significant supplement to an otherwise meager income. No one ever becomes rich playing the bow, but for many it is the difference between a modicum of comfort and the edge of poverty.

## Performance: Context into Text

The financial gains from bow singing, then, are sufficient motivation for many to compete for them. As I have described them thus far, performers might seem passive recipients and patronage an inert institution that mechanically distributes money. However, performers are more active seekers of support, and patronage is more pliable. What I find interesting are the ways singers in this Tamil tradition use performance itself to maximize patronage. In

Sometimes the group *aṇṇāvi* (guru) owns the bow and bells (attached to it), in which case he receives the extra half share.

brief, they incorporate some aspect of the context into the performance, and there they reshape it to suit their ends. Not surprisingly, the aspects of context they select are elements of the patronage system.

Bow singers carry out this general process by three major methods. In the first they incorporate audience donations into the performance; in the second and third methods, they bring the temple and then the festival of the performing context into the performed text. In the discussion that follows, these methods are described in sequence.

Gifts from the audience are not only received by the bow singers but also woven into their performance.[6] After two or three donations have been handed up to the performers' platform, the lead singer shifts out of the narrative mode and announces them. Most singers use their own fixed phraseology, but all include the donor's name, caste, village, and amount of the gift. The best singers utilize this entry of context into the performance to comment on their patrons. First, they multiply the amount of the gift by some large number, usually a thousand, sometimes a crore. The caste or village of the donor is then praised by associating it with a god or episode from classical mythology. Finally, the singer adds a special inducement to this and other donations by asking that a deity bestow favors on the donor.[7]

Below is a translation of such an expanded announcement that occurred during a performance in a local temple controlled by the Kōṉār caste (livestock breeders) in Aralvāymoḻi on the border between Kanya Kumari and Tinnevelley districts. The chief deity in the temple is Pula Māṭaṉ, a Brahmin who ran off with an Untouchable woman (of the Vaṇṇaṉ or washerman caste) and was killed, deified and now worshipped. In the announcement itself, the singer mentions that the donor is a woman from an Untouchable caste (Cāmpavar, also known as Perumāḷ). In the second part, which is sung, the gods invoked are *Murukaṉ* (Kantaṉ), Śiva

[6] Karine Schomer, in a recent paper ("Toward an Exploration of Narrative Structure in Indian Oral Epic Performance," 1982), has described audience donations in performances of the Alha epic. There is little research, however, on the various roles (narrative, performative, ritual) of such donations.

[7] Often the singer tries to associate donor and deity by some common element, usually their names; since many villagers are named after local gods and goddesses, this is not difficult.

in his form at the Neḷḷaiyappa temple in Tirunelveli town, and a local god. The singer begins in formal Tamil,

> In this great town of Aralvāymoḻi, from the Perumāḷ community which built the high dams across the Cauvery and the Vaigai rivers, in the land of many rains and cool breezes where each banana stem yields two bunches, born in that caste known for its generosity, which gives and gives when asked, and has given even its own head, in that caste of Cāmpavar, Nacciyār Aṭimai has honored us with a donation of 2,000 rupees. For her and for all her family,
>
> By the grace of Kantaṉ
> may you live for a thousand years!
> By the grace of *Murukaṉ*,
> may you prosper for a thousand more!
> By the grace of the Lord of Neḷḷai,
> may you live happily,
> By the grace of Paṭṭavaraiyar,
> may you flower forever!

Another example, occurring about an hour after the first, illustrates the gift announcement in full form. Here the donor is a man from the Carpenter caste (one of the five artisan castes known as Viśvakarma). The gods whose aid is requested are again *Murukaṉ* (whose name the donor bears) and then a local goddess. Two other donations were included in this annoucement, but the first is the most complete.

> In the great town of Aralvāymoḻi, born in the Viśva community, kings even to kings, best of all people, possessing the highest good, the caste who fashioned the rays of the sun, and made this square earth, who made crowns for poets, and lion-thrones for kings, who created humans, rajas, and the elements of nature, and who makes the *tāli* pendant for weddings, born in this caste, and bearing the sacred name of Kanpam, Kaṭampam, Poṉi Malaiyaṉ, Tiru Malaiyaṉ, Tiru Centūr Āṇtavar, Śri Cuppaiya Acāri has honored us with a gift of 2,000 rupees. For him and for his family,

By the grace of *Murukaṉ*,
  may you prosper.
By the grace of Pēcci Ammaṉ
  may you live eternally like Mt. Kailāsa.

Some of the effects such announcements have on patronage are obvious. Certainly announcing gifts encourages more of them. For one or two rupees an ordinary villager can be publicly recognized as a patron of the bow song. And this is a valued role; since the performance invokes the gods for the welfare of the community, a contribution to it becomes a small act of *dharma*.[8] The announcement stimulates patronage for another reason as well. At the end, in the song, the singers request one or more deities to show favor to the donor with a boon. The announcement thus contains, at the very least, a blessing and possibly a boon from the gods.

More subtle effects are hidden in these announcements. They praise the patrons by exaggerating the amount donated and by linking them to higher statuses: to builders of irrigation works in the first example, and Viśvakarma in the second. Each hyperbole is suggestive, and gently calls attention to the act of giving and to religious *dharma* itself. In the first announcement, the local Untouchable community is said to have performed the pre-eminent act of *dharma*: building dams.[9] They are thus likened to the Chola and Pandya kings who did build them and who are symbols of courtly patronage. Then the singers evoke the ethos of giving and generosity through a set of related images: the monsoon, fertile banana trees, and cool breezes. Finally, the Perumāḷ caste itself, as part of the vegetal yield it seems, gives its own life; and so has Nacciyār Aṭimai given to these bow singers.

The bow singer as genealogist is even more apparent in the second announcement. A carpenter who has given a few rupees is made a descendant of the Vedic god Viśvakarma. In the singer's words, however, this creator of the universe, and the artisan castes allied with him, appear like patrons, giving the sun and earth as gifts. These artisan castes as patrons is explicit in the line which claims they "made crowns for poets." This is a revealing alteration of the tradition line, praising Viśvakarma as one who "made

[8] I use the term *dharma* in this paper simply as it is used in everyday speech in Tamil, to denote giving for charitable or religious purposes.

[9] The earliest inscription in Sanskrit, the famous Rudrādaman inscription of 150 AD, praises the king for constructing an artificial lake.

crowns for kings." It is the kings, of course, who patronized poets, but here that role has been attributed to the ancestors of Cuppaiya Acāri, who has himself given to the singers.

As these examples show, announcements of patronage comment on patronage. The narrative is also used to comment on and stimulate patronage. Perhaps the most recurrent motif in bow song stories is the childless woman. Seeking to gain a child as a boon from Śiva, she and her husband make donations to temples all over South India and perform other acts of *dharma* (building roads to pilgrimage sites, planting shade-giving trees, constructing wells, sponsoring religious activities). In the end, she is rewarded, becomes pregnant, and has a child. In some performances the motif is elaborated into a major scene in the story. The journeys become longer and more numerous, the hardships more painful, the depression deeper, and the final reward of the boon more climatic. This motif, in this extended version, often garners a large number of donations from the listeners. In one performance, the lead singer received over one hundred rupees during the forty minutes he used to develop the motif.

The possibilities inherent in this motif for stimulating patronage explain why the singers have chosen to highlight it. One possibility is that by the power of suggestion, or the principle of imitative magic, like produces like. The donations in the story should produce them in the festival. Although, unlike those in the story, the gifts to the singers are not given to the gods (but are kept by the performers), they have the appearance of a religious donation because they indirectly support the festival. And like the gifts in the story, audience gifts carry the promise of a boon from the gods. A second possibility is the emotional empathy this motif evokes. When the childless couple in the story had spent all their money, had not received a boon, and were desperate, the donations flowed in from the audience. People seemed to respond to the characters' hopelessness by making the donations that they could not.

By emphasizing this narrative motif and by announcing gifts, bow singers stimulate individual donations from the audience. This is the first method used by bow singers to affect patronage. The second and third methods draw the other half of the patronage system, the community-wide collection for the festival, into performance. The second method occurs at the end of most bow song narratives when the cult of the deity is established on earth. By what amounts to a divine protection racket, the god or goddess uses its supernatural powers to harass humans with death, disease, or famine. Frightened, they go off to consult a diviner (*cōciyaṉ*) who explains to them that the troubles are caused by a particular deity, and that the only solution is to build a temple and celebrate a festival in its honor. This is done, peace is restored, and the cult established. In stories of more benevolent deities (usually goddesses), the sequence is slightly altered. The goddess descends to earth in a royal procession and displays her divinity, without violence, causing humans to worship her. The central pattern in both, however, is the same: the potentially dangerous deity is appeased and honored in a festival with *puja* offerings.

In the texts, the temple in which all this happens is either unnamed or a pan-Indian pilgrimage site in South India. In performance, however, the temple becomes that in which the performers are singing. A simple illustration of this identity between context and text is the following translation from a temple performance in a section of the Nagercôil known as Vaṭacēri. The temple is dedicated to a local goddess, Vaṇṭi Maṭicci Ammaṉ. ("The Goddess Who Stops Carts"), who is a form of the more widespread Kālī Ammaṉ. In the story, the goddess has won several boons from Śiva (including the boon to spread smallpox and scabies) and comes to earth with a retinue. She humbles a rich man and wins a loyal devotee from the bangle-selling Chetty caste, and then continues south to Kanya Kumari district. The singers bring her right into the temple at Vaṭacēri where the festival is taking place. There, she appears in a dream which prompts the local people (Cālaiyar weavers) to build a temple and celebrate a festival in her name. The singer describes this in song,

> The goddess came to Nagercoil, worshipped Nāka Ammaṉ,
> And then hurried on to the place called Vaṭacēri
> 'This will be my place, I will remain here,' she said.
> And that night, she took the form of Kāli Ammaṉ
> And appeared in the dream of the local Raja,
> And worshipped him.
> At sunrise the next day,
> The Raja awoke, confused.
> He called his diviner
> To explain what he had dreamt.

The diviner replied in a soft voice,
'Mars is in the ascendent,
And the Devi has come to this place,
Build a temple and feed her.'
The Raja ordered the temple built,
And when the foundation was set,
And the walls raised,
They boiled milk and performed the *abhiṣeka*.
They decided to celebrate a festival to the goddess.
They collected money by shares,
Each house brought a pot of *poṅkal*.
There was music, song and dance.
They fed the Vaṇṭi Māṭicci Ammaṉ her puja.
And from that day onward
Since the day the festival was celebrated,
There has been neither disease nor famine.
From inside her fortress,
The goddess protects the people.

(At this point the song ceases, and the goddess Vaṇṭi Māṭicci Ammaṉ appears through her human medium who begins to dance.)

By this second method of incorporating context in text, the temple and village (here town quarter) of the festival are brought directly into the story. In other performances, the identity between context and text is more detailed by bringing the local temple community into the story. The example below is from a performance of the Kālī Ammaṉ story in a section of Kaṭaiyanallūr town (Tinnevelley District) known as Māvaṭikāl. In this performance, the local temple community (of the Nāyakkar caste) is brought into to the text before Kālī Ammaṉ actually arrives in their settlement. A group of Nāyakkars go to Courtallam to bathe and to worship the holy places there, but on their return terrible events begin to occur in Māvaṭikāl:

On the wake night of Ammavāci, the people of Māvaṭikāl decided to go to Courtallam to worship the Lord there. They went in a caravan of twenty-one carts, worshipped all the gods and goddesses and spent the night. The next day they were preparing to return, but Kālī Amman̲, who had been watching the entire affair, said to herself, 'They worship everyone but me. They don't respect me. This isn't right.' And so, she took the form of a young child and came back with them in the caravan.

(Here the singers use a heightened style to describe the arrival of Kālī in the village.)

When she arrived, she let out the *kuravai* cry in the streets of the village. She caused disease and dirt to fall like rain. The people were confused and called the diviner (*kōṭaṅki*) who beat his drum and said, 'There's no ghost or evil spirit here; it's a devam, Kālī Amman̲ herself. Build her a temple and hold a *koṭai* for her.'

Then the men and women of Māvaṭikāl got together and built a temple in the middle of their village; they put Vairavan̲ on the north and Cuṭalai Māṭan̲ on the south. Then, in the month of Ṭai, on the third Tuesday, they celebrated a *koṭai* for Kālī with music on the bow and dance. Kālī and the other devas came to reside there and now they protect the people from harm.

As illustrated by these two examples, the second method for affecting patronage creates an identity between text and context in terms of temple, festival, and temple community. Having brought these elements of the community-based patronage system into the text, the singers can then comment on them. Text, in other words, is used to comment on context. First, the singers flatter the local community by describing its piety in going to worship at Courtrallam and its devotion and liberality in hosting a festival to Kālī Amman̲. They also give their temple status, for even though she is dangerous, Kālī's temple-presence brings glory to the little temple in Māvaṭikāl. But something else is involved: the ritual role of this identity between text and context. When the singers alter the text to bring the goddess to Māvaṭikāl in the performed story, they also help manifest her presence in the festival itself. At that point she possesses her medium. With this, the bow singers fulfil their ritual role and assure a successful festival. Only in this way can they satisfy their patrons at Māvaṭikāl and enhance the possibility that they will be invited back to next year's festival.

The third method used by the bow singers to incorporate context into the text and influence patronage is really an elaboration of the second. It is less common, but more illuminating of the issue under discussion here. Through it, the identity between context and text is detailed in terms of the festival. Some texts close not with a *koṭai* festival, but with a marriage festival; however, the parallels between a wedding and a temple festival are sufficient to allow for the context-text identity to work.

The following translation shows a skillful handling of this correspondence. This performance occurred in the same festival cited for the first translations in this paper. The performance closes with the wedding of the main characters (soon to be killed and deified), but Pakaṭai, the Untouchable father of the bride has a problem:

> As the day for the wedding got closer and closer, Pakaṭai got more and more worried. He had no money! No cash in hand and no one to borrow from. Not a rupee anywhere. But I ask you—is that anything to get upset about? Well . . . is it? Of course not. All you need to do is collect money. And where do you start? Go to every house and ask for it? No, there's no time for that. Better to start right here—right in this festival—with everyone sitting under this *pantal*!

With these words, the singer has broken the frame around the narrative and allowed context to enter the text. Context can move into text because they share the element of the festival. This commonality becomes a door between context and text that can open both ways. And, not coincidentally, the door is hinged on the issue of patronage, on the collection of money for the festival. Having brought that issue into their text, the singers can use it to comment on the patronage system that put them on the platform where they are now singing.

What the lead singer emphasizes is the necessity of community-wide support of a festival, at a wedding or in a temple. He rejects the house-to-house collection because there is no time and lays the financial responsibility on those who are listening in the festival audience. These people have already contributed to the festival, else the lead would not be singing in it; he is, in a sense, thanking them and pointing out how indispensable such patronage is to his livelihood. Then, the lead singer goes on to comment on the recipients in the patronage system. For this, the identity between context and text is strengthened by using people in the festival context as characters in the story. The lead singer continues:

> OK, we've got a little cash, now we can advance a little money to those who make arrangements for a marriage festival. And who's the first person you need?
>
> (Audience: 'A *pantal*-man.')
>
> Right! We need someone to build a *pantal*. Luckily, we don't have to go very far; in this very town there is Paramaśivam Piḷḷai.

In this way the person who built the *pantal* under which the performers and audience are sitting, Paramaśivam Piḷḷai, becomes a character in the text. He is sitting in the audience and beams with pride as the lead singer goes on:

> And so we'll go to him and say, 'Mr. *Pantal*-man, we're going to have a wedding and we need a *pantal*. How much do you want?' Now Paramaśivam Piḷḷai is not one to make a big thing out of money and he says, 'Money? Don't talk about it now. I'll do the work, then pay me.' So then we give him, say, eleven rupees advance.

This same scene is then repeated for other items necessary for a festival: food, lights and loud speakers, temple music.[10] In each scene, the name of the person who actually performed the service for the festival of the performance context becomes the character who does the same for the festival in the text. And each person, like Paramaśivam Piḷḷai, is disinterested in money and agrees to do the work out of a sense of service. Although bow singers are not among those contracted in the story, they are there by implication and also by their association with the temple musicians. The message conveyed through these scenes is clear. The recipients of temple patronage are not greedy; they perform their task for friendship,

[10] Festivals, at a marriage or in a temple, require a musical ensemble of *nākasvāram* (long oboe) and *taval* (large, double-headed, horizontal drums played with taps on the fingers), and sometimes a *pampai* (two smaller double-headed, horizontal drums, strapped one on top of the other and played with a pair of thin sticks). The whole ensemble is called a *mēḷam*.

not monetary gain. By projecting this ideal image of themselves, the singers once again use the context within the text to enhance their potential patronage.

**Conclusions**

Bow singers use performance to influence patronage in other ways (including a more elaborate presentation of self in the traditional disclaimer), but the three discussed above are interesting for their common method: the incorporation of context into the text. The first, announcement of gifts from the audience, flatters the donors. In the second, the temple in the context becomes the temple in the text allowing the singers to praise the temple and its community. The third method focuses on the festival event, emphasizing the need for communal support of such events and presenting an ideal image of the bow singers and other recipients of patronage.

All this is possible because, to reiterate the central point, the singers have first appropriated some aspect of the context into their performance. Temple in the context becomes temple in the text; festival in the context becomes festival in the text; people in the context become figures in the text. Textual world becomes congruent with the contextual, and textual time concurrent with contextual time. In sum, there is a textualization of context. Of course, this identity between text and context (just as that between local and pan-Indian gods) can be viewed from either end. Naming the temple in the story after the temple in the context can be interpreted as the familiar process of putting the text in context, or as a localization of a story to make it more relevant to an audience. However, it is more revealing of the relations between performance and patronage to look at this process as putting context into the text. From the performers' perspective, this textualization of context makes more sense, too.

Bow singers control (within some major limitations) the text, not context. The text is their best instrument for affecting context and for influencing the patronage system around them. By incorporating context into the text, they can alter it and re-present it in their own words. They can flatter patrons, highlight the patronage exchange, or comment on some aspect of it. All this is directed toward creating a context favorable to their own support.

Looking at performance in this way, we see something not always recognized about its relation to patronage. Patronage constrains performance, but performance, at the same time, creates patronage. Performers play for money and for status (as Bonnie Wade puts it, in this volume); they want to please and accommodate. Bow singers are no exception. They are sensitive to prevailing tastes of their audiences. They deliberately avoid "ugly" (*aciṅkam*) themes and omit references unfavorable to castes or lineages in the audience. But they do more than passively absorb, like litmus paper, the atmosphere around them. As I have attempted to show, they are busy creating a context supportive of them. As scholars, we have been trying to understand how context affects text; performers, on the other hand, experiment with how text affects context. If advances have been made in the study of oral tradition by putting the text in context, performers have been making their own progress by doing exactly the opposite: by putting context in the text.

## Glossary

*Cuṭalai Māṭaṉ*—a popular bow song god, born in a sacrificial fire in Kailasa.
*koṭai*—literally "offering" and name for the bow song festival.
*kuṟavai*—ululation or cry given at heightened moments of festival.
*pantal*—a roof constructed for the festival, made of thatch and decorated with flower clusters, banana bunches, lights, etc.
*poṅkal*—a South Indian sweet rice dish served to the deities during festival.
*Vairavaṉ*—(cf. Bairava, Bairon, etc.). A bow song deity who is the guardian of various goddesses in the tradition.

# The Audience as Patron: Dramatization and Texture of a Hindi Oral Epic Performance

Karine Schomer

In a widely discussed article, folklorist Heda Jason proposed a multi-dimensional model for the examination of oral literature performance that attempts to define the elements determining a work of oral literature and their interrelations. Among these are the performer's conscious shaping of the material on the one hand and, on the other, the "preventive censure" of the audience, which puts limits on the performer's freedom to depart from traditional form and content (Jason 1969:418).

* This paper is based on research conducted in North India during 1979 and 1983, with the help of a Fulbright-Hayes grant for Faculty Research Abroad, a Senior Fellowship of the American Institute of Indian Studies, and a grant-in-aid from the American Philosophical Society. The most extensive field work was done in the areas around Kanauj (Farrukhabad District, U.P.) and Mahoba (Hamirpur District, U.P.). Observations made about the *Alha* tradition elsewhere are based on brief visits and information gleaned from conversations and interviews. For help in recording, transcription and translation, I would like to express my appreciation to Sharad Chandra Ojha, Shivepal Singh Gautam and Zahir Singh. For sharing their knowledge of the *Alha* tradition and guiding me to sources, singers and locations, I am indebted to many people, especially Dr. Ramesh Tiwari, Dr. Mahendra Pratap, and Shrikrishna Chaurasia. For their hospitality in the village of Kharela, I am grateful to the entire family of Uttam Singh.

The concept of the audience's "preventive censure" was originally proposed by Petr Bogatyrev and Roman Jakobson in 1929. Their argument was that the presence of an immediate audience meant there was less freedom to innovate in oral than in written literature. In a recent re-examination of the concept, Jason suggests that there is in oral literature a constant process of reshaping by performers, but that the performer is as bound as the audience by the literary models and social conventions they share. The audience's "preventive censure" therefore applies to the quality,

The functioning of "preventive censure" is an important aspect of the relationship between performance and patronage. The role of patrons goes beyond facilitating and financing performances to influencing by their expectations everything from the specific social purpose of a performance to its most subtle artistic qualities. In this, the role of the actual patron is not sharply distinguishable from that of the audience as a whole. All are connoisseurs (to a greater or lesser extent) of the performance genre, "informed listeners" endowed with the specific competencies and expectations required to respond knowledgeably to the performance.[2].

This paper explores the question of audience "preventive censure" by comparing different regional performance styles of an Indian oral epic tradition. It focuses primarily on the most formal artistic aspects of performance: dramatization—musical accompaniment, melodic structure, rhythm, voice quality, facial expression and gesture, and texture—the grammatical structure of the language used, the prosodic features of the verbal text and the text's style. The emphasis on formal features is because regional traditions and audience expectations for a given genre differ most in this respect. There is no one standard performance style for the epic to which all audiences respond equally, but a whole range of styles. By their identification with and loyalty to particular performance styles, audiences exercise "preventive censure" and thus function as patrons of these styles.

## The Ālhā: Epic Cycle and Performance Tradition

The performance tradition examined here is the *Ālhā*, the most popular and widespread heroic epic cycle of the Hindi-speaking area of North India.[3] The *Ālhā* originated in Bundelkhand, the

---

not the nature of the performance (1988:10–13). The evidence presented in this paper lends support to both, especially in present-day situations where performers have many audiences other than the traditional ones for their genre and/or style.

[2] The notion of the "informed" reader (or listener) comes from the audience-oriented literary criticism of Stanley Fish (1972). To be an "informed" reader/listener, according to Fish, is to have all the linguistic, semantic and literary competencies required for the intended reaction to the "text", to be "sufficiently experienced as a reader to have internalized the properties of literary discourse, including everything from the most local of devices (figures of speech, etc.) to whole genres" (1972:406).

[3] For general information on the *Ālhā*, see Lutgendorf 1979 and Schomer 1989

area just south of the Yamuna and Chambal rivers with whose history it is most directly connected. It is especially popular there and in the central Doab area between the Ganga and Yamuna rivers, where much of the action also takes place. However, it is found in and belongs to a greater or lesser extent to all the sub-regions of the large Hindi heartland zone covering the present-day states of Uttar Pradesh, Madhya Pradesh, Haryana and Bihar (Map I).

The *Ālhā* is the epic narrative of the intertwined fates of the three principal Rajput kingdoms of North India on the eve of the Turkish conquest (late 12th century AD): Delhi, Kanauj and Mahoba. Kanauj is situated on the Ganga some 200 miles southeast of Delhi, and Mahoba is 150 miles due south of Kanauj beyond the Yamuna and Betava rivers, near the present Madhya Pradesh border (Map II). Delhi at the time was in the hands of the Chauhan clan of Rajputs and ruled by King Prithviraj. Kanauj was ruled by Gaharvar (or, according to some traditions, Rathor) King Jaichand, and the ruler of Mahoba was the Chandel king Paramardideva (Parmal in the epic). The heroes of the epic are brothers Alha and Udal, their cousins and other companions. Retainers of the kingdom of Mahoba, their cause is protection of Mahoba and defence of its honor. Important to the story is the fact that these heroes belong to a minor Rajput clan, the Banaphars, which is generally looked down on by other Rajputs.[4] Hence there is in all their exploits the theme of the lowly triumphing over the mighty. This theme is especially clear in parts of the cycle dealing with the heroes' marriages, each of which takes place only after a bitter combat with the unwilling family of the bride.

The epic narrative consists of a series of episodes in which the heroes confront opponents and enemies of Mahoba or the fathers

[4] Little is known about the origins or ethnography of the Banaphars. They are found today primarily in the eastern and north-central part of Bundelkhand. William Crooke described them as a clan of Rajputs who "hold only a moderately respectable rank among Rajputs" and pointed to legend material linking them to the Ahirs (1896, 1:137–39). Another theory about their origins relates them to the Huns, while yet another belief held about them is that they are the product of marriages between Rajput men and non-Rajput women. A proverbial saying about them, known throughout Bundelkhand and frequently quoted in the *Ālhā* is "*occhī jāta Banānhara kī*" ("low is the caste of the Banaphars")

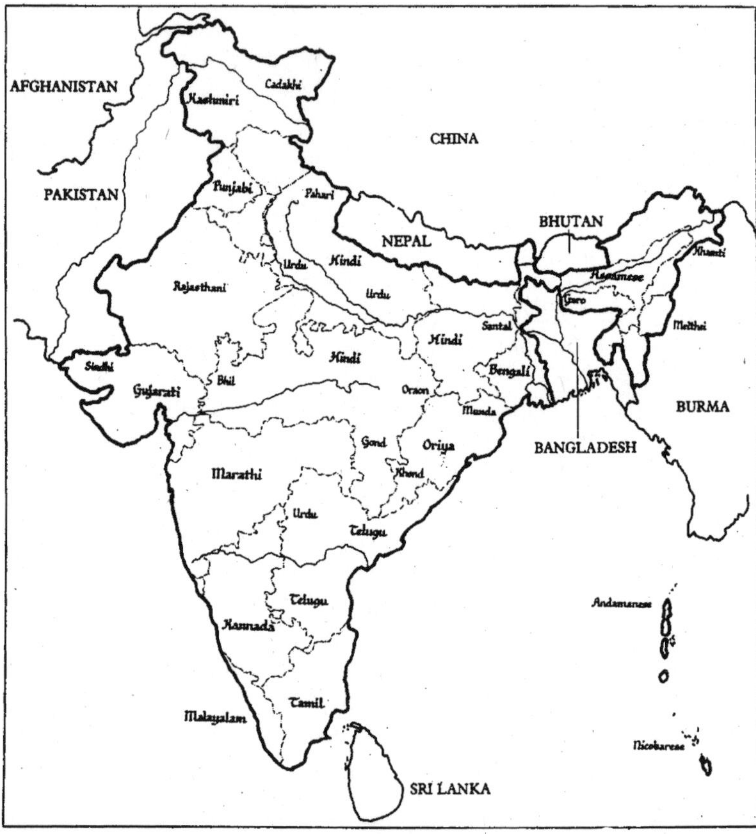


MAP I

Linguistic Regions of India, Showing Hindi-Speaking Area (from *The Living Arts of India: Indian Fairs and Festivals*, Smithsonian Institution 1986, p. 11.

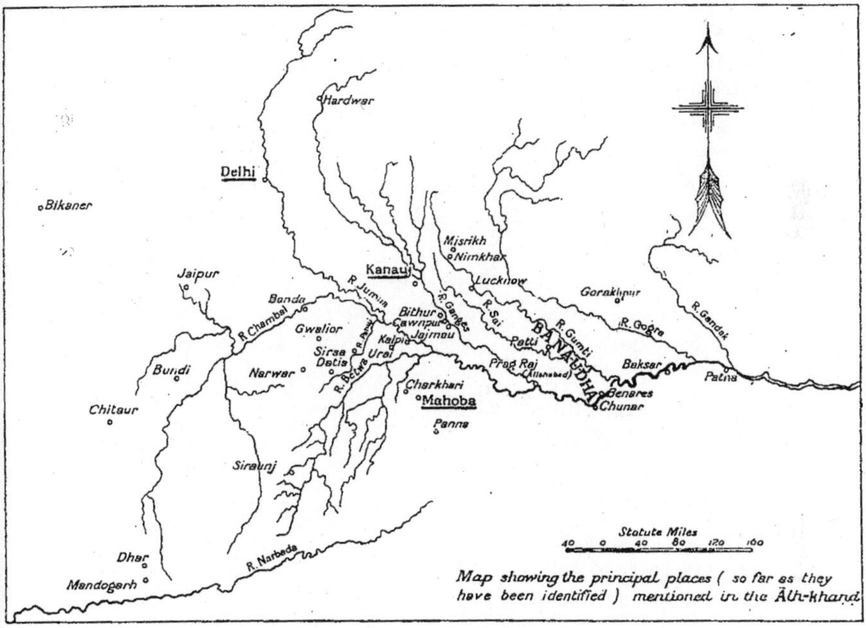


## MAP II

Geography of the *Ālhā*
(from Waterfield, *The Lay of Ālhā*,
Oxford University Press 1923, frontispiece)

of girls they want to marry.[5] Their principal enemy is Prithviraj, whose attacks on Mahoba result in major confrontations. The climax is a great battle between Mahoba and the forces of Prithviraj, which results that in the total annihilation of the Chandels and so weakens Prithviraj that he is unable to resist subsequent attacks by the Turks. This battle is probably based on the historical victory of Prithviraj over the Chandels in 1182/83, which is attested by inscriptional evidence and may have been the original traumatic event around which the epic developed.[6]

The *Ālhā* is performed primarily during the monsoon season, when agricultural work is at a standstill and the rainy weather forces people to remain close to home. There is a common belief, at least in some regions, that to sing the *Ālhā* at any other time of year is potentially dangerous.[7] Performances take place at night, out in the open. A performance traditionally consists of a single episode, referred to as a *laṛāī* (battle). A *laṛāī* can last from less than an hour to the whole night (or can even be extended over several nights), and is a self-contained unit. There is no tradition of performing a sequence of episodes, or the whole story of the *Ālhā*, over a certain number days.

There are several different performance situations:

(1) Informal performances by non-professionals for self-entertainment, unrelated to the context of any larger event. Typically such performances take place in front of homes, on the *chaupāl*s or open verandahs of houses, on rooftops and, in the cities, around lamp-posts. Like all *Ālhā* performances, they are attended only by men.

[5] The *Ālhā* cycle is said to consist of 52 episodes, though the number is a more formulaic than accurate representation of singers' repertoires. Each episode culminates in a battle.

[6] For information on the inscription, see Cunningham 1969:71 and Das 1919:7. In 1983, cultural organizers in Mahoba marked the 800th anniversary of the event by a large-scale program including a three-day *Ālhā* festival, a parade through the city with floats depicting themes from the *Ālhā*, and a scholarly symposium on the *Ālhā* tradition.

[7] The reason for this, people explain, is that the war-like emotions aroused by *Ālhā* recitation may lead to fights. In Mahoba, it is said that during the rainy-season month of Savan, Alha (who is immortal) comes and stays in the city. Because of his presence, the singing of the *Ālhā* during this period does not lead to violence, but to *śānti*, the stilling of violent emotions (Tivari 1979).

(2) Public performances for a whole village or neighborhood. These are performances by paid professionals or semi-professionals who have been specifically invited and receive a cash fee for their singing, provided either by an individual patron (usually a prominent landowner) or from subscriptions raised by the village or neighborhood as a whole. Such performances take place in public places, often the central square where most of the village's public business is transacted, or the open area in front of a temple. Audiences, consisting of males of all ages, vary in size depending on how large the village or neighborhood community is and on the reputation of the singer.

(3) Performances at weddings. This tradition does not seem to exist in all regions, and is more typical of eastern U.P. and Bihar than of Western U.P. and Madhya Pradesh.

(4) Performances at certain traditional *melās* (fairs). Though these *melās* are multi-purpose cultural, religious and economic events whose main focus is something other than the *Ālhā* tradition, their location has some connection with the *Ālhā* story. For example, the annual *melā* held at the Kiratsagar lake near Mahoba during the month of Savan celebrates the Raksha Bandhan festival, known locally as "*Bhujariyoṅ kā tyauhār*" (the Bhujariyan Festival) because of the custom of immersing in the lake small leaf baskets (*bhujarī*) in which seeds of barley or wheat have been sprouted. However, since one of the big battles in the *Ālhā* was fought on the shore of Kiratsagar during that *melā*, the *Ālhā* figures importantly at the *melā*, and regional *Ālhā* groups come to perform at that time. Likewise, in the Barabanki District of Uttar Pradesh, the *Ālhā* is performed at a *melā* associated with the Sufi saint Haji Waris Shah held every year in the town of Devan. The connection here is the tradition that the town was once conquered by Alha's brother Udal and renamed after their mother Deval.[8]

(5) Modern stage performances in towns or cities, often in the form of competitions (*pratiyogitā*) between different groups of singers (primarily semi-professionals). A new tradition which has been developing in recent times, it is sponsored by middle-

[8] The information about Devan was provided by Girija Shankar Shukla, a journalist and *Ālhā* connoisseur in Barabanki (Interview, 9/17/79).

class cultural organizers and institutions interested in the promotion of regional folk arts. The broader social motives of these sponsors range from organizing youth, to language promotion, cultural preservation, the creation of regional identity, and the promotion of tourism.[9] At the instance of these organizers and institutions, money is raised from the town elite to help with arrangements and provide cash awards to the best singers. Inspired by the economic incentive and the prospect of broader recognition, singers come to these competitions from considerable distances. Therefore the competitions have become occasions for exposure and mutual borrowings beyond traditional regional and sub-regional boundaries. Furthermore, the mixed nature of the audiences (i.e. city-dwellers as well as rural people) forces the singers to develop new performance styles that can hold listeners accustomed to the quicker pace of modern urban culture.

In addition to performances in these entertainment contexts, the *Ālhā* is used by government, political parties and even sales promotion agencies to get their messages across to the rural masses of North India (Parmar 1975). This use of the *Ālhā* as a mass communication medium involves sponsoring traditional performances in order to attract a crowd and commissioning recitations in *Ālhā* style on new themes or subjects. Historically, this is not an entirely new phenomenon. In a village near Kanauj, for, instance there is an old *Ālhā* singer who received awards and medals from the British government for his role in accompanying army recruitment teams to the villages during the Second World War.[10] Recitation of the *Ālhā* was also used by Indian nationalists to inspire courage and dedication in the Independence movement, and labor leaders have been using it for a long time in organizing the trade union movement as well.[11]

[9] In the course of my fieldwork, I have observed and recorded competitions organized by the Nehru Yubak Kendra (a social and cultural organization devoted to working with boys and young men), the Hindi Prachar Samiti (an organization for the promotion of Hindi), a small-town museum, a college, and the leaders of a local tourism development group.

[10] Prof. Ramesh Tivari, personal communication, Kanauj, 8/26/79.

[11] Ramujagar Pande, interview, Barabanki, 9/17/79. Pande, a singer in his 60s, was a retired railway worker and had been active in the railway workers' union. He related numerous occasions when *Ālhā* singing had been used to instill enthusiasm at union meetings.

## Variation in Performance Traditions

Although the *Ālhā* is known and sung throughout the Hindi heartland, it is not a uniform performance tradition. In each cultural sub-region, there are different types of performers, somewhat different patronage patterns, audiences and occasions for performance, certain favorite episodes, considerable variation in plot line and detail, some variation in linguistic texture and, most noticeable of all, a distinctly regional performance style, i.e. mode of dramatization. Dramatization may even vary within a cultural sub-region, with different guru-disciple traditions (referred to as *akhāṛā*) popularizing particular melodies, kinds of instrumental accompaniment and styles of delivery.

Thus patron-audience expectations of what an *Ālhā* performance should be vary considerably. First, different expectations exist concerning the season of performance. Though in most areas the *Ālhā* is a cultural form associated exclusively with the rainy season, there are some exceptions. Thus in the Bhojpuri-speaking eastern part of Uttar Pradesh and in Bihar, it is also performed frequently as entertainment at weddings, which do not take place in the rainy season but in winter and during the hot, dry season preceding the monsoon. In the easternmost part of Bihar (Mithilạ), the *Ālhā* may not be performed during the monsoon at all.[12]

There are also different expectations concerning who performs the *Ālhā*. As a form of self-entertainment, the *Ālhā* is sung by men of all castes except the merchant castes, and performing groups may be either of one caste or mixed. Frequently, *Ālhā* singers are also involved in wrestling, martial arts and physical fitness.[13] But while in western Uttar Pradesh (the Kanauji, Braj and Khari Boli dialect areas), it is not uncommon for Muslims to sing the *Ālhā*, in the Bundelkhand region (the northwestern districts of Madhya Pradesh and the Hamirpur district of Uttar Pradesh) this is almost unheard of. The professional entertainer communities that per-

[12] This information comes from Munnilal Yadav, an amateur *Ālhā* singer from Mithila who had come to Delhi to find work as a servant (Interview, Delhi, 12/2/79). According to Yadav, the severity of the monsoon in that region makes any kind of travel extremely difficult during the rainy season, including travel by performers.

[13] Note that the primary meaning of *akhāṛa* is a wrestling arena or a place of exercise.

form the *Ālhā* can be *jogīs* (wandering Hindu religious mendicants of the Nathpanthi sect), who are more prominent in the east, or *naṭs* (travelling acrobats), Hindu and Muslim, who prevail in the more western regions.[14] Finally, there is also variation among the semi-professionals—men who are skilled singers but whose main source of livelihood is something else. In the Bundelkhand region, semi-professionals are nowadays predominantly Rajput, though in the past Brahmin Bhats were prominent as well.[15] In the Avadhi-speaking Baiswara region east of Kanauj, Rajputs and Brahmins both perform, often together.[16] By contrast, the main semi-professional performers west of Kanauj tend to come from lower castes,[17] while in the Bhojpuri-speaking part of eastern Uttar Pradesh and in Bihar, the *Ālhā* is frequently performed by Ahirs.[18]

Patrons and audiences also vary from region to region, and also between rural and urban areas. At one end of the spectrum are intimate audiences for informal, non-professional performances

[14] The first *Ālhā* singer I encountered in the course of my research was an old Muslim *naṭ*, Shobha Khalifa, in the market town of Simbhaoli (Meerut District, U.P.). He came from a professional family tradition going back several generations. According to Khalifa, it was primarily *naṭs* who perfomed in that area (Interview, Simbhaoli, 8/20/79).

[15] According to many people in Bundelkhand, including most scholars, the original singers of the *Ālhā* were Brahmin Bhats (Brahmabhatts) attached to the court of the Mahoba kings. There is a tenacious belief, unsubstantiated so far by any manuscript but entrenched in scholarly opinion as well as popular lore, that the *Ālhā* was originally a written work, composed by the court poet of Mahoba's King Parmal, Jagnik (see, for example, Das 1919, Dvivedi 1969, Gupta 1983). Whatever the validity of the Jagnik tradition, it is a fact that there are many older singers in Bundelkhand who are Brahmabhatts.

[16] For example, I recorded and interviewed (9/17/79) a Rajput-Brahmin pair of singers from the Barabanki District of U.P. who specialized in recitations of the *Ālhā* emphasizing the comic. Thakur Pratap Singh and Pandit Ramkuber said they had been performing together since they were boys growing up in the same village. I am grateful to Prof. Dhirendra Vajpeyi for making me aware of the shared martial culture of Rajputs and Brahmins in the Baiswara region and for his own reminiscences of growing up as a Brahmin boy fascinated with the *Ālhā*.

[17] This is a statement made to me repeatedly by upper-caste singers in other regions. Though I did not have the opportunity to check on this in person, the validity of this generalization was confirmed for me by Delhi journalist Surinder Verma, a man belonging to the Kumhar (Potter) caste who had village relatives in that area (Interview, New Delhi, 10/20/83).

[18] For an account of an Ahir who sang both *Chanainī* and *Ālhā*, see Pandey 1979:22.

on the *chaupāl* or roof of a village home. Because of the residential pattern of Indian villages, such audiences often consist mainly of men from the singers' extended family and caste. Another kind of intimate and homogeneous audience situation occurs on occasions when *Ālhā* singers from the same *akhāṛa* gather around their guru or honor his memory. Here, homogeneity is not necessarily due to caste, since men of different castes sing the *Ālhā*, but to shared involvement with a particular performance tradition. In the first case, there is no real question of patronage, except to the extent that some member of the community has offered his *chaupāl* or roof for the singing session, and may provide *bīṛīs* (rolled tobacco-leaf cigarettes) during breaks. In the second, the role of patron is housing and feeding the visiting singers, and may be played by members of the guru's extended family or other local admirers of the guru. In both situations, the audiences are connoisseurs able to listen for hours in rapt attention, appreciating long digressions and poetical embellishments and responding to a host of local allusions.

At the other end of the spectrum are mass audiences at modern urban *Ālhā* competitions, events for which the patrons are members of the local intelligentsia—government officials, social workers, school teachers, college professors, literati, history buffs, civic-minded businessmen, local boosters, cultural organizers, etc. These audiences vary widely in terms of age, caste, class, place of origin and degree of familiarity with the *Ālhā*. Unlike rural audiences, their attention span is relatively short, they become restless when the singer digresses too much from the main plot, and they require non-stop excitement in the delivery.[19]

Somewhere between these two extremes are village-wide audiences for performances arranged by individual landowning patrons or collective leadership of the village. These audiences are quite familiar with the *Ālhā*, and more patient than urban ones. While varied in terms of caste, they are united in the shared village culture and its points of reference. At this kind of performance as well as in urban competitions, it is customary for listeners to show

[19] For example, at a competition held in the town of Barabanki on September 17, 1989, an *Ālhā* group led by a singer named Pramod Kumar Singh was practically booed off the stage for being too dull in its presentation. Many people in the audience got up and walked away while the singing was going on, or started conversing among themselves instead of listening with the usual quiet concentration typical of *Ālhā* audiences.

appreciation by handing up rupee notes to the singers and for singers to acknowledge donations by reciting a formulaic verse of thanks in which the donor's name is mentioned.

Because the action of the *Ālhā* encompasses all of North India, and the inner geography of the epic is not very different from the actual present-day geography of the area, it is only natural that audiences and patrons in each region and locality should have a special fondness for episodes which are most closely related to their own history and landmarks. Thus around Mahoba the favorite episode is "*Bhujariyoṅ kī laṛāī*," the story of the great battle that took place on the shore of the Kiratsagar lake. In Kaṇauj, on the other hand, a favorite episode ("*Ālhā manauā*"—"Persuading Alha to Return") takes place in that city, and another is "*Nadī Betavā kī laṛāī*" ("The Battle of the River Betava"), in which the young prince of Kanauj plays a major role. Likewise, the favorite episode around Banaras is "*Ālhā kā byāh*" ("The Marriage of Alha") because Alha's bride is believed to have come from that region, whereas in the area east of Gorakhpur, referred to in the epic as Ganjar, "*Gānjar kī laṛāī*" ("The Battle of Ganjar") is most popular. Conversely, in Baghelkhand (northeastern Madhya Pradesh) there is a particular *dislike* for "*Māṅḍo kī laṛāī*" ("The Battle of Mando"), because the villains of the episode are Baghel Rajputs (after whom Baghelkhand is named).[20] Not surprisingly, it is marriage episodes that are most popular at performances in connection with weddings.

In addition to regional preferences for certain episodes, there are regional differences in plot line and detail, on which regional audiences remain quite adamant. Among the minor differences are variants of characters' names; for example, Alha's brother is known in the west as Udal and in the east as Rudal (Grierson 1855a:210). Sometimes the names are totally different, as in the case of the princess of Mando, who is called Bijama in the west and Pauhap in the east (Grierson 1855b:257). Characters are differently identified as well. For example, the mothers of the Banaphar

Bundelkhand *Ālhā* singer Hargovind 'Vishva' related to me that he had once come to sing for the opening of the All-India Radio Station in Rewa, one of the former princely states of Baghelkhand. When 'Vishva' began to sing "*Māṅḍo kī laṛāī*," the station director frantically ordered the microphones turned off, explaining that the former raja of Rewa (a Baghel Rajput) was present with his family in the audience, and that he might lost his job if "*Māṅḍo kī laṛāī*" was performed on this occasion (Interview, Sagar, 9/9/79).

heroes are said in certain regional traditions to have been Ahir women and in others to have been the daughters of Rajput kings (Waterfield 1923:15, Grierson 1885b:255). Likewise, Alha's wife is variously identified as either the daughter (Waterfield 1923:36) or the sister (Grierson 1885a:210) of the king of Nainagarh.

Identification of locations also differs from region to region, each region wanting for itself as much of the *Ālhā* lore as possible. Thus two widely separated towns by the name of Sirsa are said to be the place where Alha's cousin Malkhan was killed.[21] Many places establish a tie with the *Ālhā* by means of minor incidents added to the main narrative.

Differences in plot can be substantial. In the "*Maṇḍo kī laṛāī*" episode for instance, *Ālhā* audiences in the east expect Udal (or, as he is called there, Rudal) to marry the daughter of the defeated king (Grierson 1885b:257), whereas in the west the tradition is that Alha orders her killed (Waterfield 1923:140). In the tradition of Baiswara (the Avadhi-speaking region to the east of Kanauj, centered in the districts of Lucknow, Unnao, Rae Bareilly and Fatehpur), there is an episode in which Alha's wife is abducted as was Sita in the *Rāmāyaṇa*, a story stoutly denied by the singers and audiences of Bundelkhand. In Mithila, on the other hand, the belief is that (like Sita in certain late versions of the *Rāmāyaṇa*), she was replaced by a false image of herself and thus was not *really* abducted.[22] Another story accepted outside Bundelkhand but denied there is that the god Indra used to come at night for trysts with the king of Mahoba's wife, and that it was his horse mating with the king's mare that gave birth to the magic flying horses of the heroes.[23]

In addition to these ancillary stories that differ from region to region, there are certain major episodes unique to particular regions. Thus around Kanauj, the well-known story of King Prithviraj's abduction of Jaichand's daughter Sanjogita is performed as an episode of the *Ālhā*,[24] while in Bundelkhand, an area with a long

[21] One Sirsa is in Bundelkhand, the other in Haryana.

[22] Munnilal Yadav (Interview, Delhi, 12/2/79).

[23] In a conversation with several Bundelkhand *Ālhā* singers (Mahoba, 9/11/83), I was surprised at the vehemence with which this story was criticized. "It's an insult to Queen Malhana to suggest she would ever have behaved that way!" said singer Chhote Singh, summarizing the group's objection.

[24] The story of Prithviraj and Sanjogita, preserved in written form in the medieval

history of resistance to Muslim military power, there is a very popular episode in which Alha at age twelve fights off an army of 100,000 Muslim Pathans.[25]

Of all the differences separating one *Ālhā* tradition from another, however, it is differences in dramatization and texture that are most marked. In every region, people refer to "the typical *Ālhā* tune" and "typical *Ālhā* drumming," which can easily be recognized even from afar. But there is in fact no typical tune or drumming pattern used throughout North India. The variety of tunes to which the *Ālhā* is sung is very large, some traditional to given regions and others more specifically linked to certain *gurus* and their *akhāṛās*.[26] Drum patterns which accompany the singing also differ from place to place and from tradition to tradition. Thus what audiences in one region consider to be "typical" melody and rhythm may sould quite strange to audiences in another.

Instrumentation is also far from standard, and the same is true of the composition of an *Ālhā* performing group. Basic accompanying instruments everywhere are *ḍholak* (two-headed drum) and *manjirā* (small brass cymbals)—the simplest and most universal of North Indian folk instruments—but there can be additional instruments as well. In Bundelkhand, the basic pattern is for one man to sing alone while playing *ḍholak*, accompanied by another man on *manjirā*. In the Kanauj area and Baiswara, by contrast, the *Ālhā* is performed by a whole ensemble: a main singer (or sometimes two), one to five accompanying singers (called *suraiyā*), a *ḍholak* player (the singers do *not* play *ḍholak* in this tradition), a *manjirā* player and, optionally, one or more players of additional rhythm

---

text *Pṛthvīrāj rāso*, was performed by the Farrukhabad *Ālhā* singers whose recitation was taken down for Sir Charles Elliott in the 1860s (see Waterfield 1923:10). This version was the basis for the first modern printed version of the *Ālhā* (Elliott 1970 [1865]) and has tended to be followed in most later printed versions as well.

[25] When I asked a group of Bundelkhand *Ālhā* singers (Mahoba, 9/11/83) what the principal episodes in the *Ālhā* were, all of them mentioned prominently the one about the 100,000 Pathans. Outside Bundelkhand, no one I mentioned it to had ever heard of it and most people insisted that it was just plain "wrong."

[26] My field recordings, which have been archived at the Archive for Ethnomusicology of the University of Washington and at the American Institute of Indian Studies Archives and Research Centre for Ethnomusicology in New Delhi, cover performances by over 65 singers. At least 25 different tunes are represented in this collection.

instruments. These instruments include *kartāl* (wooden clappers), *chimtā* (iron fire tongs with small metal clappers attached up and down each side), and *gaj* or *jhīk* (an elephant prod which is struck with another piece of metal). As one moves further towards the west, a *sārangī*-like bowed string instrument called the *chikārā* appears, playing a melodic phrase between the lines of verse.[27] Among performers who play for urban audiences, harmoniums may be added, and a famous singer of the Baiswara area has popularized the use of western clarinet as well.[28] Needless to say, audiences in each region are convinced that *their* mode of instrumentation is the superior one.

Regional traditions also differ in attention to costume and props, and in the vocabulary of gesture and facial expression. In the traditions of Baiswara and Kanauj, and in the Bhojpuri area around Banaras as well, the main singer will often have a sword that he brandishes to punctuate his singing. In the Kanauj-Baiswara region, some kind of costuming that suggests the Rajput warrior is also expected of the main singer—usually little more than a colored turban and sash tied around the waist. In Bundelkhand, on the other hand, any kind of costuming or physical prop is considered superfluous. Because the Bundelkhand singer plays his own *ḍholak* moreover, his arm and hand gestures are more limited than those of singers who perform in ensembles. His facial expressions, however, are much more varied and subtle. By contrast, singers in regions with ensemble traditions are constantly gesticulating and, not being tied down by the *ḍholak*, are free to stand up and make movements that involve their whole bodies. Facial expressions, however, are relatively underdeveloped in these traditions.

These differences in instrumentation, costume, props, gesture and facial expression are part of an overall difference in musical and dramatic style. The traditions that favor complex instrumentation and expansiveness of gesture stress action and excitement rather than emotional subtlety. Poetically, there is little

[27] This is a pattern of accompaniment that becomes increasingly common in folk music as one moves westward into Punjab and Rajasthan.

[28] His name is Lallu Vajpeyi, and he is one of the most successful *Ālhā* singers today, performing year-round and on All-India Radio. His style, flashy and dramatic, is clearly oriented to pleasing modern urban audiences.

disgression from delivery in the standard *ālhā* meter (see Chart IV), and rhythmically there is a steady, driving beat. This is the kind of performance that is expected and appreciated in Baiswara, Kanauj, and the Bhojpuri region. In Bundelkhand, by contrast, what is expected is a much greater emphasis on narrative detail and emotional expression. This is accomplished by subordinating rhythm to the demands of narrative, and bringing in a great variety of poetic material in meters other than the *ālhā* meter.

Surprisingly, linguistic differences between the *Ālhā* as recited in different dialect regions are not that great. The spoken dialect of the singer is only one of several overlapping grammatical frameworks affecting the linguistic texture of a performance. It is also affected by the local dialect of the audience (which may differ from that of the singer), the grammatical forms and pronounciation of modern standard Hindi and Urdu, patterns unique to the *Ālhā* as a genre (including the use of certain marked Bundeli forms) and, last but not least, a sort of "oral literary standard" that consists of grammatical regularities cutting across both dialectal and genre boundaries.[29] To understand the verbal content of an *Ālhā* performance thus requires much more than membership in the regional speech community. An informed listener for the *Ālhā* must be familiar with all of these grammatical frameworks as well as with the melody, rhythm, instrumentation and gestural patterns of the singers' tradition.

## Two Ālhā Performances: A Comparison

To illustrate the extent to which dramatization and texture of *Ālhā* performance vary, two performances recorded in the course of my field research are analyzed here. The first took place on August 25, 1979, in a semi-rural, semi-urban settlement on the outskirts of Kanauj (i.e. in the Kanauji dialect area). Patrons for the performance were a professor of Hindi from the local college and a doctor in the local government hospital,[30] both leaders of the

[29] I am grateful to Komal Kothari for first having pointed out to me the reality of an "oral literary standard" in the case of Rajasthani folk literature, particularly songs and poetry. The concept has not yet been explored systematically by linguists for either the Hindi or the Rajasthani area, but even a partial acquaintance with the oral literature of these regions seems to bear out the hypothesis.

[30] Prof. Ramesh Tivari and Dr. Agnihotri.

middle-class intelligentsia of Kanauj concerned with enriching the cultural life of the community. The professor of Hindi was a specialist in folk literature and interested in the *Ālhā* as a repository of regional folk concepts and values, while the doctor was an amateur archaeologist and local historian, interested in the *Ālhā* as a source for the medieval history of Kanauj. A year or so earlier, a dynamic new district magistrate had been appointed to the area who was also enthusiastic about regional folk culture, and the *Ālhā* in particular. Together, these three men had mobilized the cultural elite of the town to sponsor what was to become an annual tradition: a large-scale *Ālhā* competition, to which *Ālhā* singers would come from the district, the greater Kanauji-speaking region, Baiswara and beyond. The first competition had just taken place with about twenty *Ālhā* teams performing. It had been a great success and, in the wake of it, several local people asked singers to stay on a few days and perform in more intimate settings.

The man who was performing on August 25th, Swami Gangeshvaranand, had won third place in the competition. By profession, he had once been a primary school teacher and was now a full-time religious teacher (*swāmī*). The *Ālhā* had been his hobby for over 30 years. He was not a local man, but came from a village in the district of Unnao, in the Avadhi dialect area. He did not belong to a specific *akhāṛā* of *Ālhā* singing, but had learned in an eclectic way from hearing a variety of other people sing and from studying printed versions of the *Ālhā* of the sort sold in popular book stalls.[31]

The setting for the performance was the open courtyard in front of the Hindi professor's home. The majority of the audience of about 150 people were local laborers, herdsmen, agriculturalists, artisans and servants—the kind of people who have traditionally listened to *Ālhā* performances. Because of the sponsorship of the event, however, there were several of the town's middle-class gentry, seated to the rear on wooden chairs. The performance was formally introduced by the doctor, and Gangeshvaranand had been given careful instructions as to how long to sing (an hour and a half) and what to do: start the episode by putting it in the context of the overall story line, end it with a brief statement about himself and, most important of all, stick to the *Ālhā* story line without

[31] Swami Gangeshvaranand (Interview, Kanauj, 8/25/79).

bringing in any extraneous material. It was thus a fairly controlled performance of the type urban middle-class audiences are comfortable with, and one could perceive in the rest of the audience a certain reserve and sense of constraint because of this.

Gangeshvaranand sat on a wooden armchair. To his left, seated on the ground, were two assistant singers. To his right also seated on the ground, were the *ḍholak* accompanist, a man playing *manjirā* and a third man playing *gaj*. The episode he sang was one of the Kanauj favorites, "*Nadī Betavā kī laṛāī*," the story of the heroes' confrontation with Prithviraj Chauhan on the banks of the river Betava. The excerpt most closely examined for this paper was the duel between Lakhan, the young prince of Kanauj, and the general-in-chief of King Prithviraj, Chaunra, the duel proceeding from an exchange of increasingly provocative taunts to a fierce combat, from which Lakhan emerged victorious.

The second performance took place in August 1983, in Kharela, a village of several thousand in the Hamirpur District of Uttar Pradesh (i.e. in the Bundeli dialect area). Only an hour's journey by bus from Mahoba, and thus in the Bundelkhand heartland of the *Ālhā* tradition, Kharela has long been famous for the excellence of its *Ālhā* singing. One of the greatest *Ālhā* singers of Bundelkhand, the late Shivram Singh, was from Kharela.[32] He was the *guru* of an *akhāṛā* that popularized a particular tune throughout Bundelkhand and also developed a "literary" mode of performance in which the regular composition-in-performance (Lord 1964) is supplemented by memorized verses from various medieval literary texts in which the *Ālhā* story is found.

Once a year, right after the *mela* held on the shore of Mahoba's Kiratsagar lake, Shivram Singh's disciples gather in Kharela to honor the memory of their *guru*. The gathering lasts three to four days, during which time the disciples are the guests of Shivram Singh's oldest son, Uttam Singh, who bears all the expenses of their stay. The disciples perform daily, primarily for themselves, though anyone from the village is welcome to come and listen. The

[32] There are many stories in circulation about the power of Shivram Singh's singing. One is about a murder case in which the son of one of his relatives was involved. According to this story, Shivram Singh came and sang before the District Collector and so moved him that he dropped the case and freed the young man (Sati Din Bilthare, Interview, Mahoba, 9/7/79).

occasion is one in which, surrounded by fellow-singers who can listen critically, each man can test the limits of his ability to compose and embellish. There is no mass audience with limited attention span, nor any cultural organizer dictating when the performance should stop. As a result, each singer is free to take as long as he wants. Following a custom that began while Shivram Singh was still alive, a single episode is chosen and, with the disciples spelling each other off, that one episode is developed in the greatest of descriptive and emotional detail over the entire period of the gathering.

The gathering in 1983 lasted three days (August 27-29). Each day, towards late afternoon, all six disciples present that year (Chhote Singh, Bir Singh, Bisvanath Singh, Sultan Singh, Ram Bharosa, and Parasram) would come together in an old cowshed near the farmhouse and start singing, picking up where they had left off the previous day. The singing would continue for seven or eight hours, with listeners quietly drifting in and out and occasional breaks to smoke *bīṛīs*. In accordance with the Bundelkhand style of performance, the lead singer sat on the ground and played the *ḍholak* himself, while another man played *manjīrā*. While each man sang, the other disciples all sat around him, paying close attention, encouraging him with expressions of approval such as "*Wāh! Wāh!*", prompting him if he misremembered a memorized verse, and frequently chiming in on the last word of an especially well composed line.

The episode chosen that year was "*Bhujariyoṅ kī laṛāī*", the story of the great battle on the shore of Mahoba's Kiratsagar lake during the Bhujariyan festival, when Alha and Udal, temporarily exiled in Kanauj by king Parmal, came back to save Mahoba. Besides being the favorite episode in Bundelkhand, "*Bhujariyoṅ kī laṛāī*" is also the speciality of Shivram Singh's *akhāṛā*. As sung by the Kharela singers, the episode followed the plot line accepted in Bundelkhand, which involves a messenger from Mahoba, Arsingh, coming to Kanauj to ask for Alha and Udal's help, and the three of them together pleading and arguing with King Jaichand to let them go.

## Dramatization

Melody-wise, the two performances were very different (Charts

I and II).[33] Both tunes had a basic range of four notes, with only occasional use of higher or lower notes as embellishment or to mark a transition, but the underlying scales were not the same. Gangeshvaranand's tune was simple and straightforward, using only natural notes (no flats or sharps), as if in the western key of C-major. The Kharela tune, by contrast, used both natural and flat notes, often in chromatic sequence, which resulted in a poignant and haunting effect. Both tunes began on a high note and moved down the scale. But whereas the Kharela tune came to rest squarely on the tonic, Gangeshvaranand's tune regularly ended on the second (or alternately, on the note below the tonic), thereby creating a sense of open-endedness rather than closure.

There was also a difference in the pattern of the variations. In Gangeshvaranand's style, which is based on repetitive use of the *ālhā* meter, the variations were fixed, distinct and limited to four The first (I-1), used at stopping or turning points in the narrative, transposed the tune one note higher and ended it on the tonic. The second (I-2) simplified the melody line when it was sung at double speed. The third (I-3) was a reworking of the notes from their descending pattern to a rising and falling pattern concluding on the tonic. The fourth (I-4), used for recitative chanting, took the melody line and developed it entirely around the tonic. In the Kharela style, which is more recitative and uses a large number of poetic meters besides the *ālhā*, the variations were more numerous and somewhat free-form, differing from each other in subtle rather than dramatic ways. Thus the basic descending tune was occasionally picked up one note higher (II-1), or from below (II-2), or moved down the scale in a slightly different way (II-3, II-4). When used for recitative (II-5) or with poetic meters other than the *ālhā* (II-6, II-7), the tune was adjusted to fit the verbal material. One frequent and striking variation (II-8) was used to mark breaks and transitions. Stretching out the melody both in the middle and at the end by means of a long chromatic embellishment, it is one of the most distinctive features of the Kharela style.

Besides differing melodically, the two performances were also quite different rhythmically (Chart III).[34] The underlying *tāl* or

[33] For help in analyzing the melodies, I would like to thank Prof. Loraine Sakata.

[34] For help in analyzing the *ḍholak* and *manjirā* accompaniment of the performances, I would like to thank Pranesh Khan.

rhythmic cycle in both cases was a version of the 8-beat *kaharvā* common to much North Indian folk music. In neither style, however, was it the standard classical *kaharvā*, with its stress on the first and seventh beats (*dhā ge nā ti nā ka dhī nā*). Instead, the beats in Gangeshvaranand's performance were a syncopated *dhā gē ke nā ka dhī nā*, with the stress on the first and fourth beats. The Kharela rhythmic cycle was *te gi nā nā te gi nā nā*, with the stress on the second and sixth beats.

In Gangeshvaranand's performance, the *ḍholak* player did little more than play the basic cycle (*ṭhek*) over and over again, maintaining an unbroken beat throughout the performance, four cycles of *kaharvā* for every line of verse (or two when singing in double time). The *manjirā* and *gaj* backed it up by a steady parallel beat of their own: *tā tika tā tika tā tika tā tika*. In the Kharela performance, by contrast, the singer did *not* play the *ṭhek* while he was singing the line of verse. Instead, his drumming would pick up as he came to the last syllable of the verse and go through several cycles as an interlude or flourish between lines. His lines were not sung entirely without rhythm, however. Especially in the case of lines in *ālhā* meter, the *ṭhek* was played intermittently in the background by the *manjirā* (*tika ti nā nā tika ti nā nā*), or simply felt in the regular stresses of the recitation. Drumming therefore served differing purposes in the two performances. For Gangeshvaranand, it kept the beat, while for the Kharela singers, it served as emotional backup and punctuation. Consequently, the Kharela singers played not only the basic *ṭhek* but all sorts of variations as well, including *tihāī*s (threefold repetition of concluding phrases).

One final rhythmic difference between the two styles was in the matter of speed. Both performances began very slowly and eventually built up to an extremely fast speed of delivery (a characteristic of all *Ālhā* singing). In Gangeshvaranand's style, the acceleration was a steady forward movement, proceeding without differentiation through narrative, description and dialogue, regardless of mood or meaning. The Kharela singing, by contrast, speeded up or slowed down depending on the verbal content of the singing, using speed as yet another method of emotional underscoring.

Because the two performing groups were differently constituted, there were also differences in the voice element and in the sound of the musical accompaniment. Both Gangeshvaranand and the

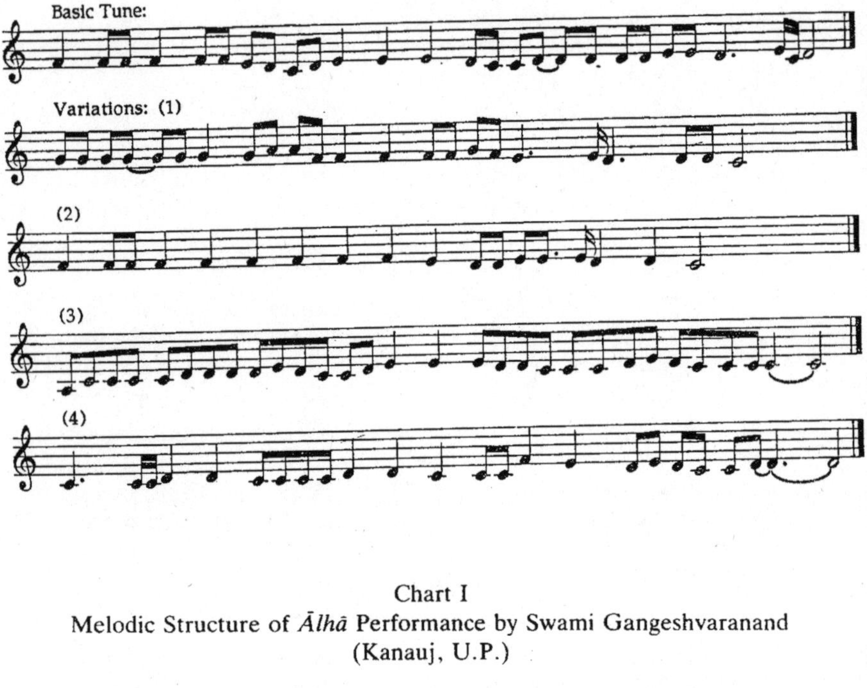


Chart I
Melodic Structure of *Ālhā* Performance by Swami Gangeshvaranand
(Kanauj, U.P.)

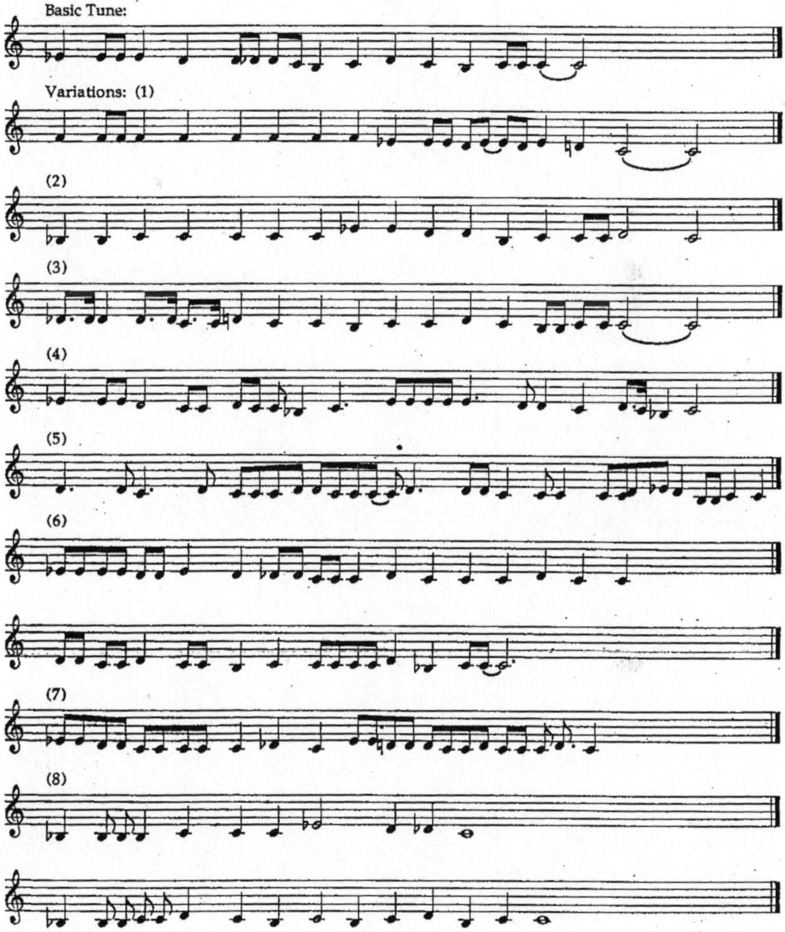


Chart II
Melodic Structure of *Ālhā* Performance by Shivram Singh's Disciples
(Kharela, U.P.)

## CHART III

### Rhythmic Structure of Two *Ālhā* Performances Compared

| | | | | | | | | |
|---|---|---|---|---|---|---|---|---|
| A. *Gangeshvaranand* (Kanauj, U.P.) | | | | | | | | |
| line of verse | e--ka | bāta yā | tum se | kahiyata, | Chauṅṛā | mā-no | kahīya | hamār |
| *manjirā* beats | tā tika | tā tika | tā tika | tā tika | tā tika | tā tika | tā tika | tā tika |
| *ḍholak* beats | dhā ge | -- ke | nā ka | dhī nā | dhā ge | -- ke | nā ka | dhī nā |
| B. *Shivram Singh's Disciples* (Kharela, U.P.) | | | | | | | | |
| line of verse | rās--tā | rvākā | vagh | Ū-dal ke, | jā-e na | pā-vai | Ma--ho-bā | gāṅv |
| *manjirā* beats | tika ti | nā nā | tika ti | nā nā | tika ti | nā nā | tika ti | nā nā |
| *ḍholak* beats | ---- | ---- | ---- | ---- | ---- | ---- | ---- | teginānā teginānā |

trikadhīnānā trikadhīnānā, dhīnādhīnā dhīdhīnānā, nātriknātrik nādhīnānā,
dhātriktriktrikdhā-- dhātriktriktrikdhā-- dhātriktriktrik dhā-

CHART IV

## Ālha Meter

| | | | | | | | |
|---|---|---|---|---|---|---|---|
| 1 2 3 4 | 5 6 7 8 | 9 10 11 12 | 13 14 15 16 | 1 2 3 4 | 5 6 7 8 | 9 10 11 12 | 13 14 (15) |
| - - - - | - - - - | -- -- | -- -- | - - - - | - - - - | -- -- | -- -- |
| khaṭa khaṭa | khaṭa khaṭa | te -- gā -- | bā -- jai -- | bo--lai-- | chhapaka chha | paka ta la | vā -- r |
| x x x x | x x x x | x x x x | x x x x | x x x x | x x x x | x x x x | x x x |
| 1 | | 2 | | 3 | | 4 | |

This verse is a perfectly regular specimen of *ālhā* meter. The first line shows *mātrā* count, the second line long and short *mātrās* (morae), the third the actual line of text, the fourth line the beats of the *tāl* (rhythmic cycle), with the first of each group of four underlined, and the fifth line the cycles of the *kaharvā* (eight-beat) *tāl*. The line is, incidentally, the single best known line of the Ālhā, an onomatopoetic one which even people only marginally familiar with the epic will know and quote to demonstrate their knowledge. It functions as a mnemonic device for remembering the structure of the *ālhā* meter. It can be translated as "Clang! Clang! go the sabers, Slash! Slash! go the swords.'

Kharela singers had the harsh voice quality and clear articulation of words characteristic of all *Ālhā* singing. But whereas the Kharela singers sang alone, Gangeshvaranand was backed up by his two accompanying singers and, from time to time, the *manjirā* and *gaj* players as well. The way they accompanied him was by coming in at the end of lines, singing the last syllable with him and then continuing on the syllable *ā-ā-ā* for two or more rhythmic cycles. This can be seen in the following example, where Lakhan swears to defeat the forces of Delhi. (Words in parentheses are sung or spoken by accompanying singers, rhythmic beats are marked by 'x').

*au karī pratigyā ham Kanauj se*
*(ā-ā-ā-ā-ā-)*
x x x x x x x x
*aba mārau bīni bīni Chauhā-na*
*(bīni bīni Chauhā-na ā-ā-ā-ā-ā-ā-)*
x x x x x x x x x x x x x
*jitane āye haiṅ gaṛhaa Dillīya se*
x x x x
*so bina ghāva e-ka na jāy*
*(ghāva e-ka na jāya ā-ā-ā-ā-ā-ā-ā-ā-)*
x x x x x x x x x x x x

I have sworn by Kanauj:
I'll pluck the Chauhan forces and kill them one by one.
Of all the men who have come from the fort of Delhi,
not a single one will return unwounded.

This drone-like vocal accompaniment continued only as long as the singing was relatively slow; when Gangeshvaranand's singing became very rapid, the accompanying voices dropped out altogether as in the following lines, where Lakhan insults Chaunra as not being a worthy opponent:

*Sunaho dulāreya Chauṅṛā e bàxasī*
x x x x
*muṅsīya suno e Āgarea kyār*
x x x x
*tumarīya hamarīya nā sarabata hai*
x x x x

*tuma charhavay Pithaurā kyār*
x x x x
•

Listen Chaunra, you darling tax-collector,
listen, you clerk of Agra!
You're no proper match for me:
you're just a hireling of Prithviraj!

Compared to other patterns of vocal accompaniment in the Kanauj-Baiswara area, in which the accompanying singers may come in on the last few syllables or even the entire second half of the lead singer's line, Gangeshvaranand's was simple and almost mechanical. In the solo performance of Kharela, there were of course no accompanying singers at all, but the performance context generated a secondary voice element of a much less mechanical nature. At points in the performance, especially when there was a particularly excellent or well-known line, singers sitting in the front row of the audience would spontaneously join the performer on the last word, shouting it aloud with great enthusiasm. There were also many interjections of "*Wāh! Wāh!*" and other expressions of approval, as well as leading questions and prompts. This can be seen in the following excerpt, in which Udal argues with King Jaichand, who has refused to let the heroes go on the grounds that they owe him a great deal for all the hospitality he gave them in exile. (*Manjirā* beats are marked by dots.)

*itanī charchā chālī jab Jaychanda ne*
• • • • |
*taba hvāṅ bvālat hai Desarāja kau lāl*
• • • • • • •
*(wāh!)*
*(mālik)*
*ek ek gehūṅ kā maiṅ nav nav daihoṅ*
*au tum kāṅ ghī kā daihoṅ chaugunā dām*
• • • •
*jitanā pānī piyo hai maiṅne torī Gangā kā*
• • •
*(wāh!)*
*au utane kāṭoṅ dūdha ke dām*
• •

*(bahut sundar!)*
*to pāī pāī āpna nṛpa kara līјai bhukatā-ā-na*
• •
*(wāhwāh!)*
*au koṛī nahīṅ chhoṛiye mālika dāya nidhān*
*(nidhān)*

When Jaichand had said this much,
then the son of Dasraj [Udal] spoke:
(Wah!)
("Master . . .")
"For every grain of wheat I'll give you nine,
and I'll pay four times the price of your ghee.
For all the water of your Ganga I have drunk,
(Wah!)
charge me the price of milk.
(Very beautiful!)
Down to the very last penny, prepare the settlement.
(Wahwah!)
Don't miss a single cowrie, O master, abode of mercy!"

In Gangeshvaranand's less intimate performance context, this element of the texture was largely absent.

In general, the voices of the Kharela singers expressed a greater emotional range than did Gangeshvaranand's. Not only was Gangeshvaranand tied to a rigid thythm that made modulation of the voice almost impossible, but his style of *Ālhā* singing was one that emphasized above all the heroic mood or *rasa*. Throughout the performance, therefore, even in passages dealing with other emotions, his tone of voice was declamatory and belligerent. The Kharela style, on the other hand, was one that emphasized the words more than the rhythm, and attached equal importance to the whole range of moods present in the *Ālhā* story. Though the dominant tone of the delivery was clearly heroic, the inflection of the singers' voices was constantly changing to express emotions of love, pathos, devotion, fear, anger, disgust, wonder, and amusement.

This difference in emotional range was also visible in the repertoires of gesture and facial expression. Gangeshvaranand sat on his armchair in a kingly pose—back straight, head held high, feet firmly planted on the ground, hands on his thighs and elbows turned outward—looking down at both his accompanists and his audience. The expression on his face was at all times stern and purposeful, conveying courage, strength and determination. As the performance progressed, this expression became more intense, tinged at times by the emotion of righteous anger or by sheer excitement in the heat of battle. He would sneer, roll his eyes, furrow his brow and make his nostrils flare—all facial expressions associated with the heroic mood. His gestures, all energetic and forceful, consisted primarily of raising one arm or the other as if brandishing a weapon, threatening to hit someone, making a proclamation or showing defiance. Occasionally, for greater effect, he would raise from his armchair/throne and pace back and forth in front of the audience, gesticulating as he sang.

The body language and facial expressions of the Kharela singers were more subdued and less histrionic. They sat on the ground, on a level with and closely surrounded by their listeners. The left leg was tucked underneath and the *ḍholak* rested on the upturned sole of the left foot; the right leg, slung over the trunk of the *ḍholak*, held it firmly in place. This position was a relaxed one that freed the hands to either play the *ḍholak* or make gestures, gave the torso flexibility, but prevented any movement away from where the singer was seated.

Since the Kharela style did not involve continuous playing of the *ḍholak*, but used it as an interlude between lines, the singers continually used their hands, arms and upper body to help dramatize the words they were singing. The vocabulary of gestures at their command was considerable. In addition to the kinds of belligerent gestures used by Gangeshvaranand, they also had gestures such as hands folded in entreaty, palms cupped to receive a gift, arms stretched out to embrace, a hand raised to the forehead in salute, the back of the fingers wiping away tears, a hand raised in the traditional gesture of blessing, fingers brought close together to express the idea of smallness, and so forth and so on.

All these gestures, though somewhat stylized, were based on those used in everyday communication, and were a direct extension of the emotions conveyed by the facial expressions. These too portrayed a broader range of feeling than was the case in Gangeshvaranand's style. The emotional expressiveness was especially apparent in passages of the story that were filled with pathos, when the facial expressions of sorrow and the gestures of pity would combine with a sob-like break in the voice to create an effect so powerful that the audience was clearly moved.

**Texture**

It is clear that the Bundelkhand performance tradition exemplified by the Kharela singers and the Kanauj-Baiswara tradition by Gangeshvaranand differ considerably in their dramatization of the *Ālhā*. Close examination of the recorded texts of their performances also reveal noticeable contrasts in verbal texture. In the grammatical structure of their language, the prosodic patterns they used and their poetic/literary style, Gangeshvaranand and the Kharela singers diverged almost as much as in the musical and dramatic aspects of their recitation.

At the level of grammatical structure, there were differences in both phonology and morphology. The phonological differences were less marked, yet clearly present. Thus both singers used the *s* sound characteristic of the regional dialects of Hindi as a whole in place of the palatal *ś* of modern standard Hindi (e.g. *sahara, Siva, sāyada, nās* instead of *śahar, Śiv, śāyad, nāś*).[35] In the case of the Kharela singers, reciting for a village audience of peers, the pattern was absolutely consistent. Gangeshvaranand, on the other hand, himself a literate man with a modern education and reciting before a partly urban middle-class audience, fluctuated frequently between the dialectal and modern standard pronunciations (e.g. *munsīya* for *munśī*, but *bādaśāha* and *śabdabedha*).

The same was true of the *z* and *x* sounds in Perso-Arabic loan words. The Kharela singers consistently assimilated them to Indic *j* (e.g. *jāhir* instead of *zāhir*) and *kh* (*khajānā* instead of *xazānā*), while Gangeshvaranand, as is typical of people educated in modern standard Hindi and who have had some contact with Urdu,[36]

[35] For a summary account of the principal dialects belonging to the Hindi language area, see Kellogg 1965.

[36] Urdu, the Persianized form of the common speech of North India, is almost identical to modern standard Hindi in its basic grammatical framework, but characterized by vocabulary derived from Persian and Arabic rather than Sanskrit.

tended more towards *z* and *x* (e.g. *taxata*, not *takhata*). Likewise, the avoidance of consonant clusters characteristic of dialectal speech (e.g. *dharam, janama, lasagara, bakasīya* instead of *dharma, janma, laśkar, baxśī*) was sporadic in Gangeshvaranand but routine with the Kharela singers—except when they were reciting memorized verses from medieval poetic texts as opposed to composing in *ālhā* meter.

Contrastive phonological features due to specific dialect included the preponderance in the Kharela singers' pronunciation of certain typical features of Bundeli: *o* vowel sounds rather than the diphtong *au*, greater nasalization of vowels (e.g. *syoṅ, jvānoṅ, pūṅcchī, sāṅchī* instead of *so, jvāno, pūcchī, sacchī*) and the frequent presence of the semivowel sounds *y* and *v* between a consonant and the following vowel (e.g. *byeṭā, lyāy, rvākā, Raṭhyauran, tyārā*). Gangeshvaranand's pronunciation, on the other hand, was not highly nasalized, fluctuated between *o* and *au* sounds, and did not have the intercalated *y/v* pattern at all.

The most noticeable phonological features of *Ālhā* recitation in general are those related to the prosodic requirements of the verbal text. First, there is a regular distortion of words at the end of lines in *ālhā* meter so they will fit the rhyme scheme (consonant + *ā* + silent consonant). Thus words like *hamārā* and *kyā* are pronounced *hamār* and *kyār*, and there is a reduction of all end of the line verbal endings to *-āy*. In addition, to fit the moraic or *mātrā* count of the poetic line, there is elongation of syllables or addition of extra syllables (e.g. *rākhoa, dharatīya, baṛeya* for *rākho, dharatī, baṛe*).

Conversely, after the manner of modern standard Hindi, there is also dropping of the word-final *a* sound following a consonant (e.g. *naulakh, mahīpālan, Lākhan, Banāphar*). The muting of final *a* was common to both performances, but the mid-line elongation and shortening was not. In Gangeshvaranand's recitation style, more rigidly bound to meter, it was very prominent, while in the recitative Bundelkhand style of the Kharela singers, it was more rare. Furthermore, the Kharela singers generally had silent final *a* at the end of words, not only because of moraic requirements but because it is the standard Bundeli pronunciation pattern.

The morphological forms shared by the two recitations included (a) those common to Bundeli, Kanauji and western Hindi dialects as a whole,[37] (b) those characteristic of the "oral literary standard," and (c) those distinctive of the *Ālhā* as a genre. The quantity of shared forms was remarkable given that one recitation was by Bundeli speakers in a totally Bundeli environment, while the other was by a man whose mother tongue was the Avadhi dialect of eastern Hindi,[38] took place in the Kanauji dialect area, and was before an audience accustomed to modern standard Hindi.

Both Gangeshvaranand and the Kharela singers used the past agentive (ergative) construction[39] for transitive verbs common to all western Hindi dialects and modern standard Hindi (e.g. *javāba Lākhana ne dīnho*, 'Lakhan replied' or *yā gata dekhī-bagh Ūdal ne*, '[when] Udal saw this situation'). Both followed the western Hindi dialectal pattern of masculine adjectival endings in *o* (tvāro, Dilliya ko versus modern standard Hindi *terā, Dilli kā*), though Gangeshvaranand used the modern standard Hindi and eastern dialectal *ā* endings as well. Similarly, both generally used the typical western dialectal past tense (e.g. *dīnho/dīnhī, bhayo/bhayī*) and future (e.g. *māraun̐/māron̐, raihon̐, pāven̐, khayihen̐*) forms rather than those of modern standard Hindi. In accordance with the general pattern of Hindi area folk poetry, and indeed of medieval Hindi poetry as well, both singers also made copious use of the unmarked verbal ending in *āy* that can be used to express any tense or mood—and happens to coincide with the *ālhā* rhyme scheme (e.g. *basāy, ḍaravāy, karavāy, pūjāy, sunāy*, etc.). Both singers used both the *ko* and the *kā* analytic postpositions (with *kā* always distorted to *kyār* in end-line position to fit the rhyme scheme).

Where the recitations differed was in the use of distinctively Bundeli forms. A striking characteristic of *Ālhā* recitation throughout the Hindi area is the use of at least a few Bundeli forms, just enough to create a certain Bundeli flavor. Gangeshvaranand's recitation followed this pattern by alternating between the locative postposition *men̐* common to most western Hindi dialects and the clearly Bundeli *mān̐*. He also made sporadic use of Bundeli

[37] For a detailed description of the western Hindi dialects, see Grierson 1968b. For the Bundeli dialect, see Jaiswal 1962.

[38] For the eastern dialects of Hindi, see Grierson 1968a.

[39] An agentive or ergative construction is one in which a transitive verb agrees in gender and number with the object rather than the subject of the sentence.

third person pronominal forms *jo/bo* (masc.) and *yā* (fem.). By contrast, the Kharela singers consistently used a large number of Bundeli forms. Thus the accusative/dative marker was always *kāṅ* instead of *ko*, and the interrogative pronouns were *kā* and *kāe* instead of *kyā* and *kyoṅ*. Past participles and past tense forms had an intercalated *y* (*rahyo, bolyo, lāgyo*) and imperfect participles had the invariable *-ata* or *-at* ending (e.g. *āvata, bvaulata, samjhāvat*). Distinctively Bundeli postpositions were used (*hūṅ* instead of *se* for 'from', *laga* instead of *tak* for 'until'), as were Bundeli forms of the possessive adjectives (*tvāro, morīya, hamarī*).

Thus while in Gangeshvaranand's recitation Bundeli forms were used sporadically, as a stylistic device, for the Kharela singers and their audience Bundeli functioned as the underlying grammatical framework. This was the case, however, only in those parts of their recitation that were in *ālhā* meter. The memorized material recited by the Kharela singers was largely in medieval Braj.[40]

Prosodically, there was a great deal of difference between Gangeshvaranand's performance and the Kharela performance. Except for an invocatory couplet (*dohā*) at the beginning, Gangeshvaranand used no meter other than the *ālhā* meter throughout his performance. In this, he was following the pattern of recitation most widespread outside Bundelkhand and most favored by patrons of modern urban *Ālhā* competitions. The Kharela singers, in accordance with the style of the Shivram Singh *akhāṛā* and Bundeli tradition in general, interspersed their recitation in *ālhā* meter with numerous fixed passages in other verse forms. These included most of the major meters of medieval Hindi poetry: *dohā, soraṭhā, rolā* and other couplet forms, four-line *kavitta* and *savaiyā* stanzas, and six-line stanzas such as the *chhappay* and *kuṇḍaliyā*.[41]

The contrast between *ālhā* meter (*ālhā chhand*) and these other verse forms is considerable. *Ālhā* meter is a single-line narrative

[40] Braj is the language of the area around Mathura and Agra. In its medieval form, also known as Pingal, it became the principal classical literary language of the Hindi area, used as a medium by poets throughout the Hindi area. For a linguistic study of Braj, see Varma 1935.

[41] For a summary description of these meters, see Pandey 1972:129-49.

meter rather than a stanzaic form. The *ālhā* line is asymetrical, consisting of a first half-line of sixteen *mātrās* (morae) and a second half-line which can be considered either fifteen or fourteen *mātrās* long depending on whether the final consonant (which is always pronounced mute) is counted as a *mātrā* or not. The rhyme scheme is unchanging: consonant + *ā* + mute consonant (e.g. -*bāt, -dām, -mār, -prāṇ, -vāy, -yār*, etc.). Though the *ālhā* meter is fairly loose, the two half-lines tend to break down rhythmically into four evenly stressed feet that coincide most of the time with the four stresses of the accompanying *kaharvā tāl* played on *ḍholak* and *manjirā*. The prosodic texture is therefore inseparable from the musical rhythm, and is in fact created by the interplay between the rhythm of the words and that of the percussion accompaniment.

*Ālhā* meter has a driving, relentless quality to it, intensified by the repetitive *tāl* played on *ḍholak* on the high speed at which singers sing much of the time—especially in the traditions of the Kanauj-Baiswara region. In Gangeshvaranand's performance, this was the sum total of the prosodic texture. In the Kharela performance, by contrast, only half of the material was in *ālhā* meter. Whereas the effect of Gangeshvaranand's performance was almost hypnotic in its prosodic regularity, the Kharela recitation was full of surprises. Just as the singer's audience would start being lulled by the repetitiveness of the *ālhā* meter, he would suddenly switch to a couplet or other stanzaic form, breaking the spell. Thus, after a long section of narrative in *ālhā* meter, in which Udal was trying to dissuade Lakhan from joining the expedition, there was a sudden switch to the *savaiyā* meter and a memorized verse in medieval Braj at the point where Lakhan declared his determination to go in spite of everything.

*au balbhara gādī kāḍhī thī Lākhan ne*
• • • • •
*gaj bhar nikal parī tarvār*
• • • •
*au aise Udal kā lalkāre*
• • • •
*Udal lauṭa jībha mūṅh ḍāl*
• • • x x x x x x x x x x x x
*Lākhana ima uccharai suna Udala mama bānī*
*o pahale janga hama karaiṅ baraiṅ apchara mana mānī*

*khaṇḍa khaṇḍa tana kaṭṭa īsa gala muṇḍa mela hūṅ*
*au pakar leṅva Prithīrāja sūra surapura kā jhelūṅ*
*(jhenūṅ)*

With all his strength, Lakhan pulled out his sword,
and drew it out a full yard.
(Wah!)
He spoke to Udal thus:
"Udal, put your tongue back in your mouth!"
Lakhan spoke thus: "Listen, Udal, to my words.
I'll be the first in battle, I'll accept whatever happens.
If my body is cut to pieces, I'll cut off my head for the sake of my lord.
I'll capture the warriors of Prithviraj and send them to heroes' heaven!"

Similarly, when the singer sensed his audience tiring from the concentration needed to follow the more complex meters (and poetic language) of his memorized verses, he would break the tension by slipping back into the familiar prosodic groove of the *ālhā* meter. The Kharela performance was thus far more richly textured in its prosody than was Gangeshvaranand's. The special audience of disciples in Kharela, and Bundelkhand audiences more generally, are trained by experience to expect this prosodic variety and challenge, whereas audiences in the Kanauj-Baiswara area expect the steady pulse of the *ālhā* from the beginning of the performance to the end.

Stylistically, the two performances also had very different textures. In general, Gangeshvaranand's was much more prosaic, a straightforward linear narrative interspersed with passages of dialogue, the plot being moved ahead step by step without much digression or poetic embellishment. By contrast, the Kharela singers' narrative meandered back and forth between action, dialogue, flashback and commentary, with poetic embellishment and digressions at every opportunity.

The principal device used to create this variety was the alternation between the leaner narrative material in *ālhā* meter (referred to by Bundelkhand singers as *sairā*) and the rich poetic material from medieval literary texts (referred to as *raiso*)[42] brought in to flesh out the narrative, create more vivid description and underscore particular ideas, feelings and words. This can be seen, for example, when Alha, Udal and Arsingh arrive before King Jaichand, and Alha first asks King Jaichand for permission to go to Mahoba, making his request in a Braj quatrain.

*Ālha Udda Arasṛnga nṛpa gaye Pangu ke pā-ā-sa*
• • • •
*au darvānī jāhir kiyo ki āyo Ālha udās (udās)*
• • • • • • •
*taba bhūpata Jaychandra kah lyāo Ālha livā-āy*
• • • • • • •
*syoṅ Arsiṃh Udal sahitā-ā-ā*
*au bangalā pahuṅcha gi jā-ā-ā-yo-o*
x x x x x x x
*(ohoho!)*
*(āyā)*
• • • • • • • • • • • • • x x x x
*āyā Alha Jaychandra juhāriyo*
• • •
*au kara bintī*
• • • • •
*(wāhwāh!)*
*(svāmihita bachana)*
*svāmihita bachana uchāryo*
• • • • • • •
*(Prathīrāja pad)*
*Prathīrāja pad dharyo āna Mahobe par chaḍḍyo*

[42] The source texts referred to collectively by the singers as *raiso* were principally three: the Mahoba section (*Mahobā khaṇḍ*) of the courtly epic *Pṛthvīrāj rāso*, the so-called *Parmāl rāso* (Das 1919), and an extremely rare text called the *Gyānī raso* (Das 1919). Though the singers in Kharela and others I met in Bundelkhand showed me manuscripts in their possession which they claimed to be one or the other of these three, there was no opportunity to scrutinize these manuscripts at length and make a determination. For a comparison between the narratives in these medieval texts and that of the oral tradition as set down in modern-day printed versions of the *Ālhā* (called *Ālhakhaṇḍ*), see Mishra 1983.

*au Māhila bhūpata chugala bhūpa batatīna bagajyo*
• • •
*ghera sahara chahuṅ ora te desa māra ujāriyo*
• • •
*(ujjāriyo)*
*au Arasiṃha āyo mama lena hita nṛpa Paramāla paṭhāiyo*
*(paṭhāiyo)*

Alha, Udal and Arsingh went before King Pangu [Jaichand]
and the doorman announced: "Alha has come, dejected."
Then King Jaichand said; "Bring Alha in,
along with Arsingh and Udal."
And he [Alha] came into the palace.
(Ohoho!)
(He came . . )
Alha came and bowed to Jaichand
and made his request,
(Wahwah!)
("Speaking for the sake of his lord . . .")
("Prithviraj set foot . . ."
"Prithviraj set foot in Mahoba and attacked it,
And Prince Mahil [the traitor in the story] goaded the king
with deceitful words.
He surrounded the city from all sides and devastated the
land.
(Devastated . . . )
And Arsingh has come to get me, King Parmal sent him."

The use of *raiso* material also contributed to a much greater range of vocabulary in the Kharela performance. While Gangeshvaranand used mostly everyday words from contemporary speech, the memorized verses recited by the Kharela singers brought in a whole archaic layer of vocabulary evoking the time period of the epic events (words like *nṛpa* for 'king' or *astra* for 'weapons', constructions like *mama lena hita*, 'to get me', verbal forms like *rissyo, subhakhyo, dunnyo*). Furthermore, even in the *sairā* portions of the performance, the Kharela singers tended towards language that was vivid, concrete and idiomatic, while Gangeshvaranand had a tendency towards statement that was general and abstract, not richly evocative. Thus Gangeshvaranand would simply state that a character was angry, or afraid. The Kharela singers, by contrast, used idiomatic expressions such as *peṭa ḍolo* ('he trembled on the inside'), *ḍoli batīsī* ('his 32 [teeth] chattered') or *mūṅh kā bolā banda par jāy* ('his speech was trapped in his mouth').

Use of traditional poetic devices (similes, metaphors, alliteration, punning, repetition, parallelism, etc.) was much more frequent and elaborate in the Kharela performance. Conversely, though all composition in *ālhā* meter makes considerable use of formulas, Gangeshvaranand's "text" was much more heavily formulaic than that of the Kharela singers.[43] While Gangeshvaranand's recitation was full of the typical *Ālhā* formulas known to singers of all the traditions (e.g. *ekai bāta yā tuma para kahiyata, so tumi māni leo kahīya hamār*, 'I've got this one thing to say to you, pay attention to my words'), the Kharela singers composed in a more individualistic way, breaking away from the formulas or playing around with them in unusual ways. In particular, they would frequently avoid a standard *Ālhā* formula and instead say the same thing using archaic *raiso* language (e.g. *taba nṛpa Jaichand boliyo ima bānī*, 'then King Jaichand spoke these words').

Another noticeable difference between the two performances was the amount of proverbial material incorporated into the recitation of the Kharela singers. Whenever one of their characters was making an argument for something, it would be backed up by a whole catalogue of proverbial precedents and statements of general principles. Thus when Prince Lakhan argued that his friendship with Udal compelled him to go on the expedition, he quoted a whole list of proverbial sayings to underscore how precious friendship is.

*Gangā kara daī hai maiṅne bagha Udal se*
• • • • •
*au chhātī lau Gange goṅv majhiyāy*
• • • •
*to bīrā vahī jo bechāra ke khaīye*
• •

[43] The recitation of the *Ālhā* in all respects follows the formulaic "composition in performance" pattern described by Albert Lord (1964). For the formulaic composition of an *Ālhā* passage, see Lutgendorf 1979.

*au hīrā vahī ghana choṭa na phuṭai*
*(uhūn!)*
*au bāja vahī jo gahai bar tītur*
*au rāja vahī jahāṅ chora na muchai*
*(muchai)*
*putra vahī jo pita ko navai*
*au mitra vahī asaneha na ṭūṭai*

"I bound myself to the lion Udal by an oath on the Ganga,
going out midstream in the Ganga, up to my chest.
A betel-leaf [i.e. a challenge] is something to take up only
upon due reflection.
A diamond is something that doesn't break even when struck.
A hawk is something that can catch fine partridges.
A kingdom is a place where a thief can't get away.
A son is someone who bows to his father.
And a friend is someone whose love is unbroken."

There were also frequent appeals to analogies from tradition. Thus when King Jaichand tried to dissuade Udal from going to the aid of Mahoba on grounds that King Parmal had insulted the Banaphars by exiling them, Udal recited a litany of all the great personages who had brought good to the world by enduring insults.

*pratiuttara kara jora kai au suno Pangu mahārā-āja*
*bvolai Bendulā kau chaṛhvaiyā*
*(dādā)*
*au je aneādara āpa kahe so kara āye par kāj*
*(par kāj)*
• • • • • •
*aneādara srī Rāma deva muni kāraja sarāyo*
*(hāṅ!)*
• •
*au aneādara Prahlāda devapura hū tama bhāryo*
*(bhāryo)*
• •
*aneādara bhaye Dhruvo aṭala padavī so pāīye*
• •
*au aneādara bhaye Pāṇḍu janga jitta adhikāīye*
*(kāīye)*

Bendula's rider [Udal] replied with folded hands:

> "Listen, King Pangu [Jaichand])!
> Those you say were insulted acted for the benefit of others.
> Because he was insulted, Rama accomplished the aims of the gods and sages.
> Because he was insulted, Prahlada removed the darkness from the heavens.
> And because they were insulted, the Pandavas won many battles.

Finally, in terms of traditional Indian poetics, the Kharela singers' performance was one that evoked many different *rasas* or aesthetic moods, while Gangeshvaranand concentrated exclusively on the heroic mood (*vīra rasa*).[44] Thus, at the level of literary style as well as grammar and prosody, the two performances diverged and called for different audience competencies.

## Conclusion

By closely examining two *Ālhā* performances by singers representative of different regional traditions, we have seen how much a "common" epic tradition can differ in dramatization and texture. The extent to which these differences are reenforced by audience expectations (i.e. "preventive censure") was dramatically illustrated by two parallel occurrences which took place during the 1983 recitation season. Because it was the 800th anniversary of the 1182/83 battle between King Prithviraj Chauhan of Delhi and King Parmal of Mahoba, cultural organizers in Bundelkhand had invited *Ālhā* singers from all over the Hindi area to come to Mahoba for a three-day *Ālhā* festival. A month after that event, the annual *Ālhā* competition in Kanauj took place on an unprecedented scale because of the interest shown by the central government's Minister of Tourism, who attended the opening session.[45]

[44] A statement frequently made by Bundelkhand singers is that the greatness of the *Ālhā* lies in the fact that it has in it "all nine of the *rasas*." Far from adhering to the classical ideal of Indian dramatic theory that *rasas* should not be mixed, Bundelkhand *Ālhā* singers delight in displaying every *rasa* from the heroic to the comic.

[45] The Minister of Tourism was Khurshid Alam Khan.

Thus in both Mahoba and Kanauj, there was opportunity to observe what happens when singers from one region perform before audiences of another. In Mahoba, the audience listened in pin-drop silence and with total concentration as long as singers from the Bundelkhand tradition were performing, but people started becoming restless whenever Kanauj-Baiswara ensemble groups came on.

In Kanauj, the audience "censure" was even more obvious in its expression. The local organizers had decided to allot a whole three-hour period of evening "prime time" to the singers from Bundelkhand, as a way of introducing their style to the local audience. Innocently, the Bundelkhand singers chose to perform one of their favorite episodes, the story of how Alha as a young boy fought off 100,000 Muslim Pathans. After a short period of tolerant attentiveness, the audience, bored with what it perceived as the musical monotony of the performance, began to titter and break into whispered comments. As the story unfolded, boredom began to be replaced by disbelief and eventually anger. Comments began to be heard: "That's not in the *Ālhā*!", "They've made it all up!" People started getting up and walking out, mimicking and making fun of the recitation style of the Bundelkhand performers. Eventually, to avoid pandemonium, the organizers had to ask the Bundelkhand singers to leave the stage and called up familiar local singers in their place. The audience had successfully exercised the preventive censure in its role as patron.

## References

Crooke, William. 1986. *The Tribes and Castes of the North-Western Provinces and Oudh*. 4 vols. Calcutta: Office of the Superintendent of Government Printing.

Cunningham, Alexander. 1969. *Archaeological Survey of India* 21, 1-2. Reports of a Tour in Rewa, Bundelkhand, Malwa and Gwalior in 1884-85. Varanasi: Indological Book House (first published 1885).

Das, Shyam Sundar. 1919. (editor) *Parmāl rāso*. Banaras: Nagari Pracharini Sabha.

Dvivedi, Loknath 'Silakari'. 1969. *Mahākavi Jagnik aur unkā lok-gāthā-kāvya Ālhā*. Sagar: Department of Hindi, Sagar University.

Elliott, C.A. 1970. (editor) *Aslī Ālhakhaṇḍ 23 laṛāī*. Farrukhabad, U.P.: Lala Chintamani Shivcharan Lal (first published 1865).

Fish, Stanley. 1972. *Self-Consuming Artifacts*. Berkeley: University of California Press.

Grierson, George A. 1885a. (editor and translator) "The Song of Alha's Marriage: A Bhojpuri Epic." *Indian Antiquary* 14:209-27.

————. 1885b. "A Summary of the Alha Khand." *Indian Antiquary* 14:255-60.

————. 1968a. (collector and editor) *Linguistic Survey of India*. Vol. 6. "*Indo-Aryan Family. Mediate Group.*" Reprint ed. Delhi: Motilal Banarsidass (first pubished 1916).

————. 1968b. (collector and editor) *Linguistic Survey of India. Vol. 9, part 1. Indo-Aryan Family. Central Group*. Reprint ed. Delhi: Motilal Banarsidass. (first published 1916).

*Gupta, Narmada Prasad. 1983. Ālhakhaṇḍ kā rachayitā mahākavi Jagnik*. In Narmada Prasad Gupta and Virendra 'Nirjhar', eds., *Ālhakhaṇḍ: śodh aur samīkṣā*. Chhatarpur, M.P.: Bundelkhand Sahitya Akademi.

Jaiswal, M.P. 1962. *A Linguistic Study of Bundeli (A Dialect of Madhyadesa)*. Leiden: E.J. Brill.

Jason, Heda. 1969. "A Multidimensional Approach to Oral Literature: A Proposal." *Current Anthropology* 10:413-26.

————. 1988. Marginalia to B. Bogatyrev and R. Jakobson's Essay "Die Folklore als eine besondere Form des Schaffens." Unpublished manuscript.

Kellogg, S.H. 1965. *A Grammar of the Hindi Language*. 3rd ed. London: Routledge and Kegan Paul, Ltd. (first published 1938; first edition published 1875).

Lord, Albert B. 1964. *The Singer of Tales*. Cambridge, Mass: Harvard University Press.

Lutgendorf, Philip. 1979. "The Alha Cycle: Oral and Written Dimensions of a North Indian Epic Tradition." Unpublished paper.

Mishra, Bhagirath. 1983. *"Pṛthvīrāj Rāso kā Mahobākhaṇḍ, Paramālrāso aur Ālhakhaṇḍ par ek tulanātmak dṛṣṭi."* In Narmada Prasad Gupta and Virendra 'Nirjhar', eds., *Ālkhanaṇḍ: śodh aur samīkṣā*. Chhatarpur, M.P.: Bundelkhand Sahitya Akademi.

Pandey, Shambhunath. 1972. *Ras, alankār, pingal*. Agra: Vinod Pustak Mandir.

Pandey, Shyam Manohar. 1979. *The Hindi Oral Epic Loriki (The Tale of Lorik and Chanda)*. Allahabad: Sahitya Bhavan.

Parmar, Shyam. 1975. *Traditional Folk Media in India*. New Delhi: Geka Books.

Schomer, Karine. 1989. "Paradigms for the Kali Yuga: The Heroes of the *Ālhā* Epic and Their Fate." In Stuart Blackburn, Peter Claus, Joyce Flueckiger and Susan Wadley, eds., *Oral Epics in India*. Berkeley: University of California Press.

Tivari, Ramesh. 1979. *Ālhā pratiyogitā Kanauj, 11-12 August 1979: smārikā*. Kanauj, U.P.: Puratatva Sangrahalay.

Varma, Dhirendra. 1935. *La langue braj (dialecte de Mathura)*. Paris: Adrien-Maisonneuve.

Waterfield, William. 1923. (translator) *The Lay of Ālhā: A Saga of Rajput Chivalry as Sung by Minstrels of Northern India*. Oxford: Oxford University Press.

# PART TWO

## Changing Patrons

# A Tradition of Change: The Role of Patrons and Patronage in the *Kathakaḷi* Dance-Drama

Phillip B. Zarrilli

## Introudction

As a performing art tradition, *kathakaḷi*, the dance-drama of Kerala, shares with other Indian traditions (religious, literary, etc.) certain general characteristics. All traditions may be thought of as dynamic systems of human action constantly in an ongoing process of generation and degeneration. A tradition exists simultaneously as (1) an inherited collection of established ways of feeling, thinking, and doing which are passed down through generations, and (2) the active and ongoing process of transmitting what has been handed down orally or through written records. A tradition, then, is created, maintained or changed by a dynamic ongoing interplay between what is received and what is passed on to the next generation. The rules, boundaries, restrictions, and process of transmission and cultural valuation of the tradition within a diachronically variable social hierarchy determine the degree of maintenance, sameness and constancy, versus variation, change, transformation, or degeneration within any tradition through time. In the dynamic interplay of individual and social forces in any culture, particular traditions may be maintained with only subtle differences, or altered in slight but significant ways, or transformed into something so totally different that only a vestige of the original remains, or absorbed completely by a new manifestation of the same tradition, or degenerate and eventually die. Indeed all of the above may be part of the 'life' of a given tradition.

A performance tradition is one type of culturally assumed and often self-consciously identified system of human action organized around a particular type of performance.[1] For *kathakaḷi*, as for other similar artistic genres, its origin, maintenance, and alteration as a culturally distinct performance tradition have been inextricably linked to its patronage. Such artistic traditions incorporate patronage necessarily, and their social and performative history are directly and indirectly related to their patrons.

[1] Performance is here defined as an active doing-in-the-moment of a prescribed set of actions, and/or an improvised set of actions circumscribed by a set of assumed conventions. A performance *per se* is any diachronically and processually performed, and conventionally framed set of such actions. Conventions consciously and reflexively communicate or implicitly convey cultural values of the social context or frame of the performance. A performance form or genre is a system of interactive phenomena, composed of determinants, conventions, sets of techniques, and aesthetic principles which collectively constitute the form. A performance tradition encompasses both the performance system in all its particularity of techniques, as well as the socio-structural network within which is is located. For the discussion which follows, each of the key aspects of a performance system may be defined as follows:

> *Performance determinants* are specific "fields of action" which collectively create a performance. Such "fields of action" include those which create sounds, visual images, and/or serve as fundamental constraints to other determinants. A major constraint for performative fields of action is a text or scenario. In *kathakaḷi* the text is an important determinant, and performative determinants or fields of action which "present" text include vocal music, percussion music, actors' sounds; performer's in-body movements and actions (including independent systems of movement such as choreography, hand gestures, facial gestures, character or interpretative gestures); visual means of presentation in the form of costumes and make-up; and finally physical means of staging (space). Each determinant is presented in performance through sets of associated techniques and conventions.
>
> *Performance techniques* are specific systems of action used to produce performance determinants or "fields of action." Techniques are the performer's methods of "doing" in each moment of performance. *Kathakaḷi* has a set of techniques for playing each percussion instrument, a set of techniques for footwork, etc. For a particular tradition to continue through succeeding generations, performance knowledge must be transmitted as systems of human action.
>
> *Performance text*, although only one determinant and constraint, is central in highly literate traditions as the 'base line' for other determinants. Text must be distinguished from *performance score*, which consists of all created and received conventions and techniques that collectively guide the complete composition. In performances like *kathakaḷi* which have text as a central element, the score is the skeletal structural arrangement of which text is one part.

The role of a patron is only one of a network of interrelated roles within the artistic tradition. The life of an Indian performance tradition is shaped by the interplay between (1) the behavioral assumptions ascribed to any given *jati* (role and function-specific group) within a tradition, (2) the socio-structural relations between these *jatis*, and (3) the techniques, conventions, and aesthetic principles which define and delimit the genre. Major roles within performance traditions like *kathakaḷi* include (1) patrons (or more recently sponsors, board members and/or administrators) who provide financial support, organize and appreciate performances; (2) artists who create the performance; (3) students who are trained in the techniques of the genre; (4) audiences for whom performances are given; and (5) craftspeople who specialize in creating the appurtenances of performance and assistants who care for costumes. Within this web of distinct artistic relationships, change or alteration introduced by any individual playing any role in any given aspect of the performance will affect the entire network of relationships as well as the fabric of the performance.

This set of artistic roles exists within the particular socio-structural and socio-economic context of a given historical period. Each artistic role traditionally exists as one role in a "role set" (Merton, 1957) associated with a particular social status within the caste

*Performance conventions* are all articulated, selfconscious, and/or assumed parameters of practice which guide and shape the use and expression of sets of techniques in performance. For example, assumed (and occasionally articulated) conventions surround the delivery style of techniques for use of the hands in *kathakaḷi*. Such conventions include the spatial area which hands may use in circumscribing and delivering *mudrās*. Conventions guide the use of stage space, such as the use of stage right by characters of higher status and stage left by characters of lower status.

*Performance frames* are the acknowledged or assumed boundaries and markers which set apart the performance from other human action. *Kathakaḷi* has a series of formal public preliminaries to the performance proper which demarcate our everyday world from the performance. A concluding delivery of verses and dance encapsulates the performance and completes its actual and symbolic action.

For a complete discussion of the structure of the *kathakaḷi* performance score, conventions, determinants, and frames, see Zarrilli, 1984a.

hierarchy.[2] The role of "patron" in an artistic tradition like *kathakaḷi* is associated only with a certain segment of the hierarchy, so also for "actors" and "craftsmen." Each artistic role is historically and contextually specific, and therefore changes through time with alterations in wider socio-structural and economic contexts.

My purpose here is to re-read the social and performative history of *kathakaḷi* in order to understand the specific roles patrons have played in the life of the *kathakaḷi* performance tradition, and how changes in that role through time have affected the tradition.[3] From the historical and anthropological literature available I examined examples of both the role of patrons within the social hierarchy, and the role of patrons within the artistic tradition itself in each of three phases of *kathakaḷi* history: (1) the formative years from its origins in the late seventeenth to the late eighteenth century, by which time the genre had evolved into what we recognize today as *kathakaḷi*; (2) the mature years from the late eighteenth to the late nineteenth century during which time there was further refining of the subtle expressive possibilities within carefully circumscribed performative limits of the tradition; and (3) the modern period beginning with a resurgence of interest sparked by poet Vallathol's establishment of an institution for teaching and preserving the genre in the late 1920's. Most attention will be given to the disjuncture between the socio-structural and artistic roles of patrons in the modern period. I conclude by asking whether the center/periphery model which emerges in the *kathakaḷi* example is generally applicable to performance traditions.[4]

[2] As Merton (1957) pointed out, any particular social status is characterized by a "complement of role-relationships" which he defined as a "role-set" or role complex. Within medieval Kerala, "patronage" was one multifaceted role within a series of social roles constituting the "role set" associated with the social status of ruler.

[3] For the specific history of *kathakaḷi* see Jones (1983), and Menon (1957). E. Easwaran Namboothiry *Bālarāmabharatam: A Critique on Dance and Drama* (1983) includes a substantive summary of the authorship and patronage of Maharaja Kartikatirunal Balarama Varma (1724-1798), a major figure in the mature years of southern style *kathakaḷi*. I depend on these three sources for my brief summary of the formative and mature years of *kathakaḷi's* development. Future research on patronage in Kerala will be aided by archival resources of the principalities and of patron families which remain largely untapped resources.

The section on the modern period is based on fieldwork conducted in 1976-77 and 1980 while on Fulbright and American Institute of Indian Studies fellowships.

[4] My use of "center/periphery" emerged over the years of my study of the *kathakaḷi* tradition, appearing in preliminary form while preparing Chapter 7 of

## The Roles of Royal Patrons in the Formative Years of the *Kathakaḷi* Tradition

The name *kathakaḷi* (story play) was first used to refer to an already existing dance-drama tradition known as *rāmanāṭṭam* (dance of Rāma), after the Prince of Kottayam (1645-1716) wrote a set of four plays based on stories from the *Mahābhārata* (authored between 1665 and 1681). Prior to this time, the dance-drama had been known as *rāmanāṭṭam* because all the plays performed in this style were based on stories about Rāma from the *Rāmāyaṇa*. The original cycle of eight *rāmanāṭṭam* plays was authored by the ruling prince of the Kottarakkara family of southern Kerala.[5] Both the Kottarakkara and Kottayam princes belonged to the highest section of the Nayar caste.

*Rāmanāṭṭam-kathakaḷi* received its earliest patronage primarily from such high-ranking ruling Nayar families, although there was also support and involvement from a few Kśatriya ruling families, such as the Venttattu Raja of the early seventeenth century (Jones 1983:18-19). Another instance of royal authorship and patronage is the closely related devotional dance-drama tradition, *kṛṣnāṭṭam*. Like *rāmanāṭṭam* it is a cycle of eight plays, although its subject is the story of Śrikṛṣna. *Kṛṣnāṭṭam* texts were composed by a member of the most powerful ruling family of the period, Manaveda, who served as Zamorin of Calicut between 1655 and 1658.

These examples show that patronage was readily accepted as one role within the 'role set' assumed by royal lineages. However, the role of patron itself was multifaceted and not limited simply to providing a disinterested means of financial support for a special group of artists in his service. Rather, it was a role in which the patron himself was often directly involved in shaping the life of the performance tradition. The multifaceted role of the early *kathakaḷi* patron was fourfold. First, there was provision for the social and

---

*The Kathakaḷi Complex: Actor, Performance, Structure* (Zarrilli 1984). Dean MacCannell's analysis of anthropology as "a dialectical tension of center and periphery" (1979:149) is similar to my use of the terms.

[5] Difficult historical questions about much of the early history of *rāmanāṭṭam-kathakaḷi*, and the relationship of *kṛṣnāṭṭam* to the emergence of *kathakaḷi* remain unresolved. Among these are the proposed dates for composition of the original *rāmanāṭṭam* plays, the range varying widely from 1484 to 1660. Jones (1983:16) accepts Menon's argument for 1555-1605 (1957:6). See also Namboodiri 1983:35.

economic means necessary to realize the art. Second, the ruler-as-patron was often an author/composer of performance texts (*āṭṭakatha*). Third, he was often directly involved in making decisions about the performative realization of his texts on stage. And finally, the ruler-as-patron was himself the ideal audience member, a *rasika* for whom the performance could serve as a means of at least temporary transcendence through his enlightened appreciative sensibilities.

### The Socio-Economic Basis of Traditional Patronage

The socio-economic basis for *kathakaḷi* patronage at the time of its origin was the fundamental unit, "house and land" (Moore 1983:273; also Miller 1954, 1955; Mencher 1966). The right to hold land was only in possession of the highest ranking non-polluting castes (Puthenkalam 1977:14)—Namboodiri Brahmins, the royal lineages (including a few Kśatriya groups and the highest-ranking title-holding Nayars, often called Samanthans), lesser ranking Nayar chiefs (*naduvaris*) and/or village heads (*dēsavaris*), and temples.[6]

[6] For a complete account of the caste structure of traditional Kerala see Fuller 1976:34; Jeffrey 1976:9-26; Puthenkalam 1977:16-25; Gough and Schneider 1961: 306-314; Moore 1983:268-289. Most sources generally agree with the following ordering of castes, listed by decreasing status as follows:

NON-POLLUTING HIGH CASTES
- Namboodiri Brahmins
  - landlords of large estates
  - lower sub-castes owning smaller estates, temple priests, physicians, household priests, cooks
- Other Foreign Brahmins
- Kśatriyas
- Samantans (and other titled royal lineages of Nayars)
- Ambalavasis (temple servants)
- Nayars
- middle ranking retainers
- various specific lower ranking serving sub-groups including serving in Brahmin kitchens, servants to Namboodiris and rulers, bearers, washermen, barbers and midwives, or funeral priests.

HIGHER POLLUTING CASTES
- Kammalas (artisan castes including carpenters, stone-carvers, blacksmiths, brass and coppersmiths, and goldsmiths)
- Tiyyars, Izhavas or Thandans,
- Chovans (tenant farmers, toddy tappers)
- Kaniyans (astrologers and agricultural laborers)

Those with the right to hold land did so by birth right (*janmam*). The majority of those working and living on the land did so by tenure (*kanam*), in service to those holding *janmam* rights (Moore 1983:281ff; Gough 1961:308-309).

The basic unit, "house and land," was ideally intended to be a self-sufficient microcosm,

> designed to contain a more or less complete set of the beings inhabiting the universe and the entire set of life-cycle events of persons who are its members . . . [T]he rest of society seems to remain solitary by means of a set of ritual relationships defined relative to it. (Moore 1982:26)

The ideal microcosm (house and land) was only realized by those at the very top of the hierarchy, Namboodiri Brahmins, the aristocratic Kśatriya or Nayar ruling lineages, or large temples dedicated to pan-Indian Puranic deities. Each house and its land provided for

> not merely subsistence, but the conduct of cultural activities (temple maintenance, festivals); and was not satisfied merely with things, but required persons of all kinds (i.e., *jatis*) who were either granted along with the land (e.g., the Cerumans) or encouraged to settle on it (e.g., the Izhavas and artisans) (Ibid:142).

Whether held by proprietary birth right (*janmam*) by a Namboodiri Brahmin, Kśatriya, or one of Nayar lineage, or by a temple, the basic unit, house and its land, supported (i.e., "patronized") those cultural activities associated with the ritual necessities of the unit as a microcosm. Most performing arts of the region prior to the emergence of *rāmanāṭṭam/kathakaḷi* were ritual arts—each was an integral part of a daily/calendrical cycle of ritual propitiation, or life-cycle or crisis ritual performances intended to prevent or alleviate disaster and disease (smallpox). Such arts

---

LOWER POLLUTING CASTES

Mukkuvans and Aryans (fishermen)
Pulayas or Cherumans (Harijan castes)
Parayas

were supported by the interdependent network of castes in service to a particular house (or temple) and its land.

Even the most aesthetic and literary virtuoso traditional Kerala theatre, the regional Sanskrit dramas *kūtiyāṭṭam*, was integrated within the socio-economic, *jati*, and ritual network of pan-Indian Puranic temples. Performers were drawn from the ranks of Ambaḷavasis, intermediate ranking temple service castes, specifically *cakyar*s and *nambyar*s. Patronage, as financial support of the network of performers and artisans necessary to put on performances, was part of the obligation of the temple as a base-unit, "house and its land." Only those temples had the right and duty to maintain performers and hold calendrical performances as "visual sacrifices" for the primary deity of the temple (Richmond and Richmond 1985:54; see also Jones 1967, Raja 1964, and Richmond 1978).

Similarly, both the right and the socio-economic means to conceive, organize, create and patronize a performance genre like *rāmanāṭṭam/kathakaḷi* or *kṛṣnāṭṭam* would *only* have been appropriate for those whose positions in the hierarchy accorded them the "rights and duties," wealth, and network of service castes necessary to realize a particular type of performance. Unlike patronage of yearly temple festivals required to propitiate deities under a family's jurisdiction, and unlike Nayar *tarvāḍu*s' commissioning *pāmbin tuḷḷal* to ensure fertility and prosperity (Neff 1987), there was initially no obligation to patronize *kathakaḷi*. At first, patronage must have been taken on for a variety of reasons, including personal devotion inspired by a general increase in Vaishnavite (Rāma and Kṛṣna) *bhakti* (Jones 1983:15); a means of accentuating the traditional role of royal patrons as protectors of the social order; and engagement in an activity appropriate to one's status, and enhancing status and prosperity. Patronizing the arts was one among many ways of acquiring "good fruits" for both family and kingdom (Moore 1983:159-168), thereby helping to ensure general prosperity.

Prompted by such motivations, *rāmanāṭṭam-kathakaḷi* was brought to the stage within the pre-existing socio-economic network of the Kerala unit, "house and land." Among those *jati*s in service to royal Nayar lineages who fostered the art were middle-ranking Nayars. They were "vassals" (*adiyar*) and formed the retinue (*akampaḍi*)—established by taking a vow to death to serve the ruler

(Zarrilli 1978:39-45). The relative power and rank of royal lineages was partially based on the number of Nayar soldiers in service to a particular ruler. Those Nayars forming an *akampaḍi* held land as tenants (*kanakkaran*) in return for service to their lords. Special titles were conferred on some Nayars, such as Panikkar (teacher, usually of the traditional martial art, *kalarippayattu*), or Kurup (material art master).[7]

These Nayars, trained in the highly energetic and fluid martial tradition, expected to actualize *vīra* (heroism) in their martial practice, became the first performers (Zarrilli 1984a:53-55). From their training they already possessed a psychophysical basis from which much of the dance-drama choreogrophy was created (Zarrilli 1978, 1979, 1984). The early patrons established a new social role, "actor/dancer" in *kathakaḷi*, as one appropriate in the role set associated with these middle ranking soldier Nayars. Eventually, the role "actor/dancer" was dissociated from that of Nayar soldier and became a primary *jati*-specific activity open to a larger group of similarly ranked service castes, but primarily associated with the middle-ranking Nayars.

Properties and costumes could easily be crafted by the artisan castes in service to the rulers. The only other people needed to complete a troupe were bearers to carry accountrements for performances outside the house compound, and washermen to care for the costumes—both *jati*-specific tasks for which traditional lower sub-caste ranks already served the house. The basic needs of performers and artisans and their families were provided for according to the pre-existing model of tenancy and service, ritually confirmed by the offering of gifts (*kazhca*, Moore 1983:273ff). Special ceremonial gifts were given in recognition of high achievement (Jones 1983:31). As long as this socio-economic infrastructure remained stable, the means of supporting the artistic tradition were within the rights and duties of land-holding royal lineages.

[7] Betty Jones notes that the leader and master of the Vettattu Raja's *rāmanāṭṭam* troupe was one Shankaran Nayar who was "also an officer of the Vettattu Raja's army" who "won a memorable victory for the Raja" in 1705 (1983:20). Two important masters in early *kathakaḷi* were Cattu Panikkar, in service of the Kottayam Raja, and Ittiri Panikkar, in service of Kaplingattu Namboodiri. Thurston (1975:6, 54) and K.P. Padmanabha Menon (1983:2, 426) have both noted that Panikkar was used for fencing-masters. It was a title given in south Malabar to those serving as master in the martial art (A. Sreedhara Menon 1972:76; Padmanabha Menon, 1983:1, 473).

The initial evolution of *kathakaḷi* into a virtuosic dance-drama depended on close artistic collaboration between royal patrons and their Nayar soldiers turned performers. The royal patrons possessed the literary capabilities and aesthetic sensibilities which shaped the art as it developed. The performers, in service to a ruler, would have been eager to please, and possessed the psycho-physical ability to realize in performance what their patrons desired.

## Patron as Author

The first *kathakaḷi* royal patrons were also authors of the first plays. However, not all plays in the post-Kottayam raja period were authored by royal or elite patrons. The patron *could* be author and he could patronize those who were authors. What are the regional sources for royal authorship, especially of the drama?

Most performing arts in the period immediately preceding the emergence of *rāmanāṭṭam* were ritual arts which by duty and place the ruler/land-holder was obligated to support. However, in the drama of the region, the precedent for kingly patronage and for artistic involvement of the ruler as author, is found in the early examples of Śaktibhadra and Kulaśekhara. It has clearly been established that Śaktibhadra authored the 9th-10th century Sanskrit play, *Āścarayacūḍmaṇi* (Jones 1984:x,3-4) and Kulaśekhara authored three 11th-12th century Sanskrit dramas (Unni 1977). Selected acts from these plays are still performed today as part of the *kūtiyāṭṭam* temple-theatre tradition. No further royal dramatists appear in the region until the emergence of *rāmanāṭṭam/kathakaḷi* and *kṛṣnāṭṭam*.

In the interim, from the *manipravālam* literature of the thirteenth to the late fifteenth centuries, we know that rulers wrote poetry and were patrons of court writers and scholars (Ramachandran Nair 1971:215-216). *Kathakaḷi āṭṭakatha* were stylistically molded from a combination of the court-supported *manipravālam* tradition and the "cantabile song-mold". From their inception the plays were characterized by a high degree of poetic conceit and the assimilation of Sanskrit (Chaitanya 1971:96). The early royal dramatists were competent Sanskritists, following a tradition of learning continued in many courts of the petty principalities from the thirteenth through seventeenth centuries.

The association of Sanskrit learning with the ruling aristocracy is in part attributable to the close relationship between ruling castes and the ritually purer and higher ranking Namboodiri Brahmins of Kerala. The legacy of Nayar/ruling class authorship as well as the eventual involvement of the Namboodiris in *kathakaḷi* is not at all surprising given the interdependency that existed between them. The Namboodiri practice of primogeniture, a method of inheritance assured by allowing only the eldest son to take one or more wives within his own caste, led to the requirement that all other males either remain celibate or form relationships with women from the ritually less pure but nevertheless high-ranking matrilineal royal castes (Mencher 1966:188). The years of interdependence affected the royal lineages.

> Namboodiri skill in Sanskrit was fostered by the local rulers who often helped subsidize Vedic sacrifices, recitations, etc. Furthermore, it was often a Namboodiri who taught Sanskrit to the children of ruling families. It should be noted in passing that, because of the close relationship between the Namboodiris and the matrilineal castes in Kerala, there was a far greater Sanskritic influence among non-Brahmins than has been noted on the east coast. Nayars, especially in Central Kerala, where the Namboodiris were most concentrated, were strongly influenced by the daily customs of Sanskrit education; in consequence the Nayars of Kerala were far more literate than their equivalents on the east coast (Mencher 1966:187).

We should not imagine that Sanskrit education went beyond the highest-ranking ruling Kśatriya and Nayar families, nor would it have been considered appropriate for the majority of Nayars in the mid and lower range service *jatis* to have learned Sanskrit.

Although this structural relationship of interdependence and Sanskritic influence existed from the inception of *rāmanāṭṭam*, at first the performance tradition had little appeal for Namboodiris. It was only after the prince of Kottayam authored his plays, richer in poetic beauty than the *rāmanāṭṭam* originals, that Namboodiri interest *and* patronage developed (Jones 1983:22). Once their interest had been aroused, Namboodiri patronage was of course possible. They possessed both the appropriate rank in the hierarchy *and* the socio-economic means of providing support for the art. As land-holders the largest Namboodiri households could support new artists recruited either from the ranks of their own service castes, *or* by bringing new individuals into their service. Thus, we find early in *kathakaḷi* history that Namboodiri patrons often brought into their service Nayars in service to royal families who had been trained in the art, as is the case of Nanu Menon, nephew of Vellattu Chattu Panikkar (Jones 1983:28). Namboodiri interest and patronage brought changes to *kathakaḷi* strengthening the movement toward literary and poetic refinement.

## Patron as *Rasika*/Connoisseur

The changes initiated by the Kottayam prince which attracted the Namboodiris led to a series of innovative refinements in *kathakaḷi*, many of which were intended to please the royal and ritual elite and provide opportunities for realization of predominant *rasas*, especially *śṛṅgāra* (erotic), and *vīra* (heroic). As patrons the royal and ritual elite also played the role of ideal audience member, the *rasika*/connoisseur, capable of savoring and appreciating the increasingly elaborate and refined means of realizing *rasa*. These refinements were certainly prompted by increased Namboodiri involvement in the art. However, even with provision for refinements, *kathakaḷi* has always maintained its popular basis, appealing to a broad spectrum of the population with the predominance of *vīra rasa* in its battles, and occasional moments of *hāsya* (comic).

## Patron as Artistic Innovator

In those traditions where ruling patrons have been directly involved as authors, they have also usually been engaged in staging their dramas. The early example of Kulaśekhara's reformation of the performative dimensions of the Kerala Sanskrit stage has been sufficiently documented to provide a precedent (Unni 1977:189, 193-194). Like Kulaśekhara, from their first involvement the patrons of *kathakaḷi* were not only authors but also innovators, helping to shape the dance-drama in its formative years into what became its distinctive style. This process of gradual evolution lasted from the authoring of the eight *rāmanāṭṭam* (late sixteenth century) and four Kottayam plays (late seventeenth century) through the end of the eighteenth century. The "new" name for *rāmanāṭṭam*, *kathakaḷi*, was a direct reflection of a major change made by the Prince of

Kottayam in the tradition he had received—namely the expansion of the repertory and inclusion of plays from epic and puranic sources other than *Rāmāyaṇa*. By doing so the Prince opened up one of the fundamental performance determinants—the content of the composed texts. *Kathakaḷi* came to designate that particular style of performing dance-dramas in which text and content were based on a general set of epic sources.

In this formative period of *kathakaḷi*'s development, the performance determinants, conventions, techniques, aesthetic principles, and even the texts and their sources were malleable. Early patrons and performers prior to and including the Prince of Kottayam and his senior performer/teacher, Cattu Panikkar, drew on numerous performance and literary sources in the formation of the genre eventually called *kathakaḷi*. During this century, among the most important performative sources for *rāmanāṭṭam-kathakaḷi*, were *kūtiyāṭṭam*; *mudiyettu*, which enacted the dramatic battle between the goddess Kali and the demon Darikan; *kaḷarippayaṯṯu*; and *kṛṣṇāṭṭam*, the devotional dance-drama based on Jayadeva's *Gīṭagovinda* (see Zarrilli 1984).

Innovation in content was one of many changes made by the Kottayam Prince in the performance tradition. Among the other modifications in text and performance which he introduced himself or in collaboration with his senior actor, Cattu Panikkar, were providing "scope for a wider range of *bhāva* or emotional mood"; using Sanskrit for *śloka*s and Malayalam for *padam*s; more careful selection of *rāga*s in creation of mood and relative place in the performance score; increasing the variety of rhythmic patterns and speeds used in performance; refinements in make-up and costuming; introduction of the language of gesture (*mudra*s) by borrowing the complex codified system of *kūtiyāṭṭam*; and introduction of many *āṭṭam*s of performative interpolations (Jones 1983:22-24; Zarrilli 1984:Ch.6).

These innovations in the *rāmanāṭṭam-kathakaḷi* performance tradition are collectively examples of the role of early patrons and their senior performers in actively creating the distinctive performance tradition eventually labeled *kathakaḷi*. Innovation continued over the next century, culminating in changes introduced by another patron-cum-performer, Kaplingattu Namboodiri and the senior actor in his troupe, Ittiri Panikkar, and consolidated as part of the tradition by Kaplingattu's retirement in 1789.

Changes and innovations became part of the artistic tradition as they were passed along to the next generation of performers. Lines of transmission from teacher to disciple are known as *sampradāyas*. *Sampradāya* has been defined as "a traditional doctrine; a family secret" (Gundert 1872:1040); "a particular cultural tradition" established "when a *guru* or set of *gurus* is recognized by a series of disciples . . . who in turn become *gurus* to the next generation" (Singer 1966:108); and in *kathakaḷi* as a "particular teacher student descent group" (Jones 1983:31). A *kathakaḷi sampradāya*, then, is constituted by the transmission of a set of techniques or conventions established by a particular artist and/or associated patron to the next generation of performers.[8]

Historically *sampradāyas* are as old as the original *rāmanāṭṭam*, the first *sampradāya* originating with the establishment of performers who enacted plays under the patronage of the Kottarakkara prince. New *sampradāyas* developed as new lines of transmission emerged which passed on a particular set of techniques and variations, innovations, and changes in techniques and performance score. A complete review of the history and intricacies of the development of *kathakaḷi sampradāyas* is beyond the scope of this paper, but by the turn of the eighteenth century when *kathakaḷi* had crystallized its technique and score under the artistic leadership of Kaplingattu Namboodiri, three distinct *sampradāyas* were in existence, the *kallatikkotan* mainly found in northern Kerala, the *kalluvazhichitta* mainly found in central Kerala, and that associated with Travancore in the south.[9]

So important were some of the innovations of Kaplingattu Namboodiri and the head of his troupe, Ittiri Panikkar, that they formed a common basis of technique with stylistic variation in different *sampradāyas*. Such was the case with Kaplingattu's expansion of the *mudrā* system to incorporate more gestures from *kūtiyāṭṭam*—a development which culminated in Ittiri Panikkar's use of the *kūtiyāṭṭam mudra* text (*Hastalakṣaṇadīpika*) as a source for use of the hands. Since its use by Panikkar it has become "the principle text followed by *kathakaḷi* actors" (Jones 1983:30-31).

[8] Given the matrilineally-based Nayar residence pattern wherein brothers continued to reside in their female parent's ancestral homes with their sisters and their sisters' children, it is not surprising that among Nayar performers many of their nephews became well-known performers such as Nanu Menon, nephew of Vellattu Chattu Panikkar (Jones 1983:28).

[9] For details see Zarrilli 1984:55-58, and Jones 1983:31-34.

The existence of multiple *sampradāya*s within a given tradition is the rule, not the exception.[10] Within *kūtiyāṭṭam*, *cakyar* lineages differ in the nuance of treatment of particular texts in performance. Cross culturally, it is typical for aristocratic and virtuosic performance traditions to develop multiple regional, court, and therefore context specific styles. Such is the case in Japanese *nō* where five different 'schools' developed—the equivalent of the Kerala *sampradāya*s. The particular and local nature of each *kathakaḷi sampradāya* identified each performer according to the teacher lineage by virtue of his training. Just as a member of a caste (*jati*) is defined by his birth into that particular group, so also an individual trained in a specific *sampradāya* has his entire performance identity defined by his lineage. The long process of training by daily corporeal repetition of techniques in a particular style indelibly imprints the peculiarities of that style on the body, consciousness, and approach of that student.

In any given present, within any particular *sampradāya*, change is *assumed* to be legitimate, even if at times controversial, when executed within the network of the traditional social and artistic hierarchy. In the *kathakaḷi* tradition only those at the apex of the artistic hierarchy within a given *sampradāya* could introduce change into the system, i.e., patrons like Kaplingattu Namboodiri and senior masters like Ittiri Panikkar. A *sampradāya*, then, is an indigenous and self-conscious method of recognizing legitimately created and transmitted variation within a cultural performance tradition.

## The Role of Patrons in Crystallization of a "Center" of the Tradition

The traditional royal and ritual elite were primary creators and innovators in the formation and eventual crystallization of the *kathakaḷi* performance tradition. By virtue of their position within the ritual, social, and economic hierarchies, many chose to assume the role of "patron" of this new performance art, providing the

[10] An interesting exception to this rule is *kṛṣṇāṭṭam* which has always existed as a single, discrete *sampradāya* performed exclusively by one troupe first patronized by the Zamorins of Calicut and later given over to the care of the Guruvayur temple. From its inception, the association of the genre with Kṛṣṇa devotionalism, and its attachment to the Guruvayur temple made it so context and function specific that it precluded transfer to other social or religious contexts.

economic and social infrastructure for its realization, authoring plays, engaging themselves in making decisions about performative realization of texts, and finally serving as ideal audience members. So crucial was the role of the early patrons that their involvement, in association with senior performers in their service, led to the development of multiple, distinct, specific artistic lineages (*sampradāyas*) associated with particularly important performers and their patrons.

The *kathakaḷi* tradition was created out of particular artistic alliances, and out of the genius of its early patrons and their performers. However, as the tradition spread throughout Kerala under the patronage of landholding families, each particular lineage with its own individual variations, was *collectively* assumed to be part of the artistic tradition for which the general appellation, *kathakaḷi*, applied. The *kathakaḷi* artistic tradition, then, consists of a set of context-specific artistic lineages (*sampradāyas*) associated with region-specific performers and their patrons, among which lineages there are basic performance techniques and conventions shared by all. These techniques, artistic and social conventions, aesthetic principles, and general stylistic traits collectively constitute the "center" of the tradition—those characteristic features which are assumed to make *kathakaḷi* identifiable as *kathakaḷi*. These now generally recognizable traits of the genre historically emerged from the specific context of art-making supported by the traditional socio-economic infrastructure at the apex of which were the patrons.

As we look back over the history of *kathakaḷi*, we see that many characteristic features of the genre today were originally at the *periphery* of the tradition, i.e., not part of the "center" received from the previous generation. Some innovations in technique, such as the use of an expanded repertoire of *mudrās* from *kūtiyāṭṭam*, became part of the "center" of individual *sampradāyas* as well as the collective center of the artistic tradition when passed on to successive generations. During *kathakaḷi*'s formative years the periphery of the tradition was constantly active, innovations being introduced from a variety of culturally available sources such as *kṛṣnāṭṭam* or *kūtiyāṭṭam*. The collective "center" of the *kathakaḷi* tradition is determined at any point in history by the dynamic interplay between what was received from the past, what is being performed in the present, and what will be passed on to future generations (Diagram 1).

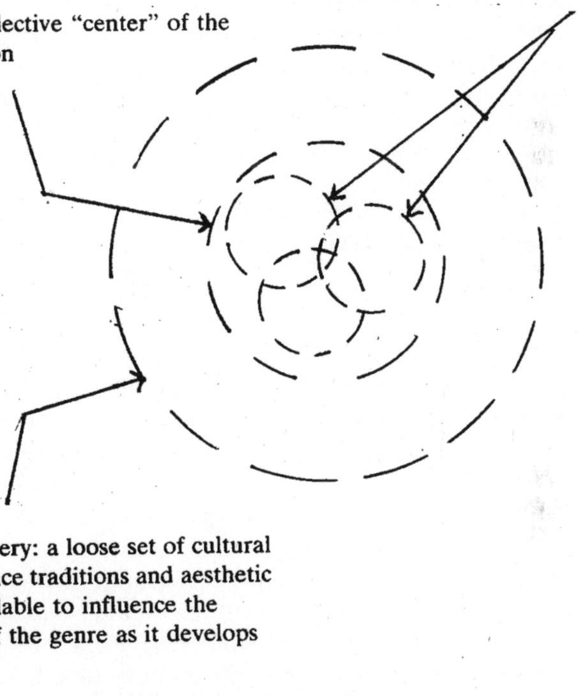


DIAGRAM 1: The Limits of the Tradition

The center of the tradition is actually a collection of individual *sampradāyas*. During its first hundred years the patrons and their senior performers set the limits of tradition by incorporating elements from genres or aesthetic ideas at the periphery.

The crystallization of the basic performance parameters of *kathakaḷi* was complete by the close of the eighteenth century. The "center" of the tradition had become relatively "fixed", i.e., the types of changes allowable in techniques and conventions took place within a more carefully circumscribed set of alternatives than had been the case when *rāmanāṭṭam* was first performed. As the stylistic and aesthetic limits became a part of the generally assumed aesthetic fabric of the performance tradition, patrons and performers in whose power further artistic change was possible limited their innovations more and more to refinements in the nuances of performance technique and to opportunities for aesthetic elaboration received within their particular *sampradāya*s from the preceding generation.

### The Primary Role of *Rasika*/Connoisseur among Patrons in the Mature Years

As the basic performance parameters of *kathakaḷi* became relatively "fixed," the limits of the collective "center" of the artistic tradition became relatively set, and the attention of patron/connoisseurs and performers turned to exploring the expressive subtleties possible within those limits. While increasing refinement characterizes the life of the artistic tradition during *kathakaḷi*'s "mature" years from the close of the eighteenth century until the mid to late nineteenth century, anything but refinement characterizes the socio-political atmosphere of the period.

Although the seventeenth and eighteenth centuries during which *kathakaḷi* emerged were periods of extreme military and political conflict prompted by colonial incursions into Kerala beginning with the Portuguese in the late fifteenth century and continuing with the arrival of the Dutch, French, and English, the traditional socio-economic infrastructure outlined above remained largely in place. The political map of the region was seriously affected by the Muslim invasions from Mysore in 1732 under Haydar Ali and Tippu Sultan. Their victories brought great social and political displacement and disruption as ruling families of the northern region fled southward (Kareem 1973; Gough 1952:78). By the time the British vanquished Tippu Sultan, evicted Muslim invaders from Kerala in 1792 and established their own political supremacy, the northern rulers were bereft of real political or temporal power as their armies were disbanded. The area became Malabar District of Madras Presidency, governed by a British Collector. Displaced royal families who had fled the area were allowed to return to their lands. In both Cochin and Travancore, maharajas continued to rule, but under the supervision of the British.

What is important for *kathakaḷi* patronage in the central (Cochin) and northern (Malabar) regions of Kerala is that displaced royal lineages were allowed to return to their lands, and therefore to their place in the socio-economic order. In spite of the political upheaval

> . . . all the royal lineages maintained their high rank and power as important landlords, together with most of the ritual paraphernalia of their former office. Such a state of affairs was possible because British contact had not yet radically changed the economy of Malabar . . . (Gough 1952:78-79).

In Malabar, as Mencher (1966b) has summarized the situation, the Namboodiris in particular were little affected:

> the replacement of the traditional political structure by a new one did not in any way curtail their wealth. They were supplanted, but without land reform or any threat to their ownership of property (190).

The basic unit of "house and land" remained intact. Wealthy landholders could continue to maintain their patronage of ritual and aesthetic performances. Perhaps performances such as *kathakaḷi* with its emphasis on *vīra rasa* served in part to assuage the ignominy of the political situation.

The situation in southern Kerala (Travancore) was quite different. There Martanda Varma came to the Travancore throne in 1729 and reshaped the political realities of the area. During his reign (until 1758) he conquered the area from Cape Comorin to the borders of Cochin, forcing submission of all Nayar chiefs in the area, and annexing their lands.

> Their land was the principal source of their economic power, and Martanda Varma's action more or less destroyed it. By annexation is meant the transfer of *janmom* rights from individual

> chiefs to the Travancore state, thus reducing them to *kanamdars* of the state . . . Martanda Varma's policies were an entirely new phenomenon in Kerala . . . he laid the foundations of a modern bureaucracy . . . (Fuller 1976:18)

In Travancore power and wealth become concentrated under the rule of the Maharaja of Travancore; the ruling family itself consolidated power in the artistic realm much as it had in the economic realm and played the role of model royal patron.

In the midst of such political turmoil, the socio-economic unit of "house and land" remained relatively constant among royal and Namboodiri families until the mid to late nineteenth century, thus providing a continuing economic and social basis for the maintenance of traditional patronage. The relative security of the system made possible the increasing tendency toward refinement. This is evidenced even in the pre-Kaplingattu Namboodiri period as texts authored and performance refinements both characterized this movement toward development of virtuosic nuance of expression to realize better the aesthetic sensibilities of the ideal audience—the patrons themselves.

A first example of the increasing refinements introduced as *kathakaḷi* matured is the series of four plays, *Nala Caritam*, authored by Unnayi Variyar. The exact dates of Unnayi Variyar are in dispute among scholars of *kathakaḷi*, some suggesting 1675-1716 (Menon 1957), others 1674-1734 (Iyer 1977:13). What is important is that four plays are even today considered the highest gem of literary expression in the repertory, and the characters in the plays, especially Nala, are considered by most to require the greatest degree of nuance in acting skill (see Zarrilli 1984:60ff; Iyer 1977).

In Travancore Maharaja Kartika Tirunal Balaram Varma who ascended the throne in 1758 on the death of Martanda Varma, is responsible for the drastic socio-economic reforms discussed above (Namboodiri 1983:26ff). The legacy of royal support in Travancore for further refinement of *kathakaḷi*'s emphasis on aesthetic realization is seen in Martanda Varma's patronage of literary and artistic figures. During his own rule Kartika Tirunal Maharaja became famous for his patronage of the arts. He himself authored six *kathakaḷi* plays, as well as an important Sanskrit work on dance and drama, *Bālarāmabharatam* (Namboothiry 1983). Three of his plays were southern *sampradāya* versions of three of the Kottayam prince's plays (Namboothiry 1983:36). His authoring of the *Bālaramabharatam* is evidence of the degree to which the Sanskrit tradition of the *Nāṭyaśastra* had influenced the elite, refined appeal of *kathakaḷi*.

Certainly plays like *Nala Caritam* and Kartika Tirunal's *Bālarāmabhartam* were written because patron/connoisseurs as *rasika*s came to expect more opportunities for actors to explore nuances of expression. Nowhere is this role of patron/connoisseurs as arbiters of aesthetic sensibility seen more than in *kathakaḷi*'s basic performance score and the types of elaboration allowable in that score. The *kathakaḷi* performance score is a complex and convoluted structure which emphasizes artistic and dramatic elaboration on and within other elaborations (Zarrilli 1984:Ch. 6). All such elaborations are expansions or interpolations within the base-line dramatic text, allowing various artists freedom of interpretation and display of consummate virtuosic artistry within the prescribed limits of the form. The purpose of all such elaborations is to challenge the limits of the expressive capabilities of performers both individually and as an ensemble, thereby providing patron/connoisseurs with additional vehicles by which to savor and relish the primary *rasa* of the performative moment. Experiencing the *process of unfolding* performance elaborations allows the essence of the juice or the *rasa* to be tasted. The story/content of the performance base-line is merely the first and most general means to the end of aesthetic realization, not an end in itself.

One such conventionalized mode of elaboration and subtle expressivity is the love scene opening many plays in which the *katti* ("knife") type is the main role. In such love scenes emphasis is on the expressive embodiment of *śṛṅgāra rasa* (the erotic or romantic flavor). Such scenes often have no direct connection with the dramatic action of that particular play. The love scene has been written into the original play solely as an opportunity for performers to expressively embody the erotic sentiment, and thereby for the audience to savor the erotic.

The refined aesthetic process of savoring *rasa* is the expressive and aesthetic backdrop of the complex structure of *kathakaḷi*'s traditional score. During this period patrons as connoisseurs placed the highest value on fulfilling this process of savoring by encouraging refinement of technique or by innovative insertion of interpolations on the text into the received score. These interpolations (*āṭṭams*) are "interior monologues" enacted by the performer and serve as opportunities for expressing the nuance of a character's interior state or condition and thereby a fuller savoring of that character's condition and of the various shades of the primary *bhāva* (emotion/mood) of his condition at the moment in the narrative. Historically, such interpolations have been made by senior performers themselves and/or by senior performers on the suggestion of, or in collaboration with, patron/connoisseurs. But in all cases, for an *āṭṭam* to be incorporated into the living performance tradition within a *sampradāya*, it must have minimally received the implicit approval of the patron/connoisseurs for whom it was first performed.

When first introduced, such interpolations are exciting innovations. When acclaimed by patron/connoisseurs, such innovations are handed on to the next generation of performers as a part of the traditional way of enacting a particular role in a particular play. An example from the twentieth century is the *āṭṭam* which Pattiyakkantoti Ramunni Menon Asan (1881-1949) introduced into Bhima's role in *Baka Vadham*, one of the Kottayam prince's original texts. The play enacts the Kauravas' attempt to have the exiled Pandavas killed in a fire. Ramunni Menon himself composed the "text" which is performed in the midst of Scene 4 of the play. The immediate dramatic context into which the *āṭṭam* was introduced is the moment when Dharmaputra tells Bhima of the trap that has been set for him and his brothers. Given Bhima's character, he responds in fury (*krodha bhāva*). In the text of the play itself, Dharmaputra begs Bhima to be patient. But Bhima begins to recall all the cruel deeds of the Kauravas, and his fury begins to mount. Ramunni Menon introduced the *āṭṭam* in order to expand on this immediate context, and to allow greater nuance in enacting Bhima's internal struggle. The one-dimensional nature of Bhima's fury contained in the original text is expanded though the introduction of the *āṭṭam* to allow the actor playing Bhima to have more scope for exploring Bhima's response to the situation. At the beginning of the *āṭṭam*, Bhima asks himself, "Why should I be patient?" The specific mood of the first line of the *āṭṭam* itself is despair over the situation. But with the enactment of each line of the *āṭṭam*, Bhima's fury begins to abate and is replaced by forlornness. Seemingly pacified, Dharmaputra leaves Bhima alone. Left alone, Bhima reflects on their condition, and again his anger begins to build until he reaches the point of wishing to destroy the Kauravas completely.

Ramunni Menon's interpolation, which became a part of the performance score passed on to all succeeding generations of performers trained in the *sampradāya* associated with the Kerala Kalamandalam, introduces for the actor the challenge of tempering Bhima's fury with a reflective despondency which comes from confrontation with his own inner thoughts. He resigns himself momentarily to his fate and to following his elder brother's orders—but for Bhima of course it cannot last long. His fury returns.

This example illustrates the changeability and flexibility of the tradition when such change is made within the limits at the center of the tradition. As *kathakaḷi* evolved in these mature years, the degree of sophistication expected by patron/connoisseurs of the emotional complexity of *kathakaḷi* characters became more pronounced. *Baka Vadham* was one of the original *Mahābhārata* plays composed by the Prince of Kottayam. Ramunni Menon's interpolation is only one recent example of the introduction of nuance and complexity into character portrayals which enrich a character like Bhima, whose relative simplicity is a legacy of the earliest days of *kathakaḷi* history.

Introduction of such interpolations is not allowed to any actor in any role. The degree of freedom of interpretation and innovation correlates directly with a performer's ranking in the hierarchy implicit among performers. The "main" roles *(ādyavasānan)* of any play, are the most complex and are played by senior or master performers. Intermediate roles (*iṭṭattaram*) or minor roles (*kuṭṭittaram*) are given to those performers ranking lower in the hierarchy. Position is implicitly determined by age, years of training and performance, and relative value placed on a actor's expressive capabilities by patron/connoisseurs. Only senior master actors are able to introduce new *āṭṭam*s into performances. This was the case with Ramunni Menon's *āṭṭam* noted above. Junior actors are expected to make their way up through the ranks to gain opportunities for taking more difficult roles with greater possibilities for expressive elaboration. An important part of the oral tradition still surrounding advancement through the acting hierarchy is that a performer is not "mature" until he reaches at least 40 years of age, a public articulation of the fact that most performers under 40 will not have many opportunities for innovation.

The subtleties of change allowed the master performer in the past and today are closely tied to the association of particular actors with particular role types. In their mature years, *kathakaḷi* performers specialize in playing particular role types, such as heroic characters, "knife" types, female roles, etc. What patron/connoisseurs look for is how well a particular actor is able to command the expressive range of character type manifest in *a* particular role. Today a patron/connoisseurs might be wondering, "how well will Gopi Asan enact Nala (a *pacca*, literally "green" or heroic role) tonight? What will he do that is new and different in *his* interpretation of *this* role on this night?" Innovation by Gopi on a particular night might come in the form of a decision to attempt a "major" change. The performer in his moments of mental preparation might have decided to change a particular dance ending (*kalāśam*) normally performed at a particular place in the performance as a conclusion to a passage of text. When he comes to this moment in the performance, the patron/connoisseurs may have expected him to dance a particular *kalāśam*. However, "unexpectedly" he performs another *kalāśam*! Should the gathered patron/connoisseurs feel that Gopi's new interpretation better fulfills the inherent expressive possibilities of that moment, then that change could become an alteration in the performance score Gopi will hand on to his own students.

The immediate respons of patron/connoisseurs during the performance may be completely non-verbal. A master actor should be capable of sensing the pulse and inner feeling tone of the audience as it responds to his performance. In addition, after the performance patron/connoisseurs may communicate directly or indirectly their response to an actor's performance. The next time Gopi teaches his own students this moment in the role, he will teach them the alternate *kalāśam* is the "correct" dance ending. Thus innovation of the master becomes part of the revised center of the tradition. Change is introduced within carefully circumscribed limits.

As illustrated by these contemporary examples, during the mature years of refinement and till today, the patron/connoisseurs have played an extremely important part in maintaining the boundaries of the tradition. Historically they have played the role of active "critics" of performers, whose favor or disfavor could determine the ultimate inclusion or exclusion of possible changes such as the introduction of *āṭṭams* or a change in a *kalāśam*. The operative orally transmitted aesthetic principle, articulated today by actors and connoisseurs as the major determinant in what is or is not acceptable in terms of innovation, is "what is appropriate to the action". The latitude allowable in defining "what is appropriate," is naturally open to wide differences of opinion. The example of the *āṭṭam* introduced by Ramunni Menon above is very closely tied to the dramatic action, and is clearly appropriate. However, it seems likely that in the past, as today, different *sampradāyas* maintained different definitions of the limits of what was considered appropriate. The common, local standard of appropriateness, however, was the guiding principle for both performers and patrons within *sampradāyas*, providing a common basis for critical and evaluative judgements shaping the local tradition.

While refinement through performative elaboration, established by the symbiotic relationship between high caste patron/connoisseurs and performers, produced the prototypical structure of *kathakaḷi* which persists today, the form never lost touch with its popular roots. Refinements and interpolations were inserted within the frames of a complete performance with wider mass appeal. The more immediate and easily engaging moments which made *kathakaḷi* popular with a general audience *continued* to be part of the performance. Certain *kathakaḷi* plays have characters who are comic caricatures of real-life "types." The court "thugs" of *Pṛahlāda Caritam* are one example. Their pratfalls easily communicate with the least knowledgeable audience member. Or, whenever Hanuman appears, his half-human half-monkey antics give him an immediate and universal appeal to all members of an audience. The concluding battle scenes (at the end of approximately 80% of all *kathakaḷi* plays) are always filled with heightened drama and excitement of madly whirling figures fighting to the death. The nearly deafening, yet totally absorbing sound-action-sensory surround created at the final moment of victory in battle continues to be one of *kathakaḷi's* most popular and compelling moments. *Kathakaḷi*, when compared with the *nō* tradition of Japan, never became as introverted and isolated from the popular public through its royal patronage. Rather, *kathakaḷi* simultaneously developed refinement and elaboration inserted into certain sections of the performance, yet maintained its incontrovertibly popular base. Even the modern period is characterized by the exploitation of elitist-oriented aesthetic of refinement as well as popular exploitation of modes of appeal to broader masses.

## The Consolidation and Refinement of the "Center" of the Tradition

The maintenance of the traditional socio-economic basis for patronage in spite of political turmoil made possible the consolidation and refinement of the tradition. Through time the aesthetic and performative parameters carefully circumscribed the tradition, allowing alteration and change only within allowable limits. The limits of change and innovation at the periphery or outer limits of the form were "tested" by a process of carefully circumscribed creative experimentation initiated by master artists or occasionally by patron/connoisseurs (Diagram 2). Once a substantive change or alternative approach to a character interpretation was introduced, it could become an accepted part of either a particular *sampradāya* or of the "collective center," or, if critical opinion among patron/connoisseurs weighed against the new practice, it would never be repeated, and eventually forgotten.

### Expanding and Redefining the Center for Multiple *Kathakaḷi* Patrons in the Modern Period[11]

As long as *kathakaḷi* existed within the confines of the traditional Kerala socio-economic infrastructure, and as long as that infrastructure remained relatively stable at the local level, change and alteration in the tradition were generated within *sampradāya*s according to traditional lines of authority: traditional elite patrons and/or senior performers introduced innovation within circumscribed limits. Although certainly an oversimplification and recognizing local/regional variation, it was with land reform and the attendant move to a job and market economy, beginning in the mid to late nineteenth century, that the "house and land" unit was no longer able to support many of its traditional responsibilities (Fuller 1976:Ch. 6). Partition and parcelling of land eroded the economic and social bases for traditional patronage. As the relationships between high-ranking landholders and *jati*s in their service began

[11] The 'modern' period in *kathakaḷi* history begins with the establishment of the first formal *kathakaḷi* training and performance institution, the Kerala Kalamandalam, in 1930.

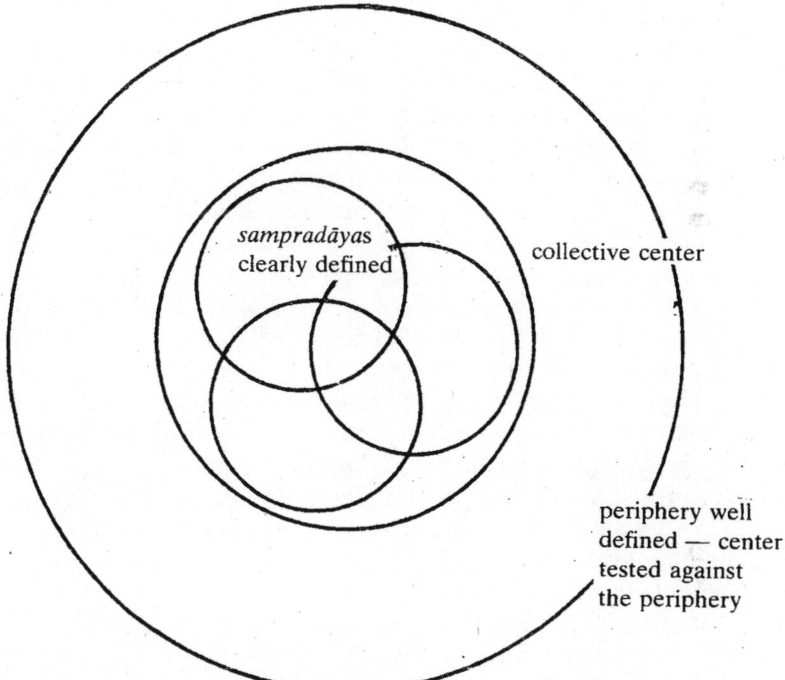


DIAGRAM 2: The Limits of the Mature Tradition

In its mature years the limits of individual *sampradāyas* and defining features of the genre became relatively set. What was permissible at the collective center is assumed and clearly understood. The tradition continues to evolve within these allowable limits. "Testing" the periphery is part of the creative process. Such tests are those of interpretation and elaboration within clearly defined boundaries.

to shift toward market-place exchange, the traditional social infrastructure on which patronage and intra-artistic relationships were based was radically altered.

In addition to the economic and structural problems facing the art by the late nineteenth century, there were additional problems of changing personal sensibilities brought by British education, especially among the Nayars (Fuller 1976). New forms of education and concomitant values altered indigenous perceptions of the value of India's cultural traditions. British rule, law, and economics both directly and indirectly forced completely new institutional and organizational structures on arenas of social action such as patronage which had previously operated according to traditional social networks. Modernization in the form of new modes of transportation, technical advancements such as the introduction of electricity, and increasing availability of marketplace commodities all placed further pressures on the *kathakaḷi* tradition during this modern period.

Although further research must be conducted on this key transition period into *kathakaḷi*'s modern era of patronage, it appears that the situation within Malabar and Cochin may have been more accute than the south with its centralized power and concentration of wealth. The collapse forced those who wished for *kathakaḷi*'s survival to find new forms of subsidy or patronage by the early twentieth century. How have all these alterations in the traditional socio-economic infrastructure and pressures of modernization affected both individual *sampradāya*s and the collective center of the *kathakaḷi* tradition?

At the center of the *kathakaḷi* tradition in the modern period, change and alteration in the performance determinants, conventions, techniques and aesthetics of the dance-drama have taken place in five major ways. First, there are alterations and changes of interpretation, performance score, etc. which are expected and allowable within the operative rules of the traditional collective center, i.e., the types of interpretative changes illustrated by the examples of Ramunni Menon Asan and Gopi Asan above. Secondly, there are changes and alterations which are a logical extension of the emphasis upon refinement, appreciation of nuance, and focus on master performers desired by the traditional patron/connoisseurs. Such changes go beyond individual interpretation to include fundamental alteration of the structure and score of modern performances. Both interpretative alterations and structural changes are *self-conscious* decisions made by those who traditionally held power at the center of the tradition—masters and patron/connoisseurs. These changes are a logical extension of the ongoing process of alteration at the very heart of the tradition. Thirdly, there are changes induced by radical restructuring of the socio-economic infrastructure supporting *kathakaḷi*. Most important here has been restructuring systems of patronage from local, personal, and relatively small loci of training and performance to the introduction of institutional structures in the early twentieth century. This fundamental restructuring of social networks governing the ongoing teaching and performance of *kathakaḷi* has meant a concomitant restructuring and shift in power structures from those located within a tightly knit and clearly articulated set of hierarchical social/service relationships to a much more diffuse institutionally-based set of relationships. These, while still hierarchical, do not presuppose the *personal* element of service characteristic of the old *jajmān* system. Many changes and alterations in *kathakaḷi* have resulted from this total restructuring of networks governing decision-making powers over various aspects of the form. Fourth, a separate set of changes and alterations have been induced by introduction of modern technical innovations which are either self-consciously or by fiat accepted at the center of the tradition: the lighting of performances with electric lights (once electricity was available), performances on proscenium stages, and the use of electronically amplified sound. Often such technical innovations were perceived as positive technical advancements, and they were accepted by fiat with no self-conscious reflection by traditional artists or patron/connoisseurs on the effect that such changes would have on the structure, techniques, and communicative power of the form itself. Finally, there are those changes which affect how *kathakaḷi* is perceived and valued as part of Kerala culture, or as a performing art form. None of these five types of changes or alterations affecting the center of the tradition and how the center defines itself exists in isolation. Rather all five exist as a network of interrelated forces which collectively constitute the field of maintenance and/or change in *kathakaḷi* today.

The most radical form of change in the socio-economic infrastructure supporting *kathakaḷi* is the complete breakdown of the "house and land" patronage system—the basis for financial subsidy of troupes, individual artists, students, and maintenance of a set of costumes and properties. Although even today there are a few families who provide subsidy support for a few artists, patronage for partial or complete companies has had to come from new sources. Beginning with the founding of the Kerala Kalamandalam in 1930 by the great Malayalee poet, Vallathol, alternative funding sources for support of *kathakaḷi* have evolved. In due course support has come from a wide variety of sources including the Kerala and Indian governments, an Ayurvedic medical factory and hospital, a major chemical and fertilizer company, cultural institutions, and even a temple for the ritual propitiation of local deities (Zarrilli 1984:Ch.7). One of the most important results of the complete change in subsidy patronage from the system of ruler/family support to institutional support has been the loss of the intimate and personal nature of relationships between artists and patrons of the past. Institutional forms of organization are based on western models superimposed on an art which had depended for its existence on the beneficent, educated, and interested involvement of the patron/connoisseur. In the past, power over artistic and pedagogical matters was clearly in the hands of the master teachers and interested patron/connoisseurs.

While such a relationship should not be idealized to the point where we assume there was no conflict of opinon or inherent struggle over particular innovations introduced, the introduction of institutional forms of management has of necessity brought, depending on the size of the school and its particular form of organization, administrators, managers, boards of directors, secretaries, and a variety of other ancillary supportive personnel into the decision-making process. While at most of these modern institutions decisions in regard to teaching specific techniques are left to the masters, boards and administrators have become involved in designing "a curriculum" and "course of study". One example has been the introduction of formal study of Sanskrit for students at the Kerala Kalamandalam. The rationale for its introduction was to give students formal instruction in the nuances of Sanskrit language since traditional texts are written in heavily Sanskritized Manipravalam (old Malayalam).

The imposition of a graded and specialized curriculum on what had previously been a much less formally structured process of training undertaken on a personal level between master and pupil (the *gurukkula* system) has led in some cases to increasing anomie among students. So specialized has the curriculum and organization of the Kerala Kalamandalam become that specific teachers are assigned to specialize in teaching students divided into classes: first year, second year, etc. While such specialization may in some respects have positive results through concentration on graded sets of skills, the structure of the new system precludes the long-term development of a close relationship-in-transmission between teacher and pupils. The continuance of particular *sampradāyas* at the local level has always depended upon imparting and implanting into the entire being of the pupil the senior master's particular style. When masters are only able to work with students over a shorter period of time, for one or two years, the indelible stamp of a particular master is lost on succeeding generations of students. At larger institutions, the clear identity of a particular *sampradāya* marked by the stamp of a particular master is giving way to collective determination of a style's defining characteristics.

The gradual process of depersonalization may also be seen in those institutions where students' living quarters have been separated from those of masters. When students trained under the old *gurukkula* system, there was more day-to-day intimate and informal contact between master and pupil and training could go on even in those interstices between the more formal training periods. While some institutions are small enough so that the degree of contact between students and teachers is similar to that of the past, in larger institutions the process of separation and depersonalization with loss of intimate contact has contributed to the anomie.

One of the most profound changes has been the disjuncture between social and artistic roles in the ranks of the patrons. The fact that the fourfold model of traditional patronage was one of the role sets appropriate to members of royal and later Namboodiri households illustrated the organic connection between involvement in and love for the art, and financial/social support of the art. Today's connoisseurs are no longer necessarily patrons, nor are those in positions of power within the newly organized institutions (the "new patrons" or sponsors) necessarily connoisseurs. In some institutions "politically expedient" appointments may be made to positions of authority. Such individuals lack traditional sensitivity to the art and the temperament of artists. Some use these positions within the institutional structure as a political and/or social means of garnering authority and power and have little or no knowledge or interest in the history, life or appreciation of the performing art itself. The anomie created in the community of actors when their art is literally used as a "political football" in the highly politicized atmosphere of contemporary Kerala politics is profound and deep among many senior artists, and among those connoisseurs who witness the erosion of respect for the art itself. It is not that such animosity and bitterness might not have existed in the past between patron and artists in his service, but certainly the structural causes for conflict were produced by different circumstances.

As long as the ideal audience for *kathakaḷi* was equated with the patron/connoisseur, there was no need to attempt to reshape *kathakaḷi* specifically to appeal to any other audience. Although *kathakaḷi* continued to appeal to many, there was no social or economic necessity for altering it to attempt to attract an audience made up of a general public unknowledgeable in the finer nuances of appreciation. The center of the tradition, maintained economically by the patrons, allowed the form to evolve and refine its techniques, assuming the presence of an audience of equals. The modern period of *kathakaḷi* history has brought an increasing dependency of *kathakaḷi* on the vagaries of a new marketplace economy. While a variety of forms of modern patronage have evolved, in no case are these full and complete subsidies. All modern schools and companies receive only a percentage of their complete operating budget from the long-term subsidies provided by the patronizing agency. The remainder of their budget comes from performances given by sponsors who invite and organize either single or series of performances on behalf of an organization or group.

The sponsors and audiences for whom the sponsors are arranging performances have become an important part of the process of change relating to modern *kathakaḷi*. In the modern period *kathakaḷi* companies must attempt to gain a maximum number of bookings in order to supplement subsidy income. The particular sponsors of bookings today fall into four broad general types: (1) those rare performances sponsored by a high-ranking family which traditionally patronized the art; (2) urban Kerala *kathakaḷi* clubs, composed mostly of those with an active and ongoing interest in following *kathakaḷi*, many of whom are traditional connoisseurs; (3) yearly temple festival committees which sponsor a *kathakaḷi* performance as part of a complete set of cultural performances during the festival periods and whose audience is usually a broad cross-section of a community; and (4) non-Kerala urban audiences who have little knowledge of *kathakaḷi*. While the majority of bookings, bringing in the most substantial portion of additional income to a troupe, comes from temple festival performances, performances for individual patron families or urban *kathakaḷi* clubs in Kerala allow performers an opportunity to perform for its most "educated" and aesthetically equal audience, and thus are valued highly by performers. In all but the first case, however, there have been substantial alterations in certain performance conventions and often in the performance score itself to accomodate the special interests and level of appreciation of a particular sponsor or audience.

Before discussing the numerous changes forced by external circumstance, it should be acknowledged that *kathakaḷi* still possesses its received and assumed aesthetic ideal of communication through realization of *rasa*, achieved through various modes of artistic elaboration. Many contemporary changes have been made at the center of the tradition. Within each *sampradāya* existing today, senior artists continue to be vested with responsibility and power of creative interpretation and expression. What differs from the past is that in many cases the new institutional forms of patronage preclude the establishment of personal relationships between particular patron/connoisseurs and senior masters. Connoisseurs, even if no longer patrons, continue to respond to the on-going process of interpretation and elaboration. The value of the interpretative and emotive skills of modern *kathakaḷi* performers is constantly in the public light. In the modern period, with the growth of modern transportation and print media, *kathakaḷi* performers are part of a larger performative and public network than was feasible in the pre-modern period. Print media including both English and Malayalam newspapers, magazines, and journals, serve as conduits for contemporary evaluation of performance skills. An outstanding example is that of K.P.S. Menon, chronicler, historian, and connoisseur of *kathakaḷi*, who has written on the modern masters. His commentaries combine biography, history of training with specific masters, identification of the *sampradāya*, role specialization in performance, outstanding roles for which the performer is known, individual traits in approaching performance in a given style, and emotional range and expressiveness. Writing of Guru Kunju Kurup, Menon called him

> a master, when it came to expressing emotions on the stage. Pathos, sarcasm, surprise, valour, anger, love were all suggested with the right kind of nuance, and with a skill matched by very few performers . . . To portray the rage of a character and to portray that the character was just pretending to be angry are two very different things and only an accomplished actor can convey this distinction . . . He towered above the others because of his ability to express transient phases of emotion in various forms: he could move from humour and valour to love, from love to rage and back to love again (1973:22).

The emphasis which Menon gives here to the subtle and refined expressive capabilities of the actor in embodying the nuance of dramatic/emotional substance has been reinforced over the years by the introduction of Western literary and dramatic values.

In addition to the self-conscious process of artistic creation accepted and appreciated at the center, there are changes in a variety of performance determinants, conventions, and techniques initiated by the center and accepted at the center in the modern period. A logical extension of the emphasis connoisseurs place on the elaborative *rasa* aesthetic has been the substantive alteration of all-night programs to focus on "favorite scenes." Nowadays some all night performances are composed of edited selections from three different plays rather than the performance of one full play. Such programs are particularly popular for audiences with many connoisseurs. In each edited selection the audience can see a senior master actor in a favorite role, whereas in many complete *kathakaḷi* plays there is only one major role. In edited programs the "less interesting" (for connoisseurs) scenes involving minor characters are pared away. A complete play's through-line of dramatic action is sacrificed for the scenes featuring roles which allow master performers their greatest technical challenge.

Changes made by choice at the center are generally viewed by traditional connoisseurs as positive "developments" of the form. They reflect the operative aesthetic of the form and thus cause little if any controversy, but rather allow a greater degree of realization of the assumed aesthetic and appreciation of the form.

Organization at the center of the tradition into multiple *sampradāyas* continues in the modern period.[13] However, the specific local and personal nature of *sampradāyas* has been affected by the superimposition of institutional structures. Greater mobility via transportation has brought more interaction between regionally varied styles. In spite of increased mobility and interaction, connoisseurs of specific modern *sampradāyas* are vocal and adamant about the relative "superiority" of the style which they champion.

In the variable contemporary performance milieu, the audience, sponsor, and social context of sponsorship for a particular performance is having an impact on the performance scored for that context.[14] For urban Kerala connoisseurs, if the program is to be all night in length, it is often arranged to include edited selections from three plays. If the program is a three hour program, a single play is selected, and an edited version is performed so that audience members arrive in the early evening and depart for home while

[13] Since 1930 three main *sampradāyas* are recognized and popularly known as "northern,' "southern," and "central," roughly corresponding to their geographical location and distribution within modern Kerala. Each is a legacy of one or more previous *sampradāyas*. The specific nature of differences between two of these *sampradāyas* clarifies local variation at the collective center of the tradition. Today the "central" style is associated with teachers produced primarily by the Kerala Kalamandalam or those who had been students of the Kalamandalam for their own training. The "southern" style is associated with the old Travancore region of southern Kerala. The southern style has persisted with much less institutional organization than is true of the central region. Only in 1974 was Margi Kathakali Yogam founded—a very modest school near the main Trivandrum temple.

What differentiates performers trained in the two *sampradāyas* today? The most important differences are: (1) The central style appears technically precise and controlled in body movement and delivery of hand gestures within a carefully circumscribed area. The southern style in contrast appears more fluid, less circumscribed, and allows use of a larger spatial area in delivering *mudrās*. (2) Actors in the central style are admonished to make sure their interpretations of a role are guided only by what is "directly relevant" to each specific dramatic moment in the play. In the southern style there appears to be more latitude in interpreting "what is appropriate" to the dramatic context. (3) Actors in the central style are told "not to play to the audience," i.e., not to play too broadly. Actors of the southern region generally are more prone to "play to the audience" to gain active response.

[14] Stuart Blackburn's paper in this volume has illustrated the important effect of context on the generation of a performance "text" (referred to here as "score"). In traditions like *kathakaḷi* where the text is a closed literary creation, context still has a profound and immediate impact on the score and on various conventions of staging even if not so overt as in the traditions Blackburn discusses. Each adjustment outlined here is an example of the subtle meshing of score and conventions with context within a textually "closed" tradition. Both are examples of strategies of engaging the patrons more directly in the performance.

public transportation is still available. In both cases substantial editing of the score has taken place, altering the received traditional score to accommodate shortened length of performance of a particular play and to allow focus on scenes most important to connoisseurs.

Alteration of the score is an implicit acknowledgement of the aesthetic values of the sponsor. Sponsors are the modern equivalent and extension of the old patron/connoisseurs at a social and aesthetic level. However, clubs are only sponsoring and not patronage organizations, which arrange monthly performances as cultural events for club members.

Proscenium stages are now the venue for such urban performances, even though the proscenium stage makes the previously close proximity of actor and audience impossible. Implicit at most urban Kerala performances is a process of educating the audience into the conventions and techniques of the form so that it can be better appreciated. At times this educational dimension becomes explicit, as when programs or souvenirs are published and distributed which introduce the plays, and discuss in brief articles aspects of performances. In addition, there are even instances of the use of "translators," i.e., an educated connoisseur speaking through a microphone and simultaneously "translating" into Malayalam the hand-gestures being "spoken" by the performers. Through the translation the audience is educated in the specific meaning of the codified gestural system.

Context also enters the conventions and score of modern *kathakaḷi* for connoisseurs in the audience/performer spatial configuration in use at the Kerala Kalamandalam's new *kūttampalam* theatre. *Kathakaḷi* is typically performed frontally, and the best vantage point for viewing a performance is directly in front of the performers. While in traditional outdoor performances audiences often wrap around the corners of a temporary stage, connoisseurs are concentrated spatially right in front of the oil lamp and stage where they have the best opportunity to see each facial expression and gesture, and to receive, "taste," and thereby commune with the performers' portrayal of characters. At the Kalamandalam the new theatre was designed as a combination of principles contained in the *Nāṭyaśāstra* and traditional Kerala temple theatre architecture. The stage is a long, wide strip stretching completely across the performance hall, divided into three sections by the centrally located covered roof of the central stage area. To the right and left are areas which *could* be used for other performances which might be staged there, but are unnecessary for *kathakaḷi* which only needs a very small centrally located area to accommodate its stage action. These "side" stage areas, which are raised to the same level as the central stage area, have become audience seating areas for *kathakaḷi* performances in the theatre. Here chairs are placed and many of the connoisseurs, visiting dignitaries, and/or members of the governing bodies of the institution are seated. They are literally "onstage," and as such become a part of the visual spectacle of performance for the audience seated on the floor of the hall in front of the raised stage. The response of the stage-seated dignitaries becomes a natural part of an audience member's peripheral vision, and at times, possibly the focus. The context here has dramatically affected the audience/performer spatial relationship.

Festival performances provide another set of substantive alterations in *kathakaḷi* which reflect matching performance with audience competencies. A few alterations concern new plays entering the repertory of companies which have gained increasing popularity with festival audiences. While festival audiences may have connoisseurs among those in attendance, the substance of the audience is drawn from a wider cross-section of the village community. The majority of audience members will not be educated in the gestural language, nuances, or subtleties of *kathakaḷi*. For a general Kerala audience, there will be familiarity with the basic epic story being enacted, but limited knowledge of the conventions of *kathakaḷi* treatment of the story. Interest, then, is usually in following the unfolding dramatic narrative, rather than subtleties of treatment of that narrative. One company in particular, the P.S.V. Natyasangham of Kottakkal, Kerala, has made a self-conscious effort to include in its repertory plays which reach a more general mass audience. They include in their repertory the *Complete Rāmāyaṇa*, a new play written in order to encompass the entire narrative of the *Rāmāyaṇa* in one all night performance! In addition, an individual highly placed in company management has authored a number of plays based on the lives of Kerala deities, including *Ayappa Caritam* (1967), one of the most beloved and popular deities of modern Kerala. These two plays are often requested for temple performances. The *Complete Rāmāyaṇa* has been authored and scored to allow introduction of several characters much closer to everyday

Malayalees and therefore more appealing to a mass audience than the somewhat more distant characters of the traditional repertory. In the *Complete Rāmāyaṇa* Manthara, the old woman, is costumed and acted as a typical old Malayalee woman. Indeed, the entire production, in the words of the senior teacher of the troupe, was "specially edited to suit the common man and does not have many technical refinements compared to other plays performed." This trend may signal continued alterations in *kathakaḷi* texts, scores, and approaches to characterization which attempt to provide *kathakaḷi* performances to match the competencies of popular audiences, so important a part of the economic vitality of competing schools and companies today. The P.S.V. Natyasangham Company continues to maintain in its repertory the traditional plays, and is trained to please traditional tastes of connoisseurs. The self-conscious alterations are an attempt to have ready at hand texts and scores which match the appropriate audience. The special attention given to alteration to suit popular tastes illustrates how the center of the *kathakaḷi* tradition has expanded to meet and accommodate changing circumstances.

The third and most recent addition to *kathakaḷi* contexts are non-Kerala urban audiences. Here again a variety of alterations may be cited as examples of how the text, score, and conventions have been substantively altered to accommodate the appreciation level of the audience. One of the most popular versions of *kathakaḷi* prepared especially for export from Kerala to urban Indian and western audiences is a complete *Mahābhārata*. An edited version prepared by the Kerala Kalamandalam linked together scenes from a number of different traditional *kathakaḷi* plays dramatizing segments of the *Mahābhārata*. The newly edited "complete" version provides a panorama of more action-packed drama than the more leisurely unfolding of each single play. In addition, in the large auditoriums the majority of an audience is unable to get close enough to see the nuances of expression.

The expanding center of *kathakaḷi* tradition has in many ways accommodated and embraced this new, non-traditional audience. The meeting of traditional dance-drama and a new, completely "uneducated public" has produced for both *kathakaḷi* and many other forms of traditional performance, several completely new forms of cultural performance—the lecture-demonstration and modern Indian dance programs. Lecture-demonstrations are "complete performances," or ancillary pedagogical activities associated with a performance by a company. In either case emphasis is on breaking down the performance score, its conventions and sets of techniques into units small enough so the audience can understand how the performer approaches and interprets his art. Simple examples are usually given of each major element which goes into training the performer, and the performance itself. In *kathakaḷi*, the most popular demonstrations are illustrations of preliminary training exercises, footwork patterns in various speeds, basic hand and facial gesture systems, and how the actor literally "speaks" with the hands. The performance score of the lecture-demonstration consists of narrated commentary explaining each element demonstrated and the demonstration itself. While lecture-demonstrations have become separate forms of cultural performance, when given by highly trained and skilled *kathakaḷi* professionals the techniques themselves are usually unadulterated. In such cases lecture-demonstrations are within the tradition in terms of techniques, yet outside it in terms of format and scoring. When performed as ancillary pedagogical activities associated in particular with international tours by major institutions and companies, lecture-demonstrations are a part of the center, widening to reach its non-indigenous audience.

All of the changes discussed thus far are accepted at the heart and center of the *kathakaḷi* tradition, although it must be recognized that those controlling the center of the tradition today include both traditional masters and patron/connoisseurs, as well as the newly included administrative personnel of modern institutions and representatives of sponsoring agencies. In the modern world, the center of the *kathakaḷi* tradition has expanded to embrace new audiences each of which possesses a different level of competency from the traditional "ideal" of the connoisseur. Often unselfconsciously *kathakaḷi*, responding to pressures of reaching such audiences, has subtly altered various aspects of conventions and score to suit their appreciation level. However, even in the midst of such changes, certain aspects of *kathakaḷi* tradition have remained inviolable and closed. At the center of the tradition since the fixing of the form in its mature years, there has never been an attempt to alter substantially basic staging conventions or sets of techniques. The alterations introduced have been editorial and compositional at the level of structure and score. At the outer edge of what is permissible and open to change, at the periphery of the tradition, exist a number of adaptations of *kathakaḷi* which have altered aspects of the dance-drama so much as to be considered outside the tradition by those at the center.

## Change at the Periphery: Creating New Forms of Performance

The collective center of the *kathakaḷi* tradition is maintained even today largely by the power and authority of the master actor/teachers who stand at the apex of the artistic tradition. Traditional connoisseurs play an important role in maintaining what is acceptable at the center through commentaries, public discussion and acknowledgement of artistic merit, and more recently through newspaper and magazine articles and reviews. Changes not accepted at the center of the tradition remain at the periphery.

Two major examples will illustrate substantive alterations of *kathakaḷi* at the periphery of the tradition. Both are self-conscious attempts by individuals to alter specific aspects of the received *kathakaḷi* tradition in order to create either a "new style" of *kathakaḷi* or an "improved" *kathakaḷi*. In both cases the progenitors of the changes believe these substantive alterations in *kathakaḷi* would allow the form to communicate with a more universal audience than an audience limited to traditional patron/ connoisseurs.

Guru Gopinath was a highly acclaimed student at the Kerala Kalamandalam during its early years. His career on the modern Indian dance stage began at age 23 in 1931 when he joined Ragini Devi for the beginning of her all-India tours in which she was presenting "*kathakaḷi* style" dances selected and adapted from the traditional repertory. After Gopinath left the company of Ragini Devi, he returned to Kerala, serving as a court dancer from 1936-45 under the patronage of the Travancore Palace where he and his newly formed company danced on request of his patrons. Eventually Gopinath founded his own school, the Viswa Kala Kendra, near Trivandrum, Kerala, where he sought to develop, codify, and transmit to future dancers his own changes and experiments in traditional *kathakaḷi*. Gopinath set out on a self-conscious path of "artistic modification" to reshape *kathakaḷi* according to an implicit new set of aesthetic principles which he had absorbed in part from his association with Ragini Devi and his exposure to the modern Indian dance-stage culture. Gopinath has spoken freely regarding the changes that he introduced into *kathakaḷi*:

> One hundred per cent of what we do is from *kathakaḷi*, but the compositions are my own. I rearrange the basic component parts according to my view of theme and situation in the dance being created. I select all movements according to theme and situation. *Bhāva*, *raga*, and *tāla* are my guides. So I make changes in *mudrās* and carefully proceed to change things according to the context of the dance.

He goes on to give a vivid example of how he has altered the delivery of specific facial expressions and correlative *mudrā*s according to his principle of "context" determining delivery:

> According to the mood of when we talk, we know that our facial expressions will have the chin in one direction or another and that is the direction of the *mudrā*s. Heaven is up; sadness is down. So there will the *mudrā*s be, according to the mood.

Gopinath has chosen to discard completely the conventional method of hand placement in delivery of *mudrā*s designating a particular spatial range in the body's surround. He has replaced the assumed spatial convention with the principle of fitting hand location for *mudrā* delivery with the "mood" of the dramatic context. Rather than remaining constant according to the received convention, the specific location of the hands is set free from tradition and must be interpreted afresh for each moment in the new composition. In addition, Gopinath reshapes all body movements to fit "the situation, theme, or emotion of the characterization."

Behind dramatic context, mood, and characterization as his operative interpretative principles in guiding use of techniques in performance, Gopinath has reshaped *kathakaḷi* according to his interpretation of what is "artistic" and "beautiful." For Gopinath, traditional *kathakaḷi* was not "artistic." Gopinath feels that his substantive alterations will "smooth out" the rough inconsistencies in *kathakaḷi*, and will develop it into an "art form." He feels that his alterations "have given an artistic way of presenting *kathakaḷi*" which can continue to develop through application of his principles of interpretation. One of the specific changes which has resulted from Gopinath's desire to make *kathakaḷi* artistic and beautiful has been in battle choreography. Gopinath states,

> There must be beauty in stagecraft, for the footwork, and for body movement. For example, for a battle scene I will keep the dancers farther apart than in *kathakaḷi*. They are farther apart according to the weapon in use. While in *kathakaḷi* there is only one relationship, in my choreography they will shoot towards each other and not at the audience.

Gopinath is referring to the fact that by accepted stage convention *kathakaḷi* is usually performed frontally, with actors facing the audience. This is even true in combat scenes when two characters may engage in battle, for example, through the use of bows and arrows. Rather than having the characters "shooting" the arrows in the conventionized, stylized manner facing at approximately a 45 degree angle toward each other, Gopinath will have them face one another and "fire" their arrows. What Gopinath is introducing is a practical extension of his earlier principles—what is best expressed as moving *kathakaḷi* toward verissimilitude. Rather than accepting *kathakaḷi*'s traditional cnventions of performance and stage use for what they are, i.e., conventions, Gopinath has attempted to bring such "inconsistencies" between stage action and life action into line with his "modern" notions of stage action and stage picture—all harmonized according to the overriding concerns of what is artistic and beautiful. All of the operative principles which guide Gopinath in reforming and creating his new style of *kathakaḷi* dance are derived from early modern Western dance and acting. He instituted a complete structural, technical, and dramatic overhauling of the received form in order to create a form of *kathakaḷi* that would communicate beyond the borders of what he felt were the restrictions of *kathakaḷi*'s regional appeal and isolation.

A second example of substantive alteration at the periphery of the main tradition is that of P.K. Devan who has also attempted in his own modifications of *kathakaḷi* to free it from what he feels are the imperfections and abominations of the past. He too is attempting to make *kathakaḷi* a 'universally' communicable art form. Devan and his family established the See India Foundation in 1969 in

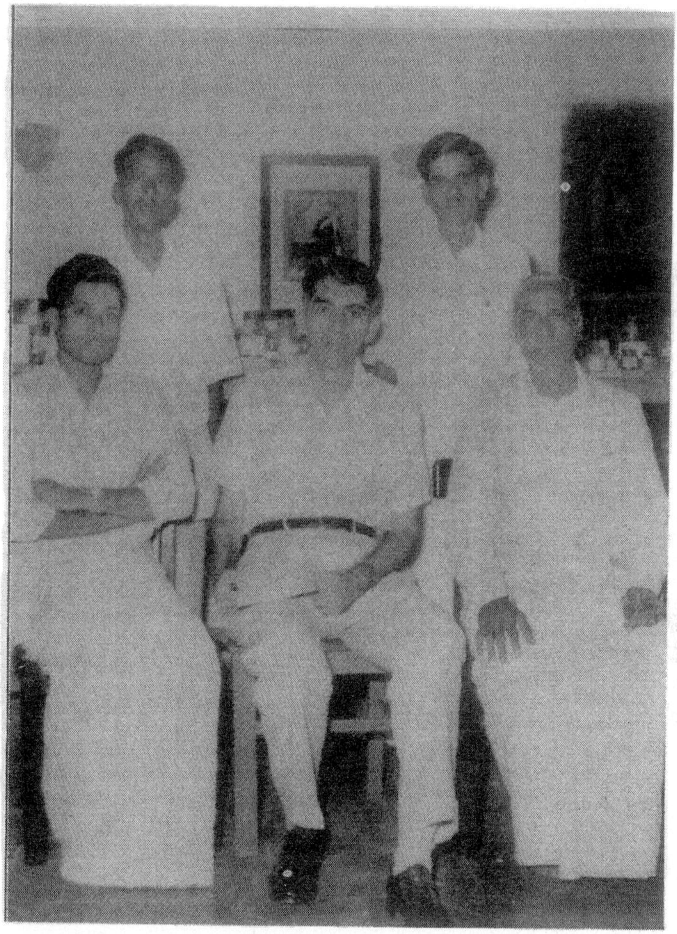

Singer 1. Milton Singer visited an ayurvedic clinic in Madraś in 1954. The ayurvedic doctor is on his left.

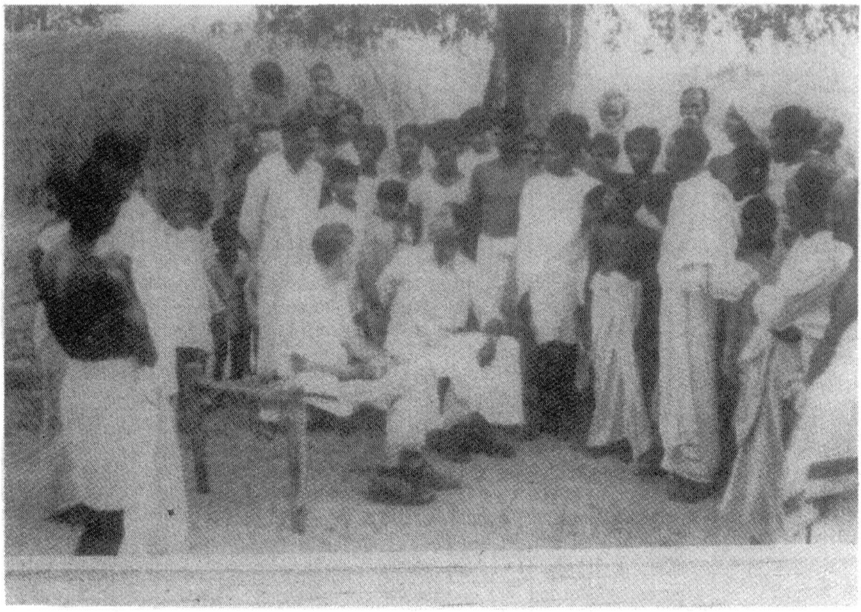

Singer 2. In 1955 Milton Singer visited an untouchable colony outside Madras.

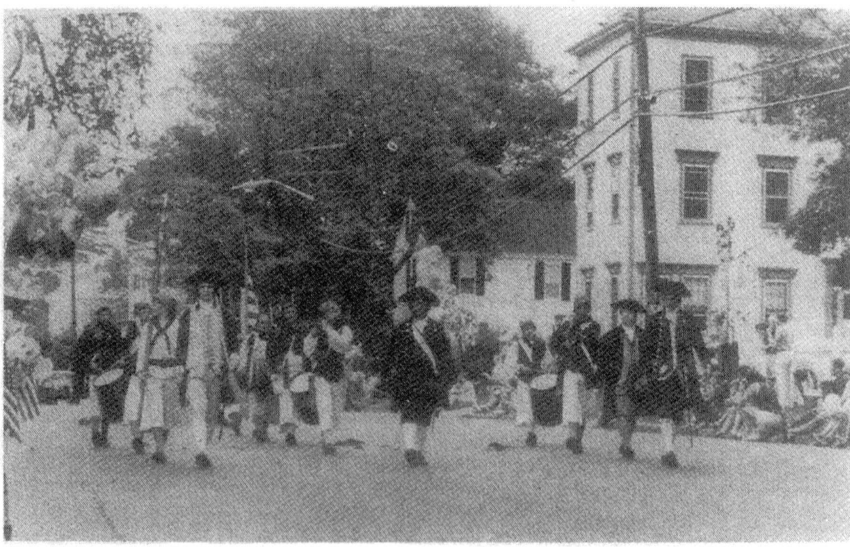

Singer 3. The Continental Navy band marches during a Yankee Homecoming Parade in "Yankee City" (Newburyport) in 1977. A voluntary ceremonial marching band, the "Continental Navy" performs for historical reenactments such as the battle of Bunker Hill and Bicentennial celebrations. Photo by Douglas Goodfriend.

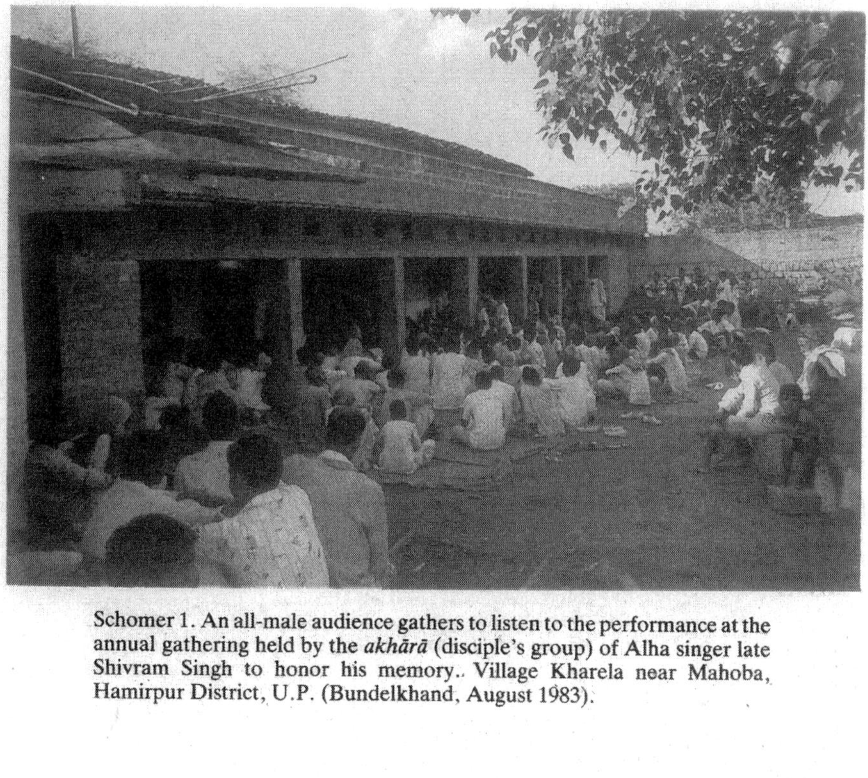

Schomer 1. An all-male audience gathers to listen to the performance at the annual gathering held by the *akhārā* (disciple's group) of Alha singer late Shivram Singh to honor his memory.. Village Kharela near Mahoba, Hamirpur District, U.P. (Bundelkhand, August 1983).

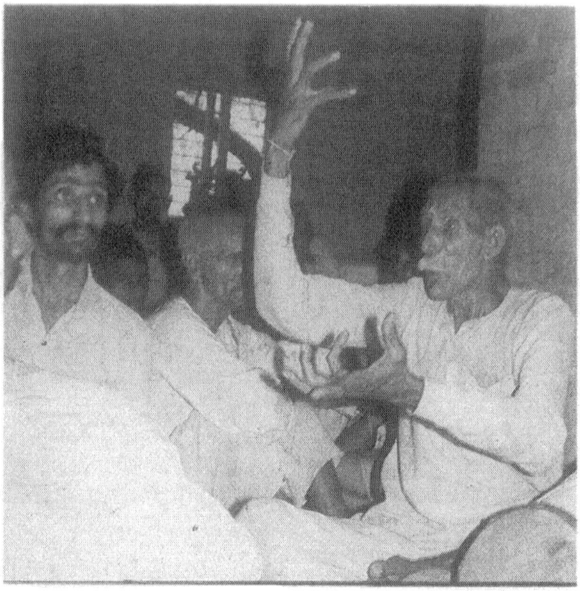

Schomer 2. Alha Singer Parasram, at 80 the oldest living disciple of Shivram Singh, sings solo, in the Bundeli style, accompanying himself on the *ḍholak*. Kharela, August 1983.

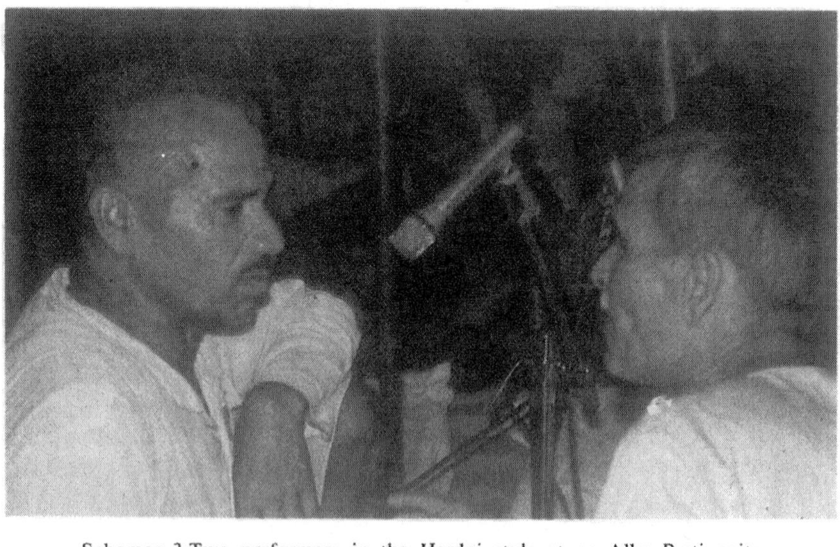

Schomer 3.Two performers in the Hardoi style at an Alha Pratiyogita (competition) in which singers from various regions sing face-to-face with full concentration to improvise together. Kanauj, August 1983.

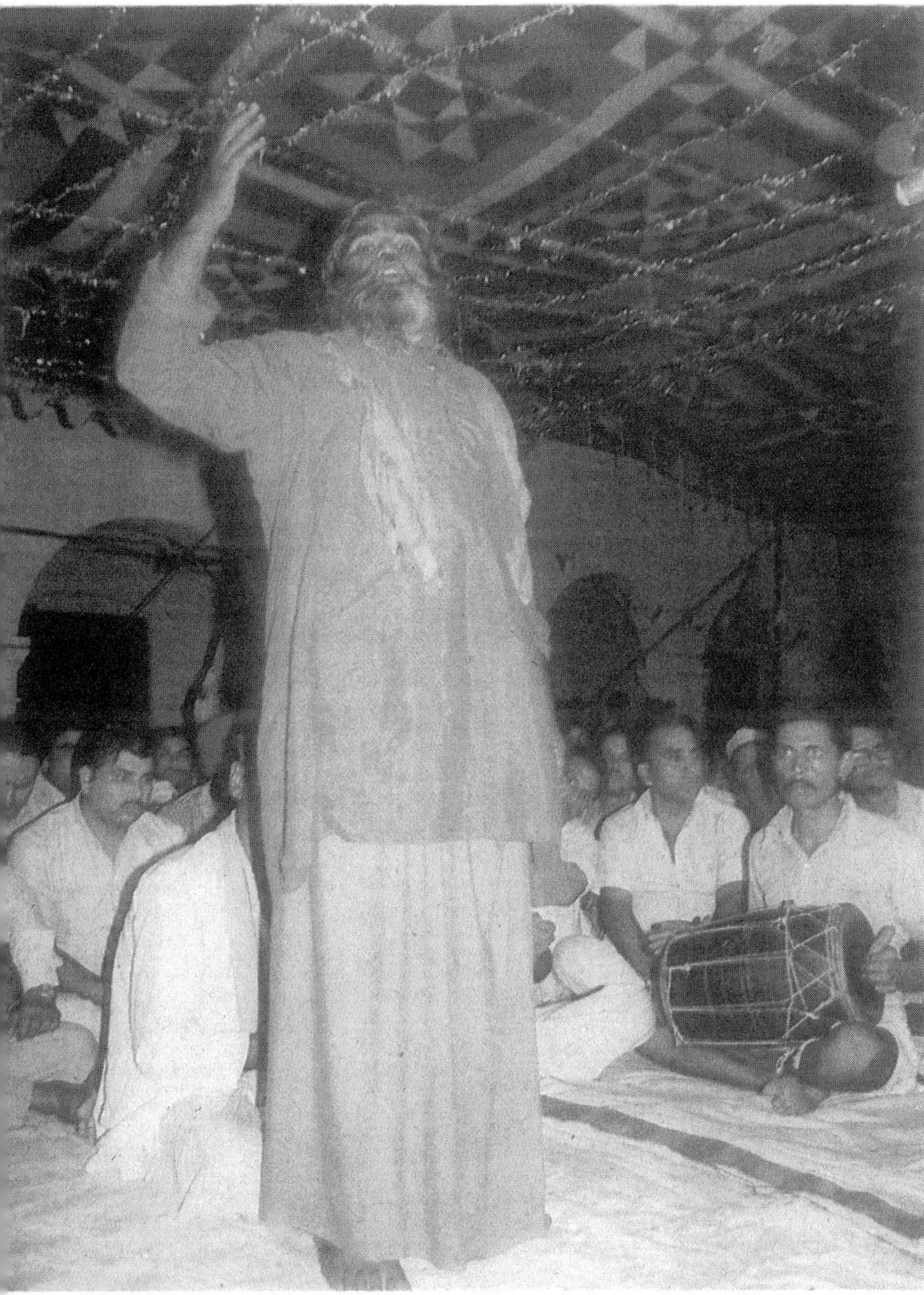

Schomer 4. Swami Gangeshvaranand performing in Kanauj, standing and using strong martial gestures, in the typical style of the Baiswara-Kanauj area. Kanauj, August 1983.

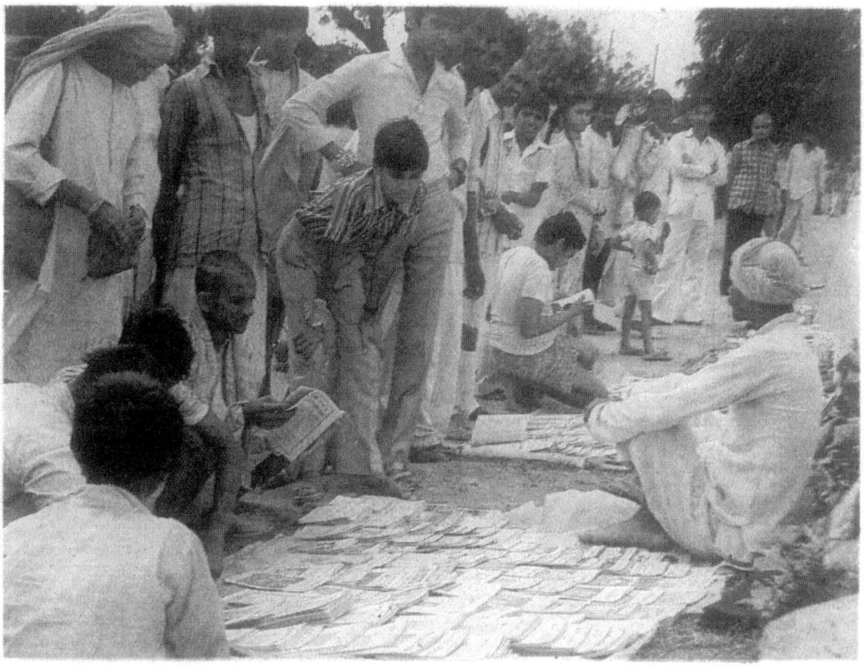

Schomer 5. At the Kiratsagar *melā* in Mahoba, roadside book and pamphlet stalls sell cheap printed versions of various Alha episodes *laṛāī*. Rainy season, 1983.

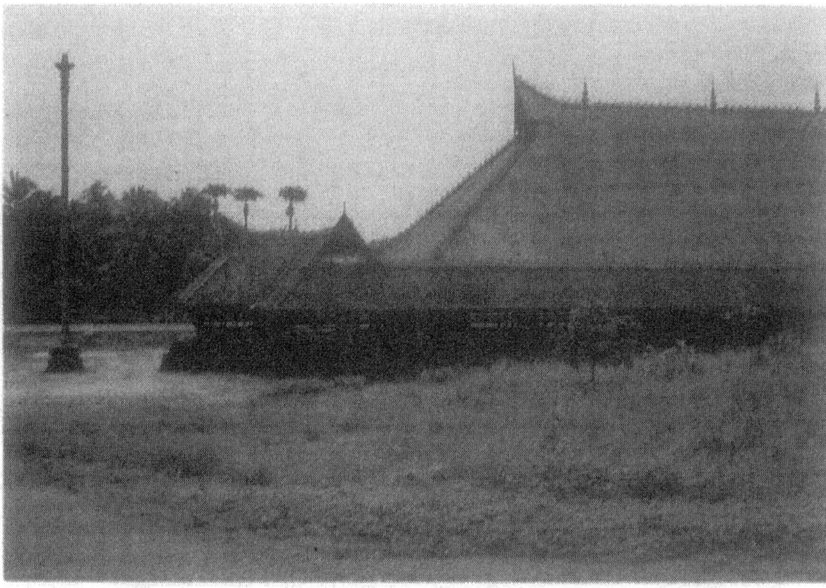

Zarrilli 1. The Kerala Kalamandlam *kūttuambalam* theatre was designed by Appakoothan Nayar for the state academy in Cheruthuruthy, Kerala. His design was based on a reading the *Natyaśāstra* combined with traditional Kerala temple architecture.

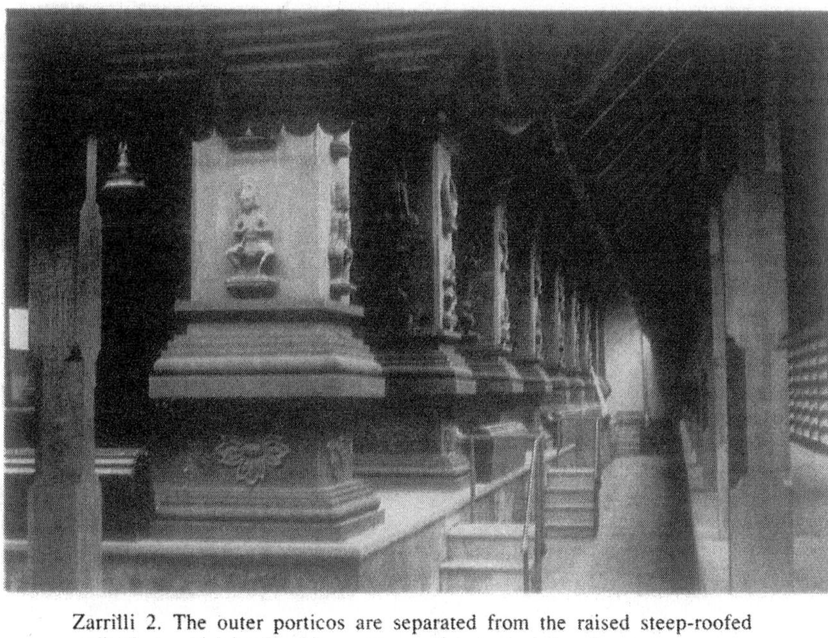

Zarrilli 2. The outer porticos are separated from the raised steep-roofed auditorium, which has hand hewn stone sculptures depicting dance poses.

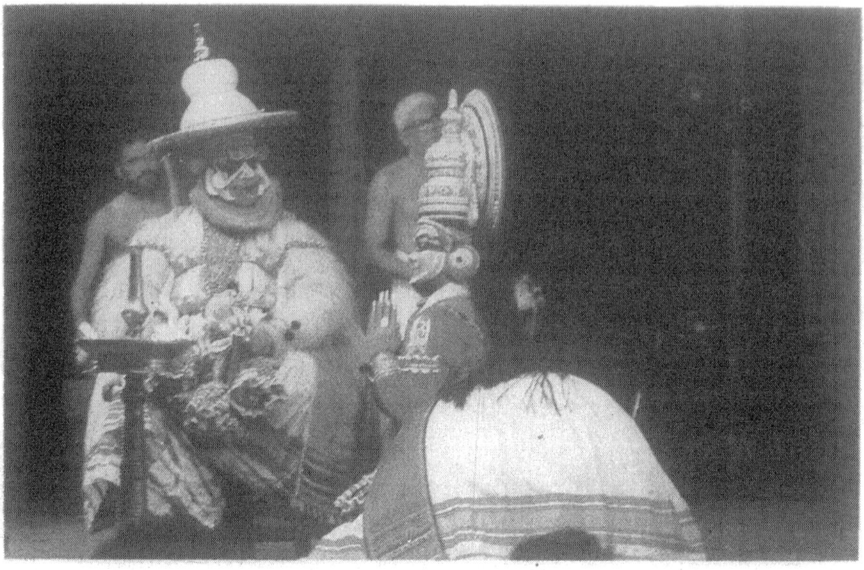

Zarrilli 3. A performance of the *Kalyaṇā Sauggandhikam* on the slightly raised wooden stage, with Bima bowing before Hanuman after he has revealed his divine form.

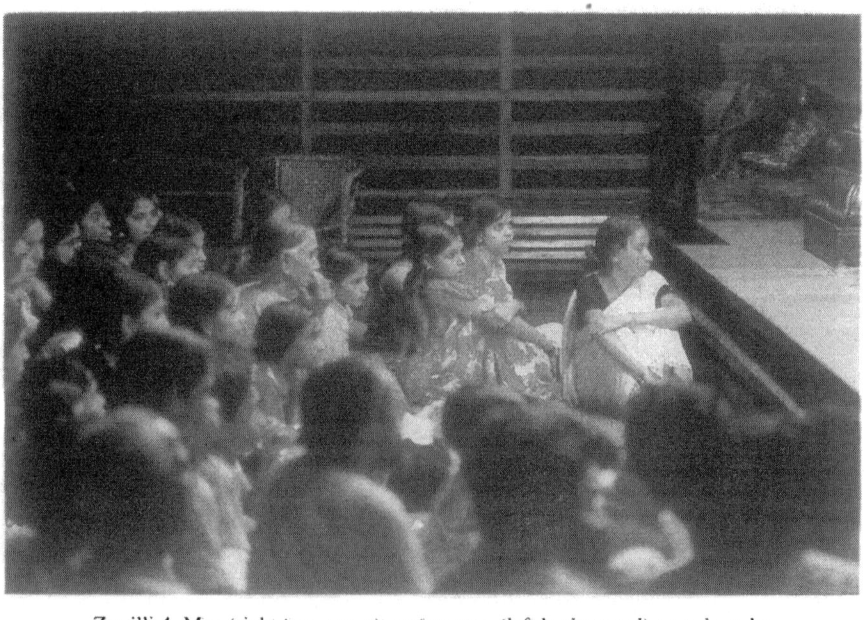

Zarrilli 4. Men (right foreground) and women (left background) seated on the audirorium floor face the raised wooden stage as they would in the traditional *kūṭiyāṭṭam kūttambalam* temple settings.

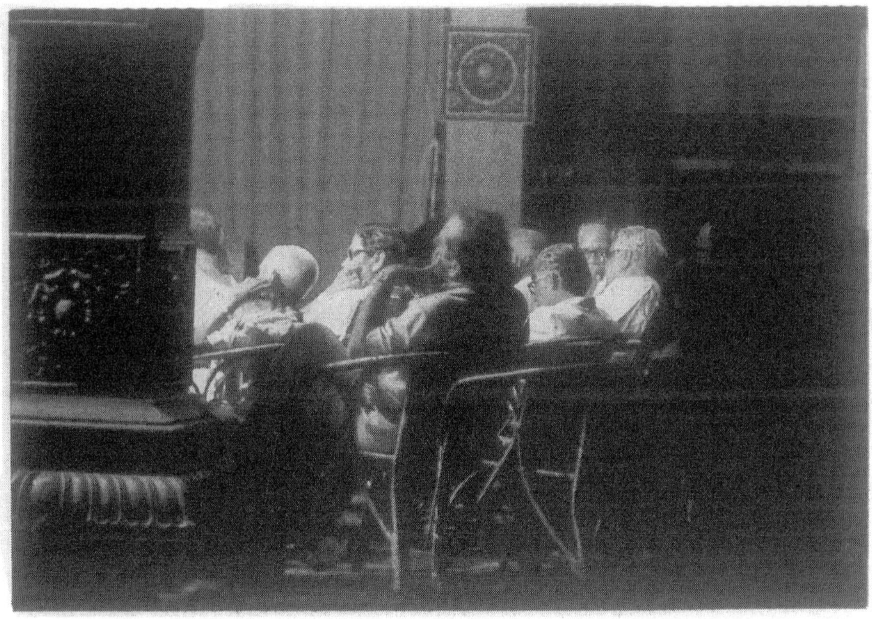

Zarrilli 5. In a new development, wicker chairs are placed on each side of the large wooden stage to accommodate important visitors, connoisseurs, and government officials. Some have fallen asleep in the early morning hours of the all-night performance.

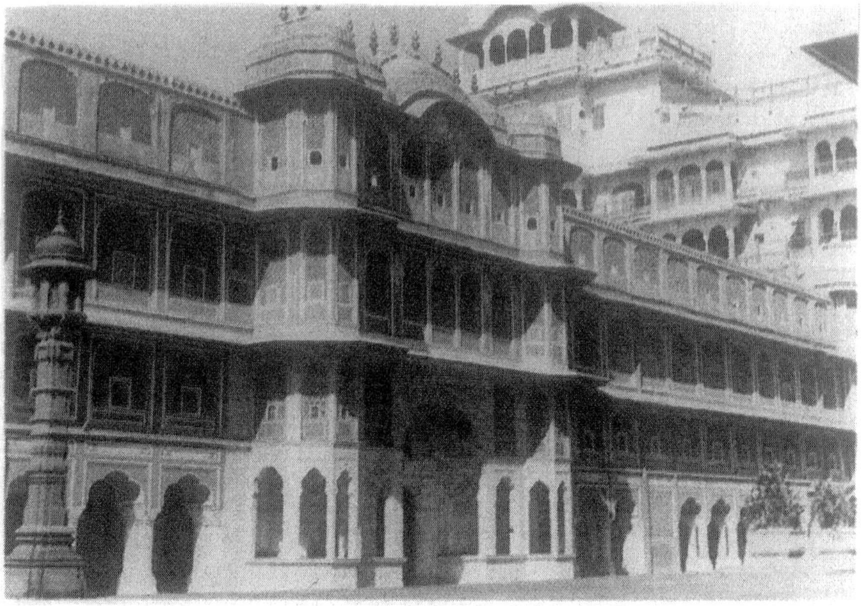

Erdman 1. In the Jaipur city palace, the *naubat khānā* was located in a room over the gateway leading from the *dīwān-ī-ām* (public audience hall) to the *dīwān-ī-khās* (private audience hall).

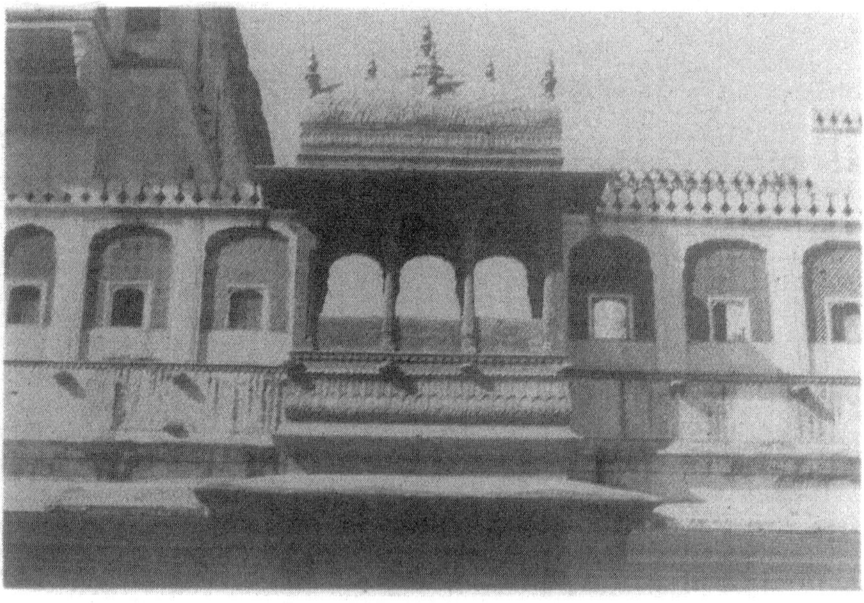

Erdman 2. On a balcony of the city palace, overlooking the private courtyard of the *mahārāja*, *Guṇījankhānā* musicians played in the Hara Mahal. The sound of their music could be heard in the Chandra Mahal and in the *zenānā*.

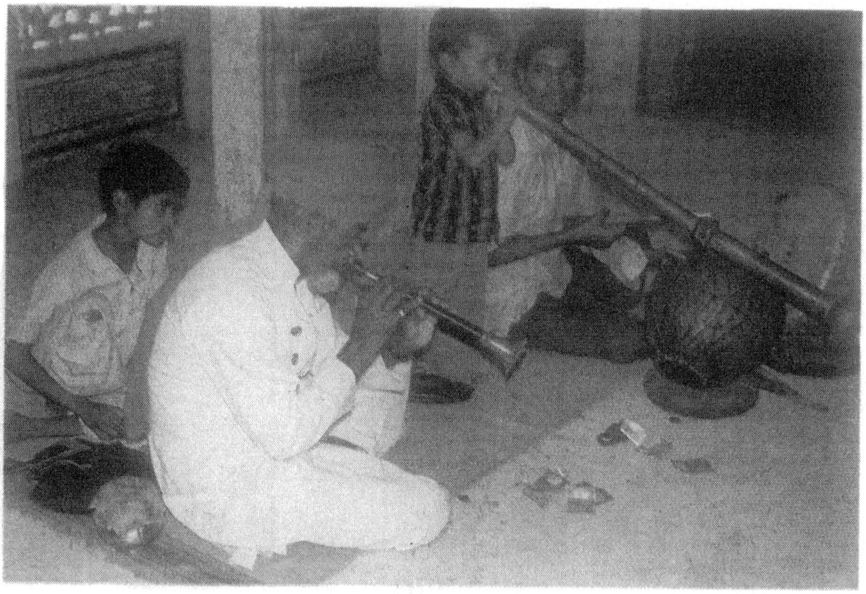

Erdman 3. Even in the 1970s the hereditary musicians of the Naubat Khana continued to play their *shehnaī* and *naggāra* on the palace balcony, behind which is a museum of armaments open to the public.

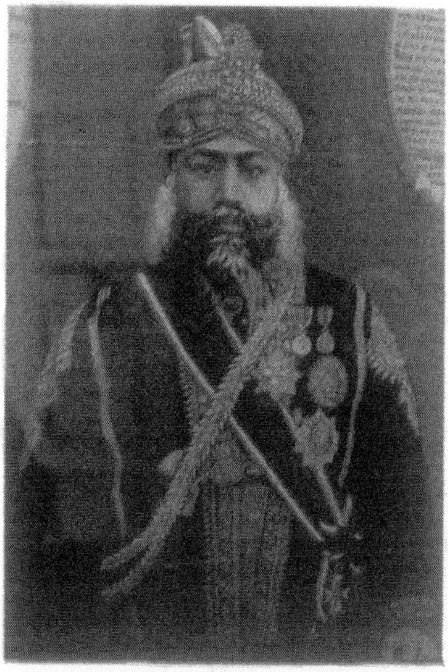

Erdman 4. During the reign of Madho Singh II in Jaipur, numerous petitions were made to the *mahārāja* by *Guṇījankhānā* artists. This painted portrait was photographed by the author at Jodhpur.

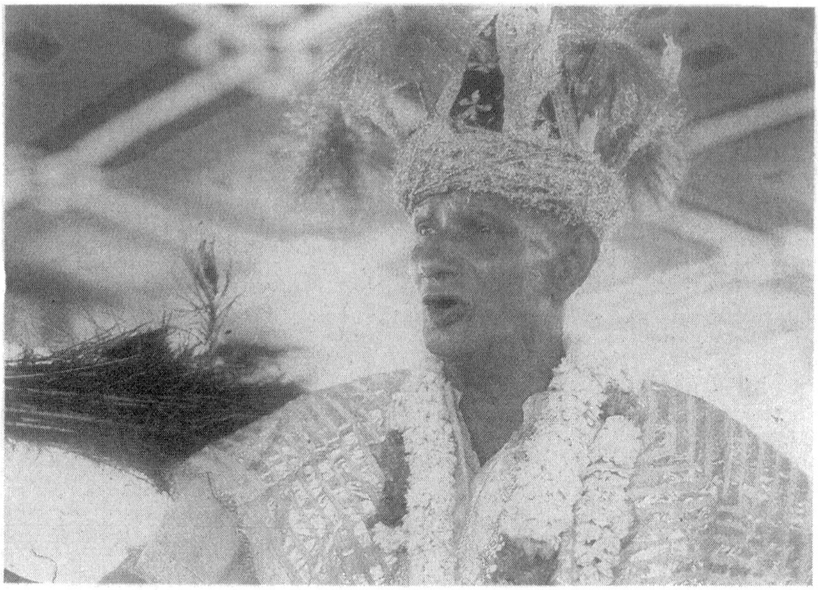

Erdman 5. Shri Gopi Bhatt, a famed *nauṭankī* player, heir to a Jaipur *Guṇījankhānā* post, performs in Brahmpuri in the northern part of Jaipur city, in April 1976. Photo by Kaushal Bhargava.

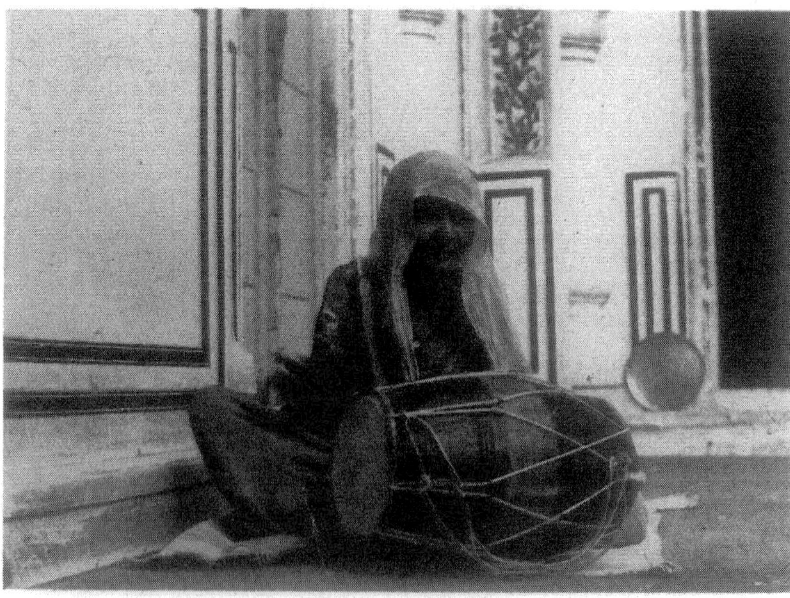

Erdman 6. A *ḍholī* woman sits with her *ḍholak* in the *zenānā* of the city palace, awaiting the beginning of the *Gangaur* singing. Jaipur 1977.

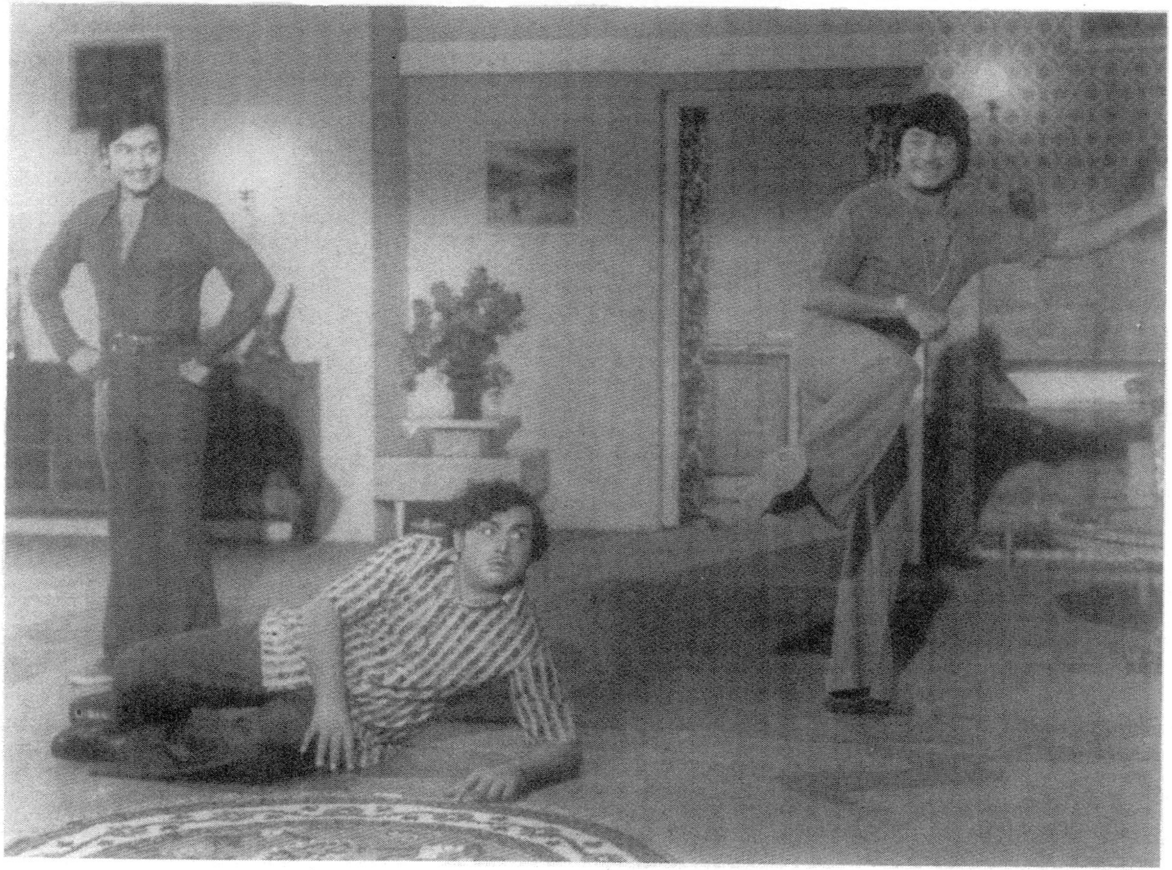

Pendakur 1. Rajkumar plays a double role in *Shakaraguru*

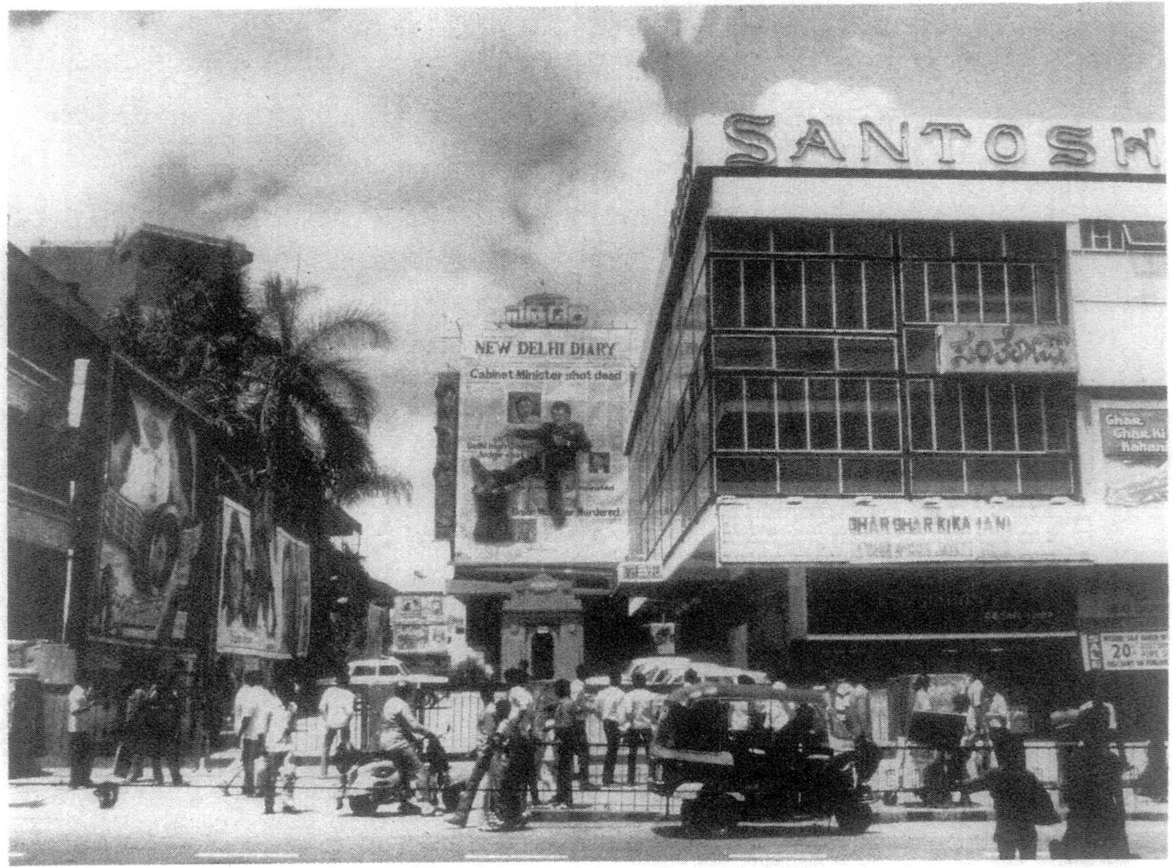


Pendakur 2. Kannada and Hindi films play adjacent theaters in Bangalore

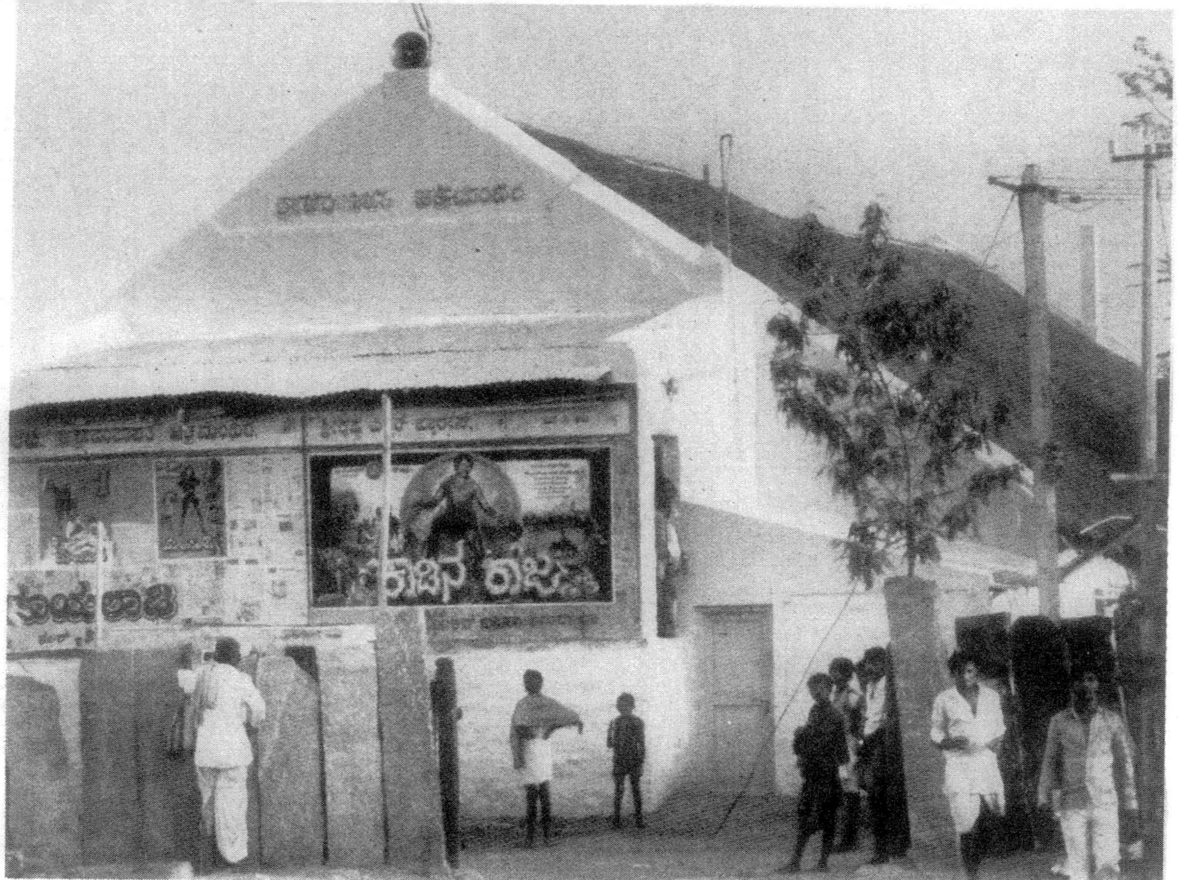

Pendakur 3. Semi-permanent theater ('c' center ) in a small town

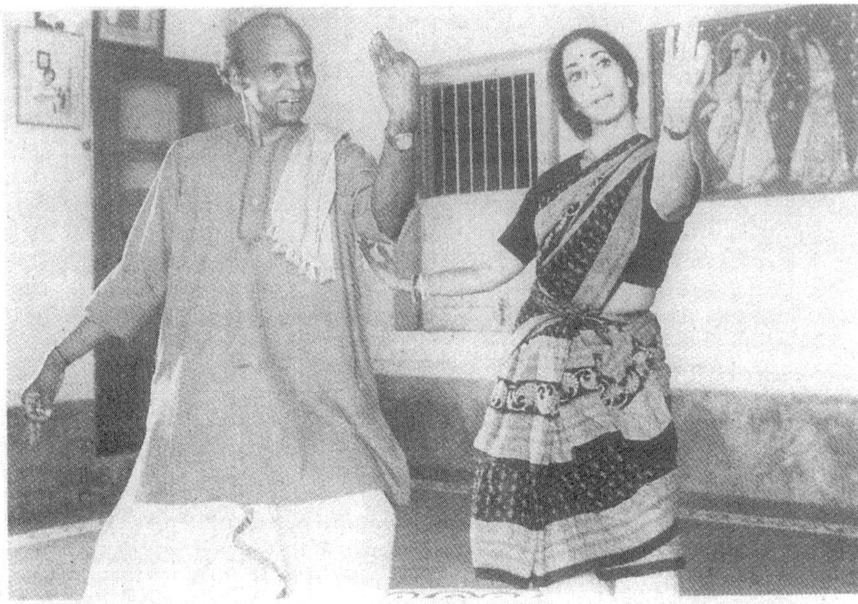

Lowen 1. Guru Kelucharan Mohapatra and Sharon Lowen work on an Odissi movement, early in her training, in the Guru's dance studio in Cuttack, Orissa. (Photo by Avinash Pasricha)

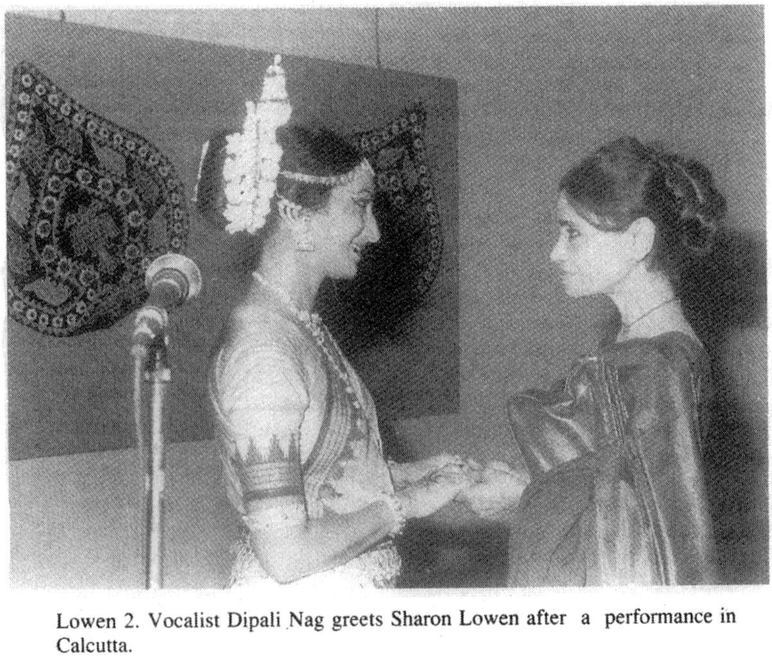

Lowen 2. Vocalist Dipali Nag greets Sharon Lowen after a performance in Calcutta.

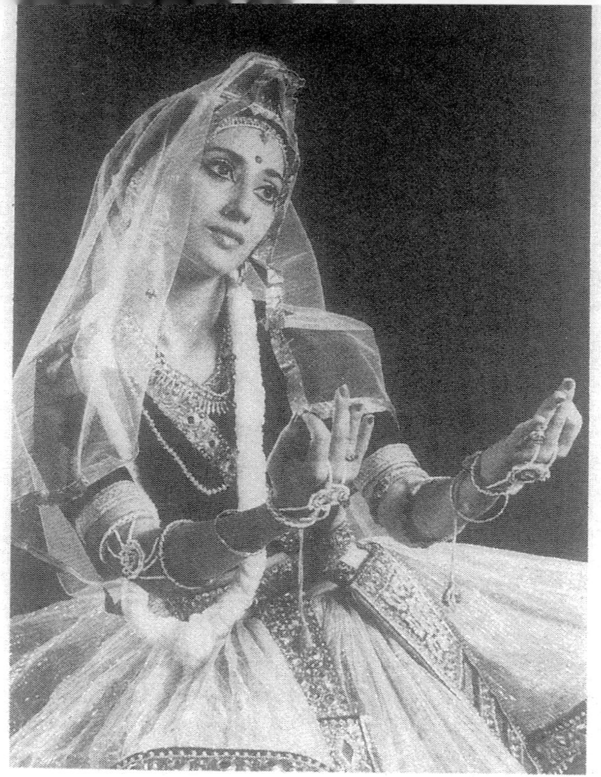

Lowen 3. Indian classical dances require elaborate and delicate costumes, which must be made by costumers and jewelers specializing in a particular dance style, to the specifications of each particular artist. Here Sharon Lowen is shown in a Manipuri dance costume.

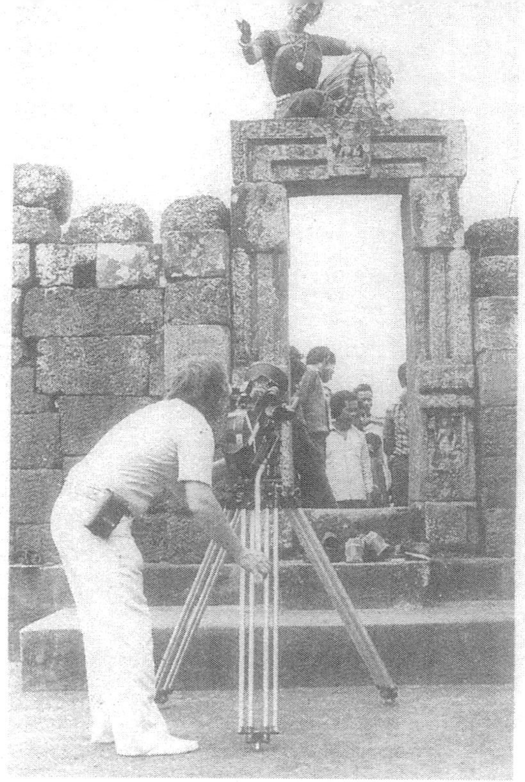

Lowen 4. During the filming of "Odissi in Odissi", a documentary on Sharon Lowen by Central Television (England), Sharon Lowen dances above a temple lintel in Bhubaneswar so the sky will provide the blue chrome to cross fade from dancer to Konarak temple structure.

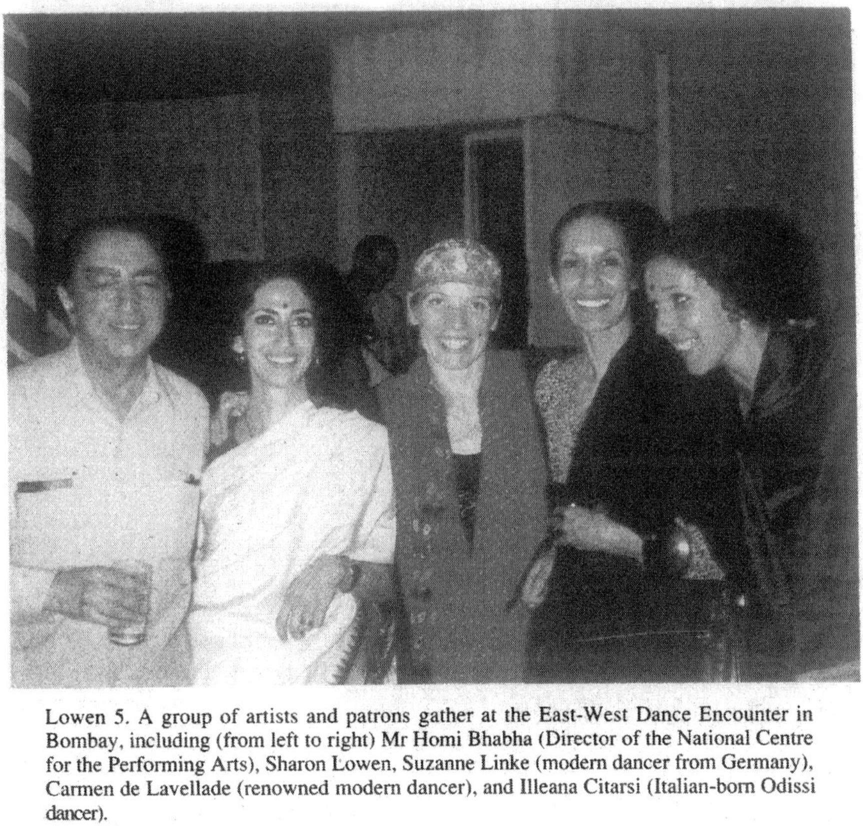

Lowen 5. A group of artists and patrons gather at the East-West Dance Encounter in Bombay, including (from left to right) Mr Homi Bhabha (Director of the National Centre for the Performing Arts), Sharon Lowen, Suzanne Linke (modern dancer from Germany), Carmen de Lavellade (renowned modern dancer), and Illeana Citarsi (Italian-born Odissi dancer).

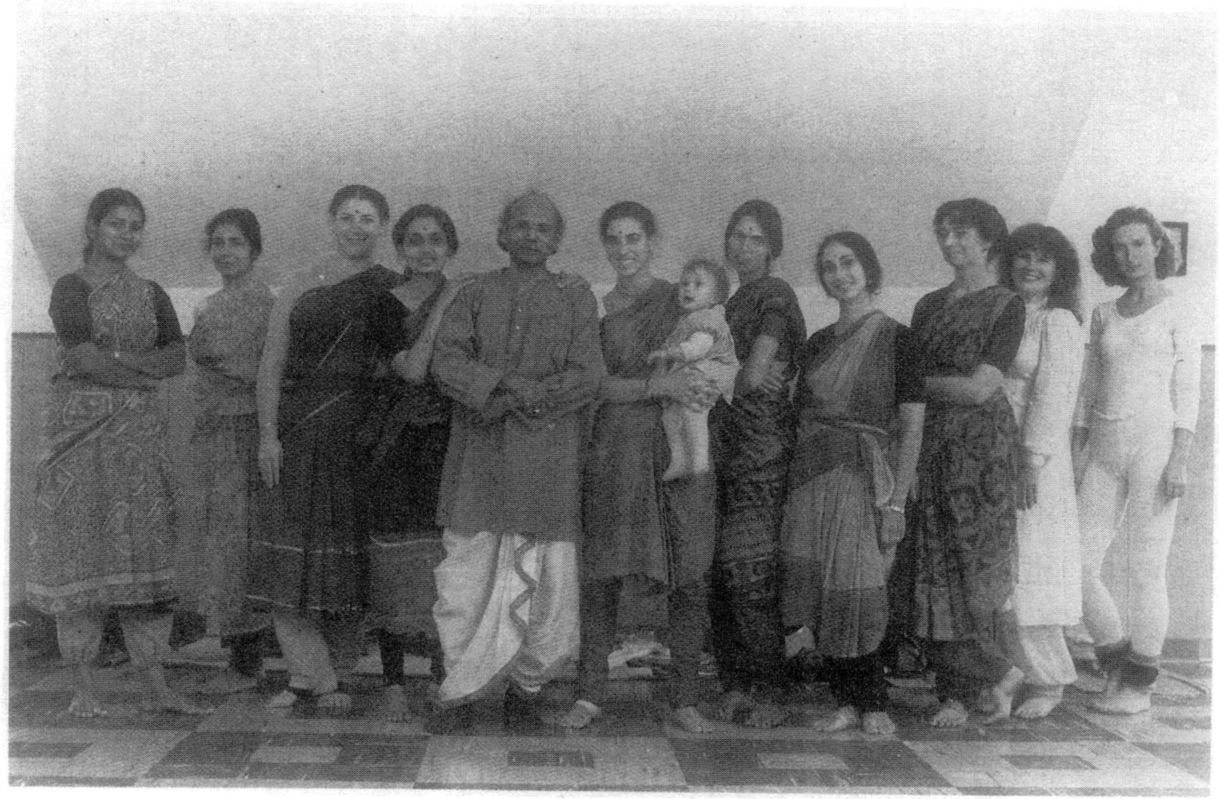

Lowen 6. During his tour of the United States with Sharon Lowen, Guru Kelucharan Mohapatra conducts a dance workshop in San Francisco.

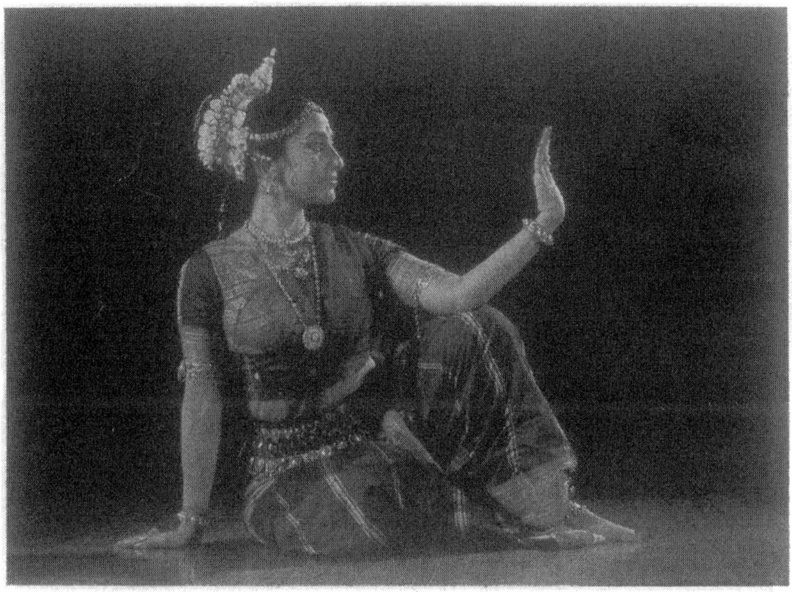

Lowen 7. Sharon Lowen as Radha, looking in her mirror to watch Krishna arrange her hair (from Kuru Yadunandana, a dance from *Geet Govind* by Jayadev). (Photo by Avinash Pasricha)

Ernakulam at the port city of Cochin, Kerala, where they offer daily performances of *kathakaḷi* especially tailored to suit tourists. Performances are given by the "Gurukulam Kathakali Yogam" which lasts approximateiy one and one-half hours from 7 p.m. Normal attendance ranges from two or twenty or more.

The performances offered to the tourist audience begin with a speech by the director which details the work of the Foundation and the "history" of *kathakaḷi*. Speaking in a highly dramatic voice the director presents *kathakaḷi* as a "2,000 year old temple art." He continues,

> Everything in *kathakaḷi* is traditional. *Kera* means coconut, and this tree is worshipped here and affects everything including our art. The costumes are ancient. The crowns that we use are more than 100 years old. There is a religious meaning to everything—the nails of the left hand are traditional from Hindu sayings. The skirt stands out wide—we believe a worshipper designed these . . .

When the introduction is complete, the performance continues as the director and his wife hold up the front curtain under the roofed shed which serves as the theatre. As the performers are revealed, the audience is told that they are seeing a "Dance of Prayer." On conclusion of the prayer dance, the director continues his commentary by describing the techniques of *kathakaḷi* performance. Finally, the short performance for the evening is presented.

In addition to the misleading interpretation of *kathakaḷi* history given in the introduction, Devan has chosen to introduce many subtle adjustments in *kathakaḷi* techniques and conventions similar to those made by Guru Gopinath. Devan's operative aesthetic principles are similar to Gopinath's, although he states them with greater disdain for what he feels are gross ethical and artistic outrages in the past tradition. The changes in Devan's form of *kathakaḷi* are based on the following principles: (1) make *kathakaḷi* artful (meaning to make it beautiful onstage, consistent, truer to life, and 'ethical,' i.e., expunging any violence and sex), (2) base choices on the common emotions so that it is universally communicable; and (3) cut down the amount of vocalization and text presentation in order to enhance communication with non-Malayalees since they do not know the language. More specifically,

Devan has chosen to completely alter the traditional *mudrā* system, feeling that "the *mudrās* in *kathakaḷi* are crude and have no roots." He has his actors make them "larger," and makes sure that those selected for presentation are from day-to-day life. He selects the minimum number of *mudrās* possible to illustrate the "common emotions" of everyday life. Quite simply, Devan has discarded the complete grammar of *kathakaḷi* through which the performer literally speaks the text, and leaves only those *mudrās* directly relevant to the emotional and dramatic context of the scene. He has deleted the very heart of the *kathakaḷi* score. The structure used to enact the *padams* or dialogue sections of the performance has been drastically transformed.

Other alterations in techniques include keeping to a "minimum singing because singing means language [Malayalam] and only a few people [i.e., not tourists] can understand it." The severely edited vocal line reflects Devan's attitude toward traditional *kathakaḷi* texts.

> In *kathakaḷi* there is not a single story which can be presented as it is. And drama means the minimum number of words to communicate the maximum of feeling. What is done in *kathakaḷi* stories is that there are too many words where they are not needed. There are romantic descriptions which do not befit to sustain the drama.

If one assumes a modern, Aristotelian, Western definition of "drama," then Devan is actually quite right in his assessment of *kathakaḷi* texts and scores. They do, as we have seen, contain love scenes which are extraneous to any direct through line of dramatic action or plot advancement—notions totally foreign to *kathakaḷi*. It is just such "extraneous" interpolations which fulfil the indigenous *rasa* aesthetic of elaboration and savoring. Devan goes so far as to propose the deletion of any vulgarity or bloodshed from the dramas—attributes of the early dramas which he feels reflect the decadent tastes of the high caste patrons who shaped the form.

> Sometimes I am ashamed to translate *kathakaḷi* songs. I deliberately avoid some of the lines written by the famous writers. I am for removing all vulgarity, bloodshed, murder, blood drinking from the *kathakaḷi* stage. Even Bharata has mentioned that

> there should be no blood shown onstage. Dussassana when presented abroad by even a top company gives a terrible impression for all art lovers. Why should a noble religious art like *kathakaḷi* present such ghastly scenes on the stage?

Devan sees *kathakaḷi* as a "noble" art which must be revised in order to allow it to communicate that nobility universally. His working definition of "noble" does not permit him to include any recognition of the popular and ritual roots of *kathakaḷi* performance— specifically the violent concluding battles and the "blood scenes" where Bhima, for example, drinks the blood of the vanquished foe in answer to his pledge. The principles which Devan uses to guide his radical revisions of *kathakaḷi* technique and stories are a mixture of Victorian disdain for the suggestive poetic eroticism of *kathakaḷi*, combined with a view of the legacy of *kathakaḷi*'s ritual drama predecessors as "vulgur," mixed with quasi-Western notions of what constitutes "the dramatic," "art," and "the beautiful". For Devan as much as for Gopinath, "art" *is* the beautiful. And the beautiful is not the indigenous understanding of "beauty" embodied in techniques and principles of *kathakaḷi* performance at the center of the tradition. Rather, what is beautiful is shaped by verisimilitude, the appearance of truth. And the appearance of truth is seen in those dramatic works which communicate "universally" through the simple emotions that all people share.

Both Gopinath and Devan operate today at the outer periphery of the *kathakaḷi* tradition. In both cases they are independent patron-managers who, with changing socio-economic circumstances, have been able to operate outside the traditional system of patronage and sponsorship. At one time, Gopinath had the patronage of the Travancore court—a temporary reflection of the acceptance of a traditional elite patron of the "modernist" aesthetic which Gopinath espoused and applied to his own creations. Each has chosen to tailor *kathakaḷi* to suit a new audience. Rather than attempting to "educate" the new audience into received conventions and traditions, they choose to alter and adapt the system itself to meet what they *think* the new audience wishes to see and appreciate. Therefore, Western and quasi-Western principles are behind both sets of alterations, though the degree of change is tempered by the views of each patron-manager.

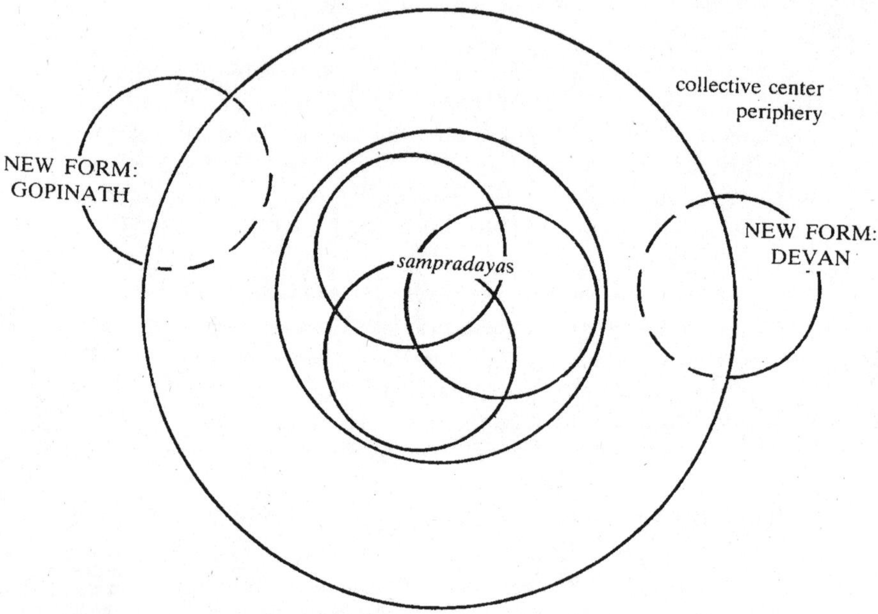


DIAGRAM 3: New Forms at the Periphery

In the modern period the collective center of *kathakali* expanded as various aspects of the form have been adjusted to suit audience competencies. Simultaneously, new forms of cultural performance have come into existence at the periphery of the tradition which are neither traditional *kathakali* as defined at the center, nor completely distinct.

At the periphery exist the "new styles" of *kathakali* created by Gopinath and Devan.

Both Gopinath and Devan began their involvement with *kathakaḷi* at the center of the tradition. Gopinath was trained traditionally in *kathakaḷi* in both the Southern style and in the composite Kalamandalam style. He has remained a noted performer throughout his life, even though he developed the new altered style taught at his own school. On the other hand, Devan's involvement in *kathakaḷi* is vicarious and indirect through his brother's traditional training as a performer and his family's long-term involvement in *kathakaḷi*. When Gopinath, and Devan's brother, Shivaram, left Kerala to begin tours and performances of modernized *kathakaḷi*-style dance under the leadership of Western influenced and/or trained modern dancers seeking a rediscovery of traditional Indian modes of performance, they stepped outside the boundaries of the center. In both cases, neither ever returned to the center from which they began. While each could give "traditional performances" if they so chose, their life vocation followed a path of development of styles at the periphery, where the interface between Western and traditional principles and forms produced the new styles of *kathakaḷi* each practices today. The existence of such modified and peripheral forms of *kathakaḷi* has only been possible with the substantive socio-economic changes of the twentieth century where new economic infrastructures support peripheral styles on a long-term basis.

How does each patron-manager view his own work? Gopinath has always publicly declared that he is developing "*kathakaḷi* style" performances. He defines himself as maintaining the core of *kathakaḷi* tradition at the level of technique, but moving outside the center in his new choreographic creations. Devan, on the other hand, presents his performances as "traditional," and therefore within the received and continuous line of development. He sees himself on a crusade to refine and improve what is the tradition and what should be presented publicly and passed on as the "correct" tradition. He sees himself as re-claiming the nobility of an art form which has become decadent and lost its pristine purity.

Those at the center of the *kathakaḷi* tradition today vary in viewpoint regarding such modifications to the *kathakaḷi* tradition made by Gopinath and Devan. As solo performers either Gopinath or Shivaram is part of the center of the tradition when performing with other traditionally trained artists in typical performances, but when they are engaged in the modified styles, they are certainly perceived as something other and different from the mainstream.

Gopinath's work falls more into the category of "modern Indian dance," that catch-all of contemporary eclecticism which has grown out of the larger interface of Western and Indian dance, while Devan's creations are an anomaly tucked away in the tourist corner of Kerala and undeserving of much discussion by masters or connoisseurs. Although they remain outside the center at the periphery, these two "new" forms or manifestations of "*kathakaḷi*" illustrate the dynamic nature of a tradition of cultural performance (Diagram 3). Without the inherent socio-economic infrastructure of Kerala society to support them, it seems unlikely that either development will be long-lived. The "creative" adaptations of Gopinath and Devan are structurally similar to the types of modifications of basic sets of techniques and forms undertaken by the early patrons and masters in *kathakaḷi*'s formative years. However, in the case of the modern examples, the patron/managers are attempting to reach a non-indigenous audience, and without the support of a societal infrastructure, there seems little chance for long-term maintenance within Kerala.

## Summary: Patronage and the Center-Periphery Phenomenon

The center of the *kathakaḷi* tradition historically began with the development of the first *sampradāya*. As local variations evolved over the years, new *sampradāya*s developed, each identified with specific individual artists and/or patrons, and by creative changes they introduced into their performance lineage. The traditional socio-economic infrastructure based on "house and land" provided the basis for local organization of the artistic tradition, emphasizing a creative and symbiotic relationship between patrons and senior performers in their service. Each *sampradāya* was constituted at its own center by the interaction between sets of patron/connoisseurs and artists, students, and craftsmen in their service and related to one another by performance lineages. The transmission of the specifics of performance knowledge to succeeding generations is the essential life-blood of the larger composite artistic tradition.

During its formative period, the periphery of the tradition consisted of those artistic innovations testing the limits of what had been received from the preceding generation. The periphery was assumed and thence consumed by the center itself, as its logical extension. Creative change at the periphery, especially up to the relative "fixing" of the basic techniques and conventions of the genre, was either accepted into the individual center of a *sampradāya*, and/or into the collective center of the tradition, or attempted in performance, dismissed and never tried again. Since the relative "fixing" of the form, numerous innovations and changes have been introduced within *sampradāya*s and are viewed as "improvements" on what is considered traditional.

The fourfold model of traditional patronage played an extremely important part in the formulation and crystallization of the essential features of the tradition, patronage which constantly moved the tradition toward refinements featuring aesthetic elaboration—hallmarks of the virtuostic identity of traditional *kathakaḷi* when pleasing its traditional patrons.

In the modern period, radical disjuncture between social and artistic roles, especially among those providing financial and organizational support, has led to separation of the four aspects of traditional patronage as one role in a role set. Connoisseurs are no longer necessarily patrons. Patrons are no longer necessarily connoisseurs. Dependency on sponsors whose performative sensibilities are decidedly pluralistic, and often populist rather than virtuostic, has led to re-constitution of the center by fiat if not by choice. Performances are altered self-consciously to suit the varied tastes of different audiences. Economic necessity as well as democratic and populist sentiments lead to attempts to appeal to wider audiences. Numerous technological changes have been routinely accepted at the collective center, subtly altering the performance tradition.

Many changes accepted at the center have substantively altered the received and still ideal aesthetic principles of the genre. The introduction of new plays for mass audiences alter the *rasa* aesthetic favored by the traditional connoisseur, replacing it with shorter scenes depending more on narrative continuity and less on opportunities for elaboration.

Although the modern tradition is still constituted by *sampradāya*s, these lineages are neither closely associated with particularly creative pairs patron/master-performer, nor are they so clearly identifiable as in the past. Today *sampradāya*s in the new institutional settings are much more diffuse collections than clear inheritances with the stamp of distinctive individuals.

And yet the limits of the collective center have been drawn

against alterations such as those of Gopinath and Devan. At present their changes are perceived as 'outside' the traditional limits of what is acceptable. The collective center now will alter and adapt to educate its alternative audiences. Plays and scenes are edited but *kathakaḷi*'s essential identifiable techniques such as the complex systems of hand and facial gestures have remained relatively inviolable. The proportion of elaboration is reduced, the proportion of improvisation curtailed, even the proportion of *padam* delivery cut; however, basic techniques and conventions remain.

With the radical change in patronage and socio-economic infrastructure supporting the tradition, the collective center has radiated outward to encompass new audiences, and has allowed each of these audiences to determine alterations in the 'ideal' mode of performance where performer skills and level of knowledge are more perfectly matched. Without compromising the basic structure of the form, alterations are introduced which maintain the score, yet allow for increased appreciation by those 'less educated' through program notes or lecture-demonstration. Performer and audience competencies are more appropriately matched.

Beyond the collective center of the tradition at the periphery are those like Gopinath and Devan transgressing the limits of change allowable at the center—modifying and altering *kathakaḷi* even more radically to suit new audiences. Producer-managers allow the principles assumed by an audience to determine changes in the techniques and structure of the genre. In response to the same socio-economic pressures impinging on the center, new satellite forms of cultural performance are created which are related to, but stand outside the mainstream of the tradition.

The traditional roles of the patron in *kathakaḷi* history have obviously been integral to its creative life. The patron was at the center of the tradition as artistic creator, and his evolving aesthetic sensibilities as a *rasika* set the circumscribing limits of the periphery. The contemporary separation of once integrally related elements of the patron's role into multiple and often independent ones, filled by individuals from a variety of socio-economic and/or caste groups, has led to a reconstitution of the center and its relationship to the periphery—a relationship that is certainly in constant tension, recontituting itself and knitting anew the network of relationships within which the art is created, and thereby altering the performance genre itself.

## References

Chaitanya, Krishna. 1971. *A History of Malayalam Literature*. New Delhi: Orient Longman.

Erdman, Joan L. 1978. "The Maharaja's Musicians: the Organization of Cultural Performance at Jaipur," *American Studies in the Anthropology of India*, pp. 342-367. Delhi: Manohar.

Fuller,C.J. 1976. *The Nayars Today*. London: Cambridge University Press.

Gough, Kathleen. 1952. "Changing Kinship Usages in the Setting of Political and Economic Change Among the Nayars of Malabar," *Journal of Royal Anthropological Institute*. 82, Pt. I, 71-88.

———. 1961. "Nayar: Central Kerala," eds. Kathleen Gough and David M. Schneider, *Matrilineal Kinship*, pp. 298-404. Berkeley: University of California Press.

Grayburn, Nelson, ed. 1971. *Readings in Kinship and Social Structure*. Berkeley: University of California Press.

Gundert, Rev. H. 1982. [1872]. *A Malayalam and English Dictionary*. New Delhi: Asian Education Services.

Higgins, Jon B. 1976. "From Prince to Populace: Patronage as a Determinant of a change in South Indian (Karnatak) Music" *Asian Music* 7,2:20-26.

Inoura, Yoshinobu and Kawatake, Toshio. 1981. *The Traditional Theater of Japan*. N.Y.: Weatherhill.

Jeffrey, Robin 1976. *The Decline of Nayar Dominance*. Sussex: Sussex University Press.

Jones, Betty True. 1983. "Kathakali Dance-Drama: An Historical Perspective," *Performing Arts in India: Essays on Music, Dance, and Drama*, ed. Bonnie C. Wade. Berkeley: Center for South and Southeast Asian Studies, University of California.

Jones, Clifford Reis, ed. 1967. "The Temple Theatre of Kerala: Its History and Description," Ph. D. dissertation, University of Pennsylvania.

———. 1984. *The Wondrous Crest-Jewel in Performance*. Delhi: Oxford University Press.

Kareem, C.K. 1973. *Kerala Under Haidar Ali and Tipu Sultan*. Ernakulam: Paico.

MacCannell, Dean. 1979. "Ethnosemiotics," *Semiotica* 27,1/3:149-171.

Mencher, Joan P. 1962. "Changing Familial Roles Among South Malabar Nayars," *Southwest Journal of Anthropology* 18, 3:230-246.

———. 1966a. "Kerala and Madras: A Comparative Study of Ecology and Social Structure," *Ethnology* 5, 2:135-171.

———. 1966. "Namboodiri Brahmins: An Analysis of a Traditional Elite in Kerala," *Journal of Asian and African Studies* 1, 3:183-196.

Menon. A. Sreedhara. 1972. *Kerala District Gazeteers: Cannannore*. Trivandrum: Government of Kerala Press.

Menon, K.P. Padmanabha. 1982. *History of Kerala, Vol. I*. New Delhi: Asian Educational Services.

———. 1983. *History of Kerala, Vol. II*. New Delhi: Asian Educational Services.

Menon, K.P.S. 1957. *Kathakaḷi Rangam*. (Malayalam). Kozhikode: Mathrubhumi Printing.

———. 1968. "Chengannur Raman Pillai," *Kalamandalam Annual* 9-11.

————. 1969. "Kruichi Kunhan Panikkar," *Kalamandalam Annual*, 17-19.
————. 1973. "Guru Kunju Kurup," *Journal of the National Centre for the Performing Arts* 2, 1:18-24.
Merton, Robert K. 1957. "The Role-Set: Problems in Sociological Theory," *British Journal of Sociology* 8:110-113.
Miller, Eric J. 1954. "Caste and Territory in Malabar," *American Anthropologist* 56:410-420.
————. 1955. "Village Structure in Noth Kerala," *India's Villages*, ed. M.N. Srinivas. N.Y.: Asia Publishing House.
Moore, Melinda. 1982. "Nalukettu: The House as Microcosm," unpublished paper presented at the 11th Annual Conference on South Asia, Madison, Wisconsin.
————. 1983. "Taravad: House, Land and Relationship in Matrilineal Hindu Society," Ph.D. dissertation, University of Chicago.
Namboothiry, E. Easwaran. 1983. *Bālarāmabharatam: A Critique on Dance and Drama*. Trivandrum: Keralasamskritam Publications.
Neff, Deborah. 1987. "Aesthetics and Power in Pambin Tullal: A Possession Ritual of Rural Kerala," *Ethnology* 26,1:63-71.
Neuman, Daniel. 1976. "Towards an Enthnomusicology of Cultural Change in Asia," *Asian Music* 7, 2:1-5.
Puthankalam, J. 1977. *Marriage and the Family in Kerala*, Calgary: University of Calgary, Department of Sociology (*J. of Comparative Family Studies*).
Raja, K. Kunjunni. 1964. *Kūtiyāṭṭam: An Introduction*. New Delhi. Sangeet Natak Akademi.
Ramachandran Nair, K. 1971. *Early Manipravalam, A Study*. Trivandrum: Anjali.
Richmond, Farley and Richmond, Yasmin. 1978. "The Rites of Passage and *Kūtiyāṭṭam*," *Sangeet Natak* 50:27-36.
————. 1985. "The Multiple Dimensions of Time and Space in *Kūtiyāṭṭam*, the Sanskrit Theatre of Kerala," *Asian Theatre Journal* 2, 1:50-60.
Singer, Milton. 1966. "Radha-Krishna *Bhajanas* of Madras City," *Krishna: Myths, Rites, and Attitudes*, pp. 139-172. Chicago: University of Chicago Press.
Thurston, Edgar. 1975. *Castes and Tribes of Southern India, Volume M-P*. Delhi: Cosmo Publications (First printed 1909).
Unni, N.P. 1977. *Sanskrit Dramas of Kulaśekhara*. Trivandrum: Kerala Historical Society.
Zarrilli, Phillip B. 1977. "Demystifying Kathakaḷi," *Sangeet Natak* 43:48-59.
————. 1978. "*Kalarippayattu* and the Performing Artist East and West," Ph.D. Thesis, University of Minnesota.
————. 1979. "*Kalarippayattu*, Martial Art of Kerala," *The Drama Review* 23, 2:113-124.
————. 1983. "A Microanalysis of Performance Structure and Time in *Kathakaḷi* Dance-Drama," *Studies in Visual Communication* 9, 2:50-69.
————. 1984a. *The Kathakaḷi Complex: Actor, Performance, Structure*, New Delhi: Abhinav.
————. 1984b. "Doing the Exercise:' The In-body Transmission of Performance Knowledge in a Traditional Martial Art," *Asian Theatre Journal* 1, 2:191-206.

# Petitions to the Patrons: Changing Culture's Substance in Twentieth Century Jaipur*

Joan L. Erdman

Performing artists were first brought to Rajasthan's princely courts as prized cultural acquisitions, appreciated by their patrons and encouraged to bring forth their creations for royal gatherings and contests. The *Āīn-I Akbarī* of Abū'l Fazl is our main source for musicians at the Mughal court of Akbar, which was probably the model for the rulers of Jaipur (Erdman 1978). "His Majesty," says Abū'l Fazl, "pays much attention to music, and is the patron of all who practise this enchanting art" (Blochmann 1965:681). Jaipur's rulers named their department of performing artists

* I wish to acknowledge the assistance of the American Institute of Indian Studies, the Fulbright Doctoral Dissertation Research Abroad Fellowship of the U.S. Department of Health, Education and Welfare, and the Danforth Foundation in supporting the studies and research for this paper. In addition I would like to thank those generous persons who assisted, advised, and encouraged me in this work, especially my assistants at the Jaipur Depository of the Rajasthan State Archives: A.K. Khan and M.L. Sharma, Nawal Patel who pointed the way to the *Guṇījankhānā* Records, and Dr. Gyanchand Sharma, In-Charge of the Archives at Jaipur; Dr. A.K. Das, Dr. Chandermani Singh, and Shri Gopal Narayan Bahura of the Jaipur City Palace Museum; Rajmata Gayatri Devi and Maharaja Bhawani Singh of Jaipur; Mohan Singh Kanota and Devi Singh Mandawa; my colleagues and teachers at the University of Chicago: Kali Bahl, Bernard Cohn, Edward C. Dimock, Jr., Lloyd and Susanne Rudolph, Milton and Helen Singer, and Phillip Zarrilli of University of Wisconsin-Madison.

*Guṇījankhānā* to reflect the virtuoso qualities of these specialists in music, dance, and other entertainments.

Jaipur city was founded in the early 18th century (Erdman 1990); we do not know when the *Guṇījankhānā* was founded. Maharaja Sawai Ram Singh II (1835-1880) learned music from one of the *Guṇījankhānā* artists, Behram Khan Dagar, and was a knowledgeable patron. But by the turn of the century, the *Guṇījankhānā* artists had acquired their penultimate patron, whose interests focussed on religion and women, rather than the exquisite arts of his household musicians. Maharaja Madho Singh II (1880-1923) and his successor Maharaja Man Singh II (1923-47) retained the department until 1942, but were "absentee" patrons, carrying out through their subordinates the administration of a department no longer of much interest to them. While not all of the *Guṇījankhānā* artists of this period were famed performers, some achieved considerable renown (Erdman 1985). But the disinterest of their patron raised issues for all the artists which allow us to ask about their lives as courtiers through records of their own making.

These issues are raised in petitions through the *Guṇījankhānā* to their royal patron, in judicial records of petitions brought by townspeople, and in departmental records of requests and decisions made by the State Council and administrators of the state departments. The petitions illustrate the concerns which were part of the conceptual framework of patron-performer relations in Jaipur in this period. Is a post (*asāmī*) granted by inheritance or merit? Is the patron a protector or an employer of virtuoso artists? Is precedence the rule for decisions in particular cases, or is the State now empowered to make rules which deny prior practice?

Embedded in these issues is the question of whether the *Guṇījankhānā*, the Department of Virtuosos in Jaipur, is a private household service to the Maharaja who is both patron and ruler, or an administrative bureau of the Jaipur State, with responsibilities governed by public officials and regulations. Since in the early 20th century Jaipur State was subject to treaties made with the British in the early 19th century, and since the two rulers of Jaipur State in the early 20th century were both adopted and ruled under British advice, affirmation, and guidance, the familial connections of servants and rulers were broken. Jaipur State reforms, begun by Maharaja Sawai Ram Singh II during his long rule, were continued.

The movement from household and servants to state and servant-employees in Jaipur in the late nineteenth and early twentieth centuries is reflected in the *Guṇījankhānā* petitions.

## Guṇījankhānā: A Department of Performing Artists

In Jaipur the *Guṇījankhānā* was the department which maintained artists for religious, social, and domestic services, as well as the cultural institution which supported artists, professional musicians and dancers who were individually known and appreciated for their artistic performances.[1] As one of the royal household departments, the *Guṇījankhānā* had offices in the square contiguous to the maharaja's palace, within the same compound. The performers resided mainly in the city neighborhood directly east of the palace compound, and came to the palace for their duties and service at appointed hours. No schools for performing artists existed; training was by apprenticeship in families, and took place at the performers' residences.

In the palace music was provided from dawn to dusk by a series of musical parties in the Hara Bangla, a gateway in an open courtyard of the Chandra Mahal, as the maharaja's residence is known. Dancing took place daily in the Rajarajeshwari Temple, adjacent to the *zenānā* (women's quarters). On special occasions, such as the entertainment of visitors, religious festivals, birthdays and other family celebrations, performers were called, and sometimes given special rewards for their performances. But ordinarily the *Guṇījankhānā* was an administrative bureau, under the direction of a *dārogā*, which functioned as the supplier of traditional performance services to the *zenānā* and *mardānā* (men's quarters) of the royal family.

*Guṇījans*, or the virtuosos of the *Guṇījankhānā*, were usually related to other household servants, often in the *Guṇījankhānā* itself. Inheritance of a post by a son or adopted disciple or daughter or *tawā'ichi* (dancer's adopted student) was frequent, but performers were also accepted from outside the Jaipur lines of artists. Two

This description of the *Guṇījankhānā* of Maharajas Madho Singh and Ram Singh is based on interviews with elderly palace servants in Jaipur in 1976-77 and 1978, and readings in the records of this department in the Jaipur Depository of the Rajasthan State Archives.

trends are notable in the artistic composition of the *Guṇījankhānā* in the early twentieth century: (1) the variety of types of posts was reduced, with such specializations as *khartālī* (clappers) and *rāsdhāri* (performers of the *dhāri* or *dhāḍi* caste who danced the round-dance of Krishna called *rās*) being dropped or reduced in number; and (2) recruitment of particular types of artists, e.g., Hindu *tawā'ifs*, was undertaken in order to allow traditional performances to continue despite retrenchment of *Guṇījankhānā* artists for budgetary reasons, and the refusal of Muslim artists to participate in Hindu processions or performances during their own celebration of Muhurram. In addition, there was a continual reduction in the number of persons in the *Guṇījankhānā* (artists and administrators) as well as the amount budgeted for payment to them between the early 1900s and the 1940s (although the real value of the monies is difficult to determine).

Between 1905 and 1933 there was a reduction in the persons holding posts in the *Guṇījankhānā* (chart I). Payments to

Chart 1. Selected *Guṇījankhānā* Posts[2]

| | 1905 | 1933 |
|---|---|---|
| *Kalānaut* | 44 | 21 |
| *Tawā'if* | 33 | 20 |

artists are more difficult to compare because of lack of comparative incomes, knowledge of the purchasing power of the currency in this period, and a shift in coinage between 1905 and the 1920s. The budgets and application records, including artists' petitions, establish the bureaucratic practices of the period. Lists of employees, their *asāmīs*, the sources of their allowances, and the payments made to them, are available for each year, as are periodic budgetary proposals and departmental evaluations. By 1933 widows of *Guṇījankhānā asāmīs* are transferred to the Welfare Department. Dancers originally called "*bhagtaniya*" are recorded as "*tawā'if*" in the early 20th century. Of course the *Guṇījankhānā* is part of a wider system of household management and state rule in Jaipur, and is not unaffected by the particular maharaja who rules, or by events outside Jaipur State. The patronage of the performing arts is a social relationship which occurs in a cultural context, where both

From the budgets of Jaipur State for the *Guṇījankhānā*, 1905, and 1933 A.D.

the patrons themselves, and the cultural expectations about patronage are evidenced.

*Guṇījankhānā* artists in the early twentieth century argued for their interests in concrete cases, in terms of immediate needs and rights. They requested the continuation of their right to an *asāmī* (post) as ancestral or hereditary, meaning that it went back in their family for many generations, and was (for them at least) the property of the family through inheritance and custom. Just as one patron-ruler succeeded another through generations, so also the artists argued, they succeeded one another, each line continuing its respective succession in the princely household, parallel and complementary.

In 1928 Ashiq Hussein Pakhawaji, in a petition, stated that he was maintained and supported by the late Maharaja Ram Singh, who gave him on the occasion of the *Chāti* ceremony, clothes and gold decorations, and that it was ordered that when Ashiq Hussein had a son the same award should be given. Ashiq Hussein said that now, 57 years later, he has served also the late Maharaja Madho Singh, and trained the *bai*s (ladies) of the *zenānā* (women's quarters of the palace) in the art of music. But now he has been refused both the award and the *zenānā* appointment. After noting his 45 years of loyal and diligent service to the state, he asked for appointment to a post equivalent to that sanctioned by Maharaja Madho Singh, and presentation of the promised award to his son.[3] Ashiq Hussein's petition combines aspects of being "like a son" to the Maharaja, serving the state loyally, and expecting both his service and his family-like relationship to continue through generations of maharajas and his family. Other petitions similarly stress these parallels, more like an English "upstairs-downstairs" single system family unit, than a manager-employer organization of labor. From the viewpoint of the artists, we can learn what they considered to be their rights, and how they expected their patron to support them.

Jaipur's maharajas and their representatives, on the other hand, argue in this period that it is important to maintain the quality of excellent performances in the court, and extraordinary artists are required to carry on their cultural tradition in Jaipur. In 1934 Hari Singh, Superintendent of the *Karkhānejāt* (royal departments),

Jaipur *Mahākmā Khās* Records GI7/100, Pt. II (1928).

stated in an order that the post of a man who was expert in his art has been transferred to one who is not, and he doesn't want to encourage such fellows, so the applicant can't be granted his ancestral post.[4] An order of May 1941, probably from the Superintendent, stated that it was necessary to add good female singers to the *Guṇījankhānā* "of a class superior to those presently employed . . ."

Communications between patrons and performers in early twentieth century Jaipur suggest that the parallel lines of inheritance, which granted participation in the same system to royal rulers and royal performing artists, have become asymmetrical. Rulers are adopted by blood relationships (both Madho Singh and Ram Singh were chosen from royal families) but artists are to be selected by qualifications. Furthermore, testing and retrenchment of performers in this era and comments on their performances suggest that excellence became a bureaucratic rather than an artistic matter. *Guṇījankhānā* artists were evaluated by non-connoisseur patrons and their administrators, and rewarded by salary increments and privileges for satisfactory fulfillment of their duties, rather than granted income from villages and honors for their especially the brilliant performances.

## Reviewing the Records of the Past: Historical Anthropology

The records of the past can be reviewed through the interests and biases of the present, or they can be seen historically in terms of their own time and place.[5] To these approaches "historical anthropology" has now been added, which is the review of accounts, records and other data, and through them communicative events,[6] in which a singular historical chronology is insufficient to describe the variety of alternatives from which participants in a particular socio-cultural system, in a particular time and place, made choices

[4] Jaipur *Mahākmā Khās* Records GI7/100, Pt. XIV (1936-37).

[5] See Stocking 1968, in which he contrasts the historian's commitment to the past, which is "historical interpretation proper" with commitment to an interpretive context of present-day polemic, i.e., "Whiggish history."

[6] See, for example, the use of visual data in studying the "dialectic of past and present" in Ariès 1962.

and decisions. Seeing themselves as part of a whole, socially and culturally, participants offer, in their own words and descriptions of their own actions and pasts, access to a system which they, as participants, have no need to describe to observers. Yet, as performers present in their own times, their selection of terms, setting of issues, and relating of expectations allows an observer using participants' data to become a participant-observer in the recent or distant past. The texts are an objective fact; to enter the subjective world of the participants one must know their codes, their expectations, and their range of alternatives.[7]

A statement close to the intentions of historical anthropology is Marc Bloch's *The Historian's Craft* (1963), in which he evokes the processual aspect of observing past events. Rather than separating the past from the present, Bloch sees historical time as "a concrete and living reality with an irreversible onward rush . . . the very plasma in which events are immersed, and the field within which they become intelligible (Bloch 1963:27-28). Such a conception of historical time allows understanding of the *Guṇījankhānā* artists, who themselves see the past and present as a continuity rather than an opposition, and whose actions stress both the expectations of their predecessors and the problematic of confronting a cultural structure which gives priority to reform rather than to traditions long kept.

Thus the questions of the *Guṇījankhānā* artist were concerned with why the present should be unlike the past, why a patron who has been like a father should reject them, and how they could be considered dispensable employees when their forefathers had always been part of the family household. These issues of change as evoked by the performers of Jaipur's *Guṇījankhānā* mark our entrance into their conceptual world.

The ethnographer's effort is, as Geertz suggests, "to uncover the conceptual structures that inform our subjects' acts, the 'said' of social discourse," but also and furthermore "to construct a system of analysis in whose terms what is generic to those structures, what

[7] A study by Bernard Cohn on British power and Mughal authority in India investigates the significance of symbolic procedures and exchanges in the Mughal court, and the systematic misunderstanding and learning processes involved in attempts by Mughals and Britishers to communicate. The study focuses on the "rush of reality", events as they happened, thickly described.

belongs to them because they are what they are, will stand out against the other determinants of human behavior" (Geertz 1973: 27). What our subjects said is important to us, and the terms they used to say it, and finally, how those terms, embedded in contexts for which we can construct an analytic frame, suggest the ways the structure influenced and endorsed choices and decisions. The terms are signs in a system of relational meaning. Recognizing that an initial perception of these signs is not necessarily extended from the conceptual system of the sign-maker, we attempt to discover the terms of his system, the sign-maker's experience of his own signs.

In the study of the changing substance of culture in Jaipur, the ethnographer starts from a set of verbatim records, purposefully written by participants at the time, addressed by patron to performer, and by performer to patron directly or indirectly through the *dārogā* (administrative head of the *Guṇījankhānā*) and superintendent of the administrative departments. Using these records as indicators of the terms, issues, and expectations of the participants in the system, we note the particulars of the dialogical exchange, bringing issues into our view. The values and priorities of the performers and patrons, as proposed and restated, give us an entrance into their conceptual world.

Entering the past as an ethnographer, in order to understand how the artists regarded and courted their patron in a princely court, is possible only if there are available accounts of events and conversations. The bureaucratic organization and record-keeping of Jaipur State from the latter part of the 19th century provides an opportunity for an ethnographer to seek the lives of the artists in their own words, preserved in files in depositories in Jaipur and Bikaner. The organization of the Rajasthan State Archives after independence (Erdman 1979) has placed these records within reach of scholars and students.

**Petitioning the Patrons**

Our most direct evidence of the changing patronage of musicians and other performing artists in early 20th century Jaipur comes from the archival records of the *Guṇījankhānā*, which is the major department for performing artists in Jaipur State. While the *Pātarkhānā* (female dancers in the women's quarters), *Naubat*

*Khānā* (gateway drum and shenai ensemble), State Band (for ceremonial western style music), and *Rozan Chowki* (daily time-keepers) also produced dance and music, their performances were specific and they are not the bases for today's performing artists, either musically or socially.[8]

The records of this department are neither anecdotes nor texts; they are not narratives to be performed. Rather they were written communications, official conversations from written sources in the past. But these written sources were more like dialogues, for the artists, who were usually illiterate, dictated their petitions to writers, who recorded the spoken applications and requests. When read aloud, they combine the distancing of written formal texts with the authenticity of contextual conversations, and illustrate the directness, cleverness and skill which speakers in a primarily oral and aural tradition developed in speech, rather than in writing.

Maintained in the Rajasthan State Archives in Jaipur and Bikaner, the records on which this study is based are primarily for the period 1904-1946, in the categories of Finance, *Mahākmā Khās* (State Council)-*Karkhānejāt* (Departments), and Judicial. Some files, with interesting titles like "Conversion of the post of carpenter into that of Harmonium-*wālā* in the *Guṇījankhānā*,"[9] and "Order requesting the new employees of the *Guṇījankhānā* to attend the Gangore and Teej processions and follow the old procedure in this connection,"[10] have been destroyed. The remaining records include petitions for leave, dismissal and appointment; requests for granting privileges and the righting of oversights; budgets of the department; and pleas for special consideration. The documents are in four languages: Persian, Hindustani, Dhundari (the local Jaipur dialect) and English.[11] The lexicon of the Jaipur records has some

[8] A more complete description of household departments in Jaipur can be found in Erdman 1978 and Bahura 1976.

[9] Jaipur *Mahākma Khās* Records G17/100/1608 (1935).

[10] Jaipur *Mahākma Khās* Records G17/670 Pt. V (1928).

[11] Since I do not know either Persian or Dhundari, I have worked closely with the archivists and a translator who is familiar with the languages of the archives and with local usages of the period studied. While the need for translation is a limitation, the reading of the records aloud and discussion of key terms in them has added to my understanding of the place and circumstances of their recording. I appreciate the assistance of Dr. Gyanchand Sharma, A.K. Khan and M.L. Sharma of Jaipur for their cooperation in arranging for the translation of the archival records used in this study.

unique features, which must be understood in the context of local conventions and the history of record-keeping in the State. The entire record was read, and most of it translated, with the exception of routine leave petitions, which were noted and translated only when they provided special additional information.

Through these petitions, the performers sought to preserve their rights, motivate remedies for wrongful actions, or enhance their positions. These purposes, stated in the documents themselves, were pursued by varying means, including the invocation of rights, recall of privileges granted in the past and to past generations, and changes due as an extension of external causes. As communications between artists and their patrons, the petitions offer access to issues relevant to the on-going social organization of tradition in Jaipur. Yet the performers did not call them petitions—they were applications or letters—since they did not view them as records, but rather as communicative events. Why have I chosen to characterize these documents, preserved as records of the state, as petitions?

A petition is a solemn supplication or request to a superior authority, an entreaty, and it is also a formal written document requesting a right or benefit from a person or a group in authority.[12] It may be an application for a position, stating the qualifications of the petitioner, or it may be an attempt to solicit, through persuasion, some desired end. The etymological root of petition is in seeking or demanding, and its route of action is purposeful. Whether pursuing self-interests or protecting the rights of the petitioner as a member of a class, the argument of a petition asks for some action, which has not been granted in the usual course of events. Thus a petition signals either (1) the breakdown of ordinary ways of accomplishing things; or (2) the creation of new routes to new or old ends.

The petitions considered here are both entreaties and formal requests for rights, but not the routine applications for posts which were also included in the *Guṇījankhānā* records of Jaipur State.[13] Individual petitioners to their ruler-patron, in Jaipur, sought both

[12] Definitions are based on *The American Heritage Dictionary of the English Language*, 1973 edition.

[13] Routine applications for posts are charts answering standard questions: name, community, address, age and health, education, relations in Jaipur State service, and remarks by the *dārogā* (department head).

special privileges and argued rights in their communications. What was "fair" or "just" from their perspective, was not necessarily backed by precedent, but might have been the outcome of new policies or changing criteria for status in a wider context.

A question to be asked here is whether these petitions, as signals of interference with ordinary routines of action, indicate a break-down in the social organization of the maharaja's musicians, or the creation of new routes to unchanging goals within a continuing social organization of tradition. And if the conclusion is that the petitions are creative, we must ascertain whether the goals of the petitioners were the same as those of performers of an earlier era, or different from them. That is, we must identify the goals in the petitions, and discover whether they suggest alternatives to accepted goals for performers in the maharaja's household.

But since the petitions are also our main resource for describing the ordinary events and relationships of patron and performer, we must pay special attention to statements which described the usual or commonly encountered expectations for performers and their tradition. Still, there will be rules or exceptions which are not known to us through the petitions themselves. It is indeed very difficult to develop a picture of the "normative" occurrences in the *Guṇījankhānā* without sets of written rules and regulations, such as are said to exist for the *Kalāvantkarkhānā* of Baroda State.[14] Neither historical accounts nor oral history from surviving *Guṇījankhānā* performers has produced such a set of regulations, and it is evident from the petitions that precedent and privilege, custom and traditions, were the basis for arguments about rights, rather than laws or rules. These are not "legal petitions," which could inform us about a formal system of rules, and which have been subjected to scrutiny by a professionalized set of specialists trained in a common code of law.

Despite the fact that the *Guṇījankhānā*, as one of the *Karkhānejāt*, or state departments, was at the bottom of a hierarchical bureaucracy, including the department *dārogā*, the *Karkhānejāt* super-

[14] In 1975 I was told that the record for the *Kalāvantkarkhānā* of Baroda was retained by the ruling family after independence as part of its personal record, but that there was a "book" containing printed rules and regulations for the functioning of the department. Unfortunately I have been unable to locate a copy of this publication.

intendent, the State Council member-in-charge, and finally the royal patron-maharaja, there was no regulation of their rights and obligations except customary behavior.

Recommendations which climb the hierarchical pole are based on specific incidents, particular cases, and momentary problems. Only in a 1930s leave application, where the level of granting permission came into question, is there an indication of a change in procedures endorsed by the State Council.

> The *dārogā*s of the *Sileh Khānā* [Armory] and *Guṇījankhānā* in support of their request for being delegated with powers to grant casual leave to their subordinates, say that the procedure observed at present is much too hard for those who apply for casual leave in unavoidable circumstances. It is not strictly followed as the applicants first avail themselves of the leave they require and then apply for it, saying the leave applied for was due, and there is no option but to recommend sanction thereof. The employees of these *berās* [departments] are comparatively low paid servants and it is obvious that they often require leave in peculiar circumstances to earn something from other sources. The refusal of leave or detention of the applicants until sanction of the leave applied for is obtained would mean material loss to them which they cannot afford. Hence it is necessary that the *dārogās* should have powers to grant casual leave to men and artisans working under them.[15]

This document was signed by the Home Minister, Chandra Pal Singh, a month later, after clarifications regarding the current powers of these *dārogā*s, their respective pay, and the number of employees subordinate to each officer, as well as an approximation of the number of recommendations for granting leave during a month from each department. His decision above the signature was that

> it will be in the fitness of things if the *dārogās* of the *Guṇījankhānā* and *Sileh Khānā* are delegated with the powers to sanction one week's casual leave at a time.[16]

[15] Jaipur *Mahākma Khās* Records G17/42 Pt. Ve (1934), dated 18.8.1936.
[16] *Ibid.*

Thus this regulation extended the affirmed powers of the *dārogās* to coordinate with on-going practices.

### The Art of Petitioning

The written conversations of the *Guṇījankhānā* artists with their patrons are, in whichever language, couched in terminology appropriate to the court language of the period. This court language might be called a "bureaucratic-patrimonial code" in terms of its function, which was dual. This code incorporated terms from both the rule-governed relationships between authorities and petitioners, and the patrimonial traditions of Rajput households in Rajasthan. The code was used strategically and tactically, with speakers combining a highly Persianized Urdu with local Dhundhari terms, and introducing English lexical items where particularly purposeful. "Financial stringency," for instance, is spelled out in the Devnagri or in the Persian script, entering the twentieth century Jaipur records as a conceptual shorthand for a set of circumstances which didn't arise when social reform was not an activity of the royal court. Such additions are in line with other findings which suggest that Indian languages have a syncretic capacity, as do perhaps all languages in use, so that new ideas, problems and innovations of a technological type are named with terms brought into play through oral communication.

Reading these petitions suggests that three kinds of linguistic efforts are made by the artists. First, there was the choice of language for the petition. While Urdu was Jaipur's official language until the end of the State (Roy 1978:83), there was an agitation in 1943 for shifting to Hindi, which resulted in both being declared official languages. Yet the lexicon of the petitions of the *Guṇījankhānā* artists included many Persian words and phrases, and in the 1930s and 40s some petitions were written in English and Hindustani (Devnagri script). Literacy in Jaipur State (as in most of Rajasthan) was very low, and was blamed, by Jaipur's Director of Public Instruction in 1905, on the use of Urdu as a State language despite not being the language of the people, as well as on the apathy of the landlords for educating their people (Roy 1978:128). Urdu was the preferred language for most of the Muslim musicians who were descended from artists previously at the court of the Mughal emperor; local Rajasthani artists, however, spoke the particular dialects of their native places, so that Urdu was learned only as necessary, and then only aurally.

But even in English the petitioners manage to convey the sense of their relationship with their patron, and their own view of their status and role in the tradition. A letter in English from Mohanlal, addressed directly to "His Highness Mahārājā Sahib Bahadur" in 1933, is a poignant example.

> May it please your Highness. This humble and devoted servant begs to approach your distinguished feet with some heartfelt stern facts for favourable and cordial consideration.
>
> That I am an unfortunate creature, struggling against adverse fate and unsympathetic circumstances, disease, death, and degradation.
>
> Disease, death and degradation I repeat, these powerful forces have all at once, completely victimized my life.
>
> My father, Chauthmal Sarangia (Fiddle Player) mothered by the late Highness, was a well-known fiddle-expert and a good singer. Disease laid palsied hand upon him and he passed away to the world of immortality, leaving me his only heir to enhance his fame and glory. But my high and noble aspirations have been brought to a sudden shock of arrest for the post of my father has been relegated to a certain son of *Fadali*[17] contrary to hoary state traditions according to which the post of the father should be assigned to the son in case he is found competent in all respects and satisfies all the conditions.
>
> On the sad demise of my father I applied for his post and was ordered to be examined by the *Dārogā Guṇījankhānā*, who reported to the effect that the examinee in question had not only distinguished himself in Fiddle playing like his father but also in other branches of vocal and instrumental music.
>
> This being the shining result of my examination I am denied the fruits of it and deprived instead of my legitimate bread and butter.
>
> Thrice did I apply and thrice my attempts have been failed [sic]. Heaven only knows as to why my applications do not find their destined end and are lost in the way. That is why I have taken the royal road to approach your Highness, that knows no

[17] I have not been able to find out the meaning of "*Fadali*" in this context.

thwarted desires, unsatisfied longings, and undeserved sufferings, to make clear of the whole matter and to expose the reality of things. My claims and qualifications when pitted against the so-called son of a *Fadali*, who was illegitimately usurped my father's place, are null and void. An ability test be again held before your Highness and the one who proved himself competent enough to be given what is his due.

I have invincible faith and optimism in Your Highness' catholicity of mind, sanity of judgement, sense of kindness and generosity and fervently hope that justice would be done to my case by appointing me on my father's post (which is my birth right) or on that of Liyakat Hussain or Vijeera, who have also left world leaving no heir behind them.

I shall be highly thankful and shall supplicate Almighty to grant you happiness, success and length of days.

I beg to remain sir,
Your Highness' obedient servant,
[signed in Hindi] Mohanlal
Saukiyon ka Rasta, Jaipur[18]

The flavor of supplication and the seeking of redress for wrongful action pervade this petition. The fact that it was addressed directly to the Maharaja is unusual, but the terminology of emotional distress, rational understanding of his rights according to tradition, and ability which can be examined, was typical of many artists' petitions. Pleading with the patron to accept his birthright, his faith in royal justice, and his need, as well as his ability, Mohanlal juxtaposed the timeless beneficence of the Maharaja with the particular injustice done to him through no fault of his own. A similar supplication would be addressed to a deity in requesting a favor, though not justice. The Maharaja, a living presence, was asked to serve as judge of both the rights of the petitioner and his ability to perform the required arts. Faith in the ways of "heaven" is replaced by faith in the "royal road." For a Hindu, of course, the Maharaja was regarded as embodying the divine through his selection and affirmation.

But the Maharaja, unlike the deity, was a living person, who

[18] Jaipur *Mahākma Khās* Records G17/100 Pt. XI (1932-33).

could be addressed directly with hope of a direct response.[19] So multiple routes to a solution of the difficulty were suggested: testing his ability again, or appointing him to another vacant post—despite the fact that Mohanlal is arguing that as heir to his father, the post of his father is his birthright. In addition to the direct plea for legitimate rights and justice, the petition contained a pragmatic attitude towards action, embedded in Mohanlal's choice of terms. Even irony entered into it: "this being the shining result of my examination I am denied the fruits of it and deprived instead of my legitimate bread and butter." The imagery of denied food was contrasted with the imagery of light (shining result), suggesting that royal glory and economic reality were not in line, or were somehow out of balance. Mohanlal was clearly not merely a humble servant begging for favor from his master; he was also a sharp operator, utilizing every strategy he could conjure to convince his patron that he deserved the requested result.

Thus this son of a fiddler, communicating in English, conveyed the gist of his plea in terms both petitioning and bargaining. His use of English terms suggested that he was pleading for an English justice; yet his imagery was that of a servant pleading with his patron, trying to please him through terms of honor and the exchange of service for food. Contemporary reality, that is Mohanlal's denial of his father's post, and timeless tradition, namely the inheritance of posts by sons of the deceased, were coming apart, no longer reflecting each other's actions.

In a petition originally in Urdu, Azim Bux, underage, but the only son of Maula Bux, indicated the familial relationship of patron as protector and supporter of his servants.

> [This *asāmī* (post)] has been served by my relatives since the foundation of Jaipur. Now my father has died, and there are no relatives but me, the only surviving member of my family. The *dārogā* of the *Guṇījankhānā* has recommended me for *parvārish* [allowance] and the Superintendent of the *Karkhānejāt* has also been informed of this. My father had the post of *gānebajānewāllā* [singing and playing on instruments]. I'm the only person surviving and I deserve the post of my father

[19] The Maharaja was also expected to answer as a person, without becoming a medium for the divine, unlike mediums who sought to provide communication with a divine who is beyond living persons.

> May I be granted the post of my father. Take pity on my condition. You are my *Mā-Bāp* [mother and father], my only protector. If you don't help me, it will be difficult for me to live. I prefer long life and prosperity. In fact, I deserve two posts, one of my grandfather and the other of my father. So the vacancy created by my father's death should be restored to me.
>
> At present I am living with my *Māmu* [maternal uncle].[20]

Azim Bux, in whose name this petition was submitted, was only five years old. His relatives offered a substitute, Subhan, son of Hussain Khan, to work against the post until Azim Bux attained maturity, and was trained. But the *Mahākma Khās* (State Council) of Jaipur State was not convinced that inherited right was a sufficient criterion for granting Azim Bux the *asāmī* of his father. Azim Bux's proposal was that Subhan would divide the salary with Azim, so that the latter could support himself and give fees to an *ustād* (teacher) who would train him in his father's arts. Thus the *ustād* would give the training usually rendered by father to son in the musical arts.

Azim Bux's petition is an example of the second kind of linguistic effort in the petitions: terms which are not indigenous to the linguistic medium are introduced to enhance the argument and give strategic momentum to the petitioner's desired success. Here, for instance, the point that "You are my *Mā-Bāp*, my only protector," was used to double the effectiveness of the petition. The Maharaja was both the patron-protector whose duty it was to look after his servant-family, and he was also the person who stood in place of the orphaned petitioner's deceased parents. "*Mā-Bāp*" is a domestic term rather than a court term, a Hindi usage rather than Persianized Urdu, and has an emotional power that more formal terms cannot convey. So both relationships, Maharaja as patron and Maharaja as parent, are called forth in conjunction with the emotionally laden term, used to sway the recipient of the petition in the petitioner's favor.

However such petitions do not at this time go directly to the Maharaja who is both patron and protector, but rather are submitted by the *Dārogā* of the *Guṇījankhānā* with a recommendation to the

[20] Jaipur *Mahākma Khās* Records *Karkhānejāt-Guṇījankhānā* V.S. 1967/7 (1910 A.D.).

Superintendent of the *Karkhānejāt*. In response to the *dārogā*'s recommendation that Azim Bux be given his father's post, the Superintendent writes to the State Council that

> in the *Guṇījankhānā* appointments are for artists expert in their art, and this is not a department where orphans are brought up. Experienced and trained persons are employed in the *Guṇījankhānā*. Underage people are not recruited . . . so the *dārogā*'s suggestion of a substitute is not worthy of consideration.
>
> But again the *dārogā* has written. He asks what sort of arrangement is made for underage sons and daughters of those who have served the *Guṇījankhānā* for many years. These sons, he says, are in pitiable condition and they deserve encouragement. When they are underage, someone else is appointed to perform their duties of singing and dancing, and when they are fit for service, they are taken into service . . .
>
> Such underage persons also support the widow, mother, and grandmother, and they pray for the prosperity of the government. . . . How can they live their lives? . . . For four generations his father and forefathers have served the State . . . for 100 years. If the underage are not given opportunities, then where will they go and what will happen to their widows? Will they lead their lives by licking the ash? The generations[21] of other candidates will be broken, and they'll be disappointed. . . . Pity these poor people, and their family's services should be taken into consideration. Long live the gracious maharajas and may your kingdom prosper. If some money is given to underage people, then when they're big they'll also serve the State. In the *Karkhānejāt*, youngers are given the chance on the death of their elders. So the *dārogā* says this boy deserves *parvārish* [allowance] and should be sanctioned in the post.[22]

Apparently swayed by this appeal to precedence, practicality, and potential for loyal service, the council members suggested that Azim Bux be given the post of his father, and Subhan be allowed to perform his duties. But an order from Chandra Mahal signed by

[21] The word used is "*pusht*" which refers to the "backside" of generation, i.e., ancestry or generations.

[22] See note 31.

Maharaja Sawai Madho Singh, which came only four months later, stated that a post cannot be sanctioned to an underage person.[23]

The outcome of this petition, unlike that of Mohanlal which was investigated and finally filed without any action, was a statement of a general rule by the patron-maharaja. The royal lack of regard for precedent (stated in the *dārogā*'s recommendation) that posts are inherited, paralleling his royal succession, and for the potential for continued an loyal family service, which was a tradition in the Rajput household of the Jaipur ruler, is documented in his order. Is the status of Madho Singh as a Maharaja different from that of his predecessors? Certainly he implied in this order that the parallel successions of rulers and servants in the royal household must now be distinguished. And patronage would thus move from *in loco parentis* to a new regulation regarding inheritance of *asāmī*s.

Azim Bux was not asking an extraordinary favor in requesting that he be placed in the post of his father, albeit with a substitute acting for him until he was trained and came of age to serve. When, shortly after the death of Maharaja Madho Singh II (in 1922), and the designation of Maharaja Man Singh II as his adopted heir, a listing of the *Guṇījankhānā* appointments was made, there were 140 posts, of which 67 were inherited, 31 were not inherited, 7 were new, 4 officials, and others either vacant or in the process of becoming inherited posts. Maharaja Man Singh II was himself underage when he was designated as heir to the throne of Jaipur. A regency ruled in his stead, as was common in the Rajput states.[24] About half of the posts of the dancing girls, or *tawā'if*s, were inherited, and two thirds of the posts of *kalānaut*s (artists; see Erdman 1978) had also been inherited.[25]

Each artist, in this *Guṇījankhānā* listing, was also rated on performance. *Tawā'if*s were, for example, characterized as doing "good work", or "ordinary work," or having daughters who are expert in performance, or intelligent. *Kalānaut*s were said to know their job well, to perform ordinary singing, to be weak in singing and therefore to be considered for pensions or, though old and

[23] See note 31.

[24] See, for instance the career of Sir Prâtap Singh of Jodhpur, who was regent for several underage Jodhpur rulers (Rudolph and Rudolph, forthcoming).

[25] Jaipur *Mahākma Khās* Finance, Budget 77, V.S. 1980 *Guṇījankhānā* (1924).

knowing the job well, having an intelligent son who could perform the official duties for the appointee.

Azim Bux's service chart shows that he has no education, that his *bhai-bandh* [family group] are *kalāvathan* (artists) in the Raj service, and that although he held no previous post, the post is his by his father's right ("*Apne bāp kā huk chhata hai*").[26] The term "*huk*" carries the idea of authority of attachment, and its use has a logic intended to convey the rightful order of succession in the *Guṇījankhānā*. Thus the choice of lexical item in the petition or application form indicated the relationship which was to be recognized in granting the request of the performer.

There is a third kind of linguistic effort in the petitions, which is not separable from the first two, except analytically, since it depends upon both the petitioner's choice of language, and the lexical items selected to plead his case. This effort, which I shall call "terminological" to indicate that it includes not only the existence of the word but also its usage in a particular context, occurred when words which had been used to indicate something in particular were extended or altered with regard to reference, but without changing their performative aspects in a grammatical context. Such usage can be distinguished from "*Mā-Bāp*" of the petition of Azim Bux, which recalled expectations and obligations of patron-rulers towards their dependent servants and invited an emotional response to this case.

The name "*Guṇījankhānā*" itself serves to illustrate this third kind of linguistic effort. What, exactly, is a "*Guṇījankhānā*"? How can we understand an institution which is a "Department of Virtuosos?" There is no institutional parallel to the *Guṇījankhānā* in Western performing arts, even in the European courts, although closer comparison might bring further insights. The *Guṇījankhānā* can be seen in India as a predecessor to contemporary performance organizations, such as All-India Radio, which produces ordinary and expert programs, has a regular staff, hires special artists for particular programs and provides continuous employment for per-

[26] That is, he wants the "hook" of his father. *Huk* which means hook, binder or fastener, was used here multi-vocally. It had, in compound forms, the idea of order and authority, as in the frequent responses to a landlord's or guest's request in a landlord's (*thakur*'s household, "*hukm*" ("order"), or in the word for an obedient servant or dependent "*Hukm Bardār*". A *hukmnāmā* is a written order, or decree.

forming artists during their lifetimes. But such an extension does not offer us insight into what the *Guṇījankhānā* of Jaipur State provided for the performers of the artistic tradition, in their own view. Nowadays in Rajasthan, persons who remember the days of princely rule have explained the *Guṇījankhānā* as follows.

(1) *Guṇījankhānā* was the department of those who know the art. From the 17th century to the end of Jaipur State it existed. (Interview, Jaipur, July 1975.)
(2) There was a department of music in state times, but it wasn't called the *Guṇījankhānā*, but the *Rundīkarkhānā*. (Interview, Jodhpur, August 1975.)
(3) It was called *Guṇījankhānā*. *Rundīkarkhānā* was the usual name people used, but it wasn't the formal one given. (Interview, Udaipur, August 1975.)

"Those who know the art" was given as a gloss for *Guṇījankhānā* by the first respondent in Jaipur. A more literal translation would explain that *gunī* refers to qualities or virtuosities, *jan* is an individuating plural, and *khānā* refers to a room or department. *Rundī* is glossed as "prostitute" or "pross" by today's Rajasthanis, and *kar* indicates the doer or maker of that which precedes it. All the speakers are referring to the department of the Maharaja's household which housed the instrumentalists, vocalists, and dancers, as well as other performers (sometimes jesters, acrobats, wrestlers and dramatists). While the informants share the manifestation—the object which existed by observing, they do not share the same experience with respect to the performers and performances. Are these terms, *Guṇījankhānā* and *Rundīkarkhānā*, compatible? How can the relationship between the two terms be shown? These seemingly contradictory experiences of the same manifestation must be reconciled in terms of a theory of language use. Native speakers see no contradiction between the two words *Guṇījankhānā* and *Rundīkarkhānā*, in terms of what might be called "a common sense view of Rajasthani culture."[27]

Alternatively labeling the experience of the manifestation of the department as "*Guṇījankhānā*" or "*Rundīkarkhānā*" may result

[27] See Geertz 1975. Silverstein (1976) has used the term "ethnometapragmatic" to describe the culturally limited commentary on the use of terms.

from (a) differences in the departments in Jaipur, Jodhpur, and Udaipur; (b) the particular social positions of the speakers which produces differing perspectives with respect to this princely household administrative department—(1) was a Rajput patron, (2) a *Baniya* arts administrator, and (3) a Muslim musician; or (c) the fact that while the three speakers belong to the same speech community (i.e., sharing a pragmatic system of signification), they belong to different linguistic communities (i.e., groups defined by a normative basis for experience).

The speakers are using the same language, and can understand each other; but their ideological bases for meaningfulness derive from different viewpoints. Being from Jaipur, Jodhpur, or Udaipur is inadequate as an indicator; certainly the departments in these places were different, but clearly persons in each place had an idea of a department of performing artists. The speakers have different socio-economic roles, but correlations of social status and experiential data are redundant. The possibility (c above) of the same speech and differing linguistic communities is, however, explorable, particularly in the *Guṇījankhānā* records. In the petitions and applications there are statements about the nature and function of the *Guṇījankhānā* of Jaipur state, expressed in terms of expectations, traditional behavior and action, and obligations. If we look particularly at the *tawā'if* (female dancers and singers), we can clarify the issues and understand the efforts of the performers to state their cases in their terms.

In 1912 the *tawā'if* Gohar Jan, a resident of Jaipur, applied for a post in the *Guṇījankhānā* in Jaipur. She said that she belongs to Jaipur, has high attainments in music[28], and has been tested many times and is ready at the moment to be tested again. She belongs to a respectable family, her petition stated, and she has no means to maintain her livelihood.[29] When interviewed and tested by the *Guṇījankhānā's dārogā*, she appeared well dressed, wearing ornaments, and was extraordinary (*nāharukt*—undefeatable) in singing and dancing. Eventually she was appointed (after being turned down several times) and given *parvārish* in 1913.

In 1925 Gohar Jan submitted another petition, to the President of the *Mahākma Khās* (State Council), saying that

[28] She uses *musiqi*, the Persion word.

[29] Jaipur *Mahākma Khās Karkhanejāt-Guṇījankhānā* S.V. 1969/29 (1912 A.D). File partially destroyed by white ants.

> Among the musicians and dancing girls employed in Jaipur State service, I claim to be the most skilled in my art, as has been acknowledged not only by the local experts, but outside also. But the grade of pay given to us is fixed in a very arbitrary way. Those who are only novice get high pay, while the older and expert receive very low Thus I am getting a salary of only Rs. 30/- per month, which is very insufficient, and meagre in consideration of my skill and family responses.[30]

Furthermore, she wrote, if she is required to go outside on professional calls, and "for earning livelihood . . . by display of musical genius," the *dārogā* imposed heavy on her fines and asked explanations of many charges. She asked that her pay be increased, and that the *dārogā* be directed not to molest the *tawā'if* in trivial matters. She was always prompt, she said, and it is "unjustifiable" to be put under difficulties without any reason.

Eventually given a pay increase, Gohar Jan and her sister Kamal were ordered, in 1933, to instruct the *Bāis* (women) in the *Zenānī Deohrī* (the women's quarters of the palace household), in addition to their usual duties. For this service they were given additional allowance of Rs. 20/- per month.[31] In the same year, Gohar Jan and Kamal Jan, who serve in the *khās* and *ām* (private and public audience halls) as well as the *Zenāni Deohrī*, stated that these are manifold duties and requested that they "be exempted from ordinary (*Mandir* and daily) and other temple duties, festivals, Teej and Gangore services."[32] Although research by court officials showed that no *tawā'if* had been exempted from daily services before[33], the State Council ordered Gohar Jan and Kamal Jan to be exempted from daily service, except in the *Zenāni Deohrī*. In 1937, on the basis of an application and a medical certificate from Dr. John Huben, Director of Medical Services for Jaipur State, Gohar Jan was exempted from ordinary services except at special occasions and durbar.[34]

[30] Jaipur *Mahākma Khās* Records G17/100 Pt. I (1923).

[31] Jaipur *Mahākma Khās* Records G17/100 Pt. X (1933).

[32] Jaipur *Mahākma Khās* Records G17/100 Pt. Xii (1933-34).

[33] In 1929 Gohar Jan's and Kamal Jan's mother, Nanne Jan, and also Munna Jan, had been exempted from Teej and Gangore Mataji by order of the Home Minister Gopinath Purohit.

[34] Jaipur *Mahākma Khās* Records G17/100 Pt. XIV (1936-37). She had requested full exemption from dancing.

Her superiority and status were confirmed in a 1941 note from the *dārogā* to the Home Minister in charge of *Karkhānejāt* saying that

> the necessity for the addition of really good female singers to the *Guṇījankhānā*, of a class superior to those at present employed, and *something approaching Gohar*, is a necessity . . ."[35]

Throughout her tenure as a *tawā'if* in the *Guṇījankhānā*, Gohar Jan was treated as an artist of high stature and an expert in her art. Servants still employed at the City Palace in 1977 reported that she was very highly regarded, and that her house in Ram Ganj east of the Palace was a gathering place for ministers and officials. Petitioners used to gather in the square below her veranda, awaiting the departure of the most important men in Jaipur. She participated in music conferences outside the State on many occasions, and was respected as a woman of culture and manners, expert in singing and communicating the *rasa* (aesthetic experience) of the Rajasthani music she performed.

Not all *tawā'if* of the Jaipur *Guṇījankhānā* were so respected or well paid. A letter in the Judicial Department addressed to the Finance Minister of Jaipur State dealt with the matter of a house purchase by a dancing girl Chagan. Written by residents of Rasta Kalyan ka Chowkri in 1939, the letter asked that "in the interests of public morality" the matter of Musamat Chagan's purchase be reconsidered.[36] The petition was couched in terms of "the interests of justice and protection of the *izzat* [honor] and character of loyal and respectable subjects of His Highness." They said they are respectable householders, and in their quarter "there is not a single house owned by any dancing girl." Recently however a dancing girl named Chagan had "deceitfully purchased the house of one Kailan Kallavat" and permission of the Council for a permit to register the sale deed was pending in the office of the minister addressed.

The residents went on to say that the Municipality reported that no other house in the locality is owned by a dancing girl and thus under restrictions for purchase of house property, the "prostitute" should not be permitted to purchase the house. Thirdly,

[35] Jaipur *Mahākma Khās* Finance Department G17/1781 Pt. II (1941).

[36] Jaipur *Mahākma Khās* Records Judicial Department 6/75 (1935), Registration of Documents.

> . . . on inspection of the said site the Education Minister was showed how the *Izzat* and honour of so many citizens will be affected by residence of a dancing girl in the midst of their houses but on that occasion on account of the propagandist activity of the dancing girls who had gathered here at the instigation of Musamat Chagan, the intending purchaser, a wrong impression was given to the Education Minister that the said locality was inhabited by dancing girls, although as a matter of fact not a single dancing girl owns any house in this street and the whole of this quarter is inhabited by respectable Hindu and Muslim families.

Furthermore, they said, if the Council gives permission for the dancing girl to purchase the house, "hundreds of respectable people will have to quit their homes and suffer great hardship and privation." The proposal of the minister that permission be given to Chagan to purchase the house was made

> without paying any attention to the real facts disclosed by the Municipal Report and without paying any consideration to the repeated representations made by the respectable Hindi and Muslim Purdah families in this quarter.
>
> . . . It is submitted that while a very enlightened administration is taking very keen measures to avoid residence of prostitutes and dancing girls in the quarters inhabited by respectable people in order to safeguard public morality the Education Minister is not at all mindful of the public grievance and with closed eyes is recommending for purchase of house by a *pros* in a street, the whole of which is inhabited by respectable people.[37]

Despite this elaborate petition, copies of which were sent to the Judicial, Education, and other ministers, the house purchase was sanctioned, suggesting a different view of dancing girls from the vantage of the court and administrative council.

In other petitions, the same townspeople say that "the late His Highness the Maharaja Sahib Bahadur [Madho Singh]" gave orders on June 3rd, 1892, which clearly stated "that no pross be allowed to purchase house in the close vicinity of the High caste people."

[37] *Ibid.*

"When they are being turned out from the Bazars even," the petition goes on to say, "it is quite improper and contrary to the resolution of the council of state to allow them to inhabit in such a *mahālla* [neighborhood] as [Kalyan Kon Ka Mahalla]."[38]

The equation of dancing girl and prostitute is clear in these documents. The distinction between a *tawā'if* who is a respected artist and a *tawā'if* who is not, is not made in neighborhood petitions by their writers. These townspeople are not connoisseurs or even devotees of the courtly arts of singing and dancing; they are concerned about their status as reflected by the social standing of persons living in their neighborhood. For them the role of dancing girls as artists is subordinated to the status of dancing girls as prostitutes. Whether or not Chagan is indeed a prostitute is never the issue: the fact is she is a dancing girl, and dancing girls are, in the definitions of the self-named "high-caste" inhabitants of Kalyan Kon Ka Mahalla, of low status, since they are prostitutes.

But inside the *Guṇījankhānā*, a *tawā'if* is an artist, who sings and dances in the temples and the court of the maharaja, providing special songs for birthdays and visitors, and dancing in the religious processions honoring Gangore, a goddess to whom young virgins and married women pray for a husband who is kind and will outlive them.[39] Whether the artists were virtuosos or prostitutes depended on the perspective of the speaker and the values of the signification system in which the assessment was made.

To the Rajput patrons, the *tawā'ifs* were court entertainers, capable of evoking the heroic and romantic moods of their Rajput heritage.[40] To Brahmins in the Kalyan Kon Ka Mahalla, *tawā'ifs* were prostitutes, not artists at all. Women who were paid for singing and dancing, and who performed for men, were "public women." A married woman, of respectable status, would take the veil and be in purdah, and she would dance and sing only in the *zenānā* (women's quarters) for women only, and if coaxed, for the

[38] Jaipur *Mahākma Khās* Records (English)-Judicial 6/75 (1935), Registration of Documents.

[39] See Erdman 1980, Chapter III on Recreations and Subtle Performances, for a full description of the Gangore procession.

[40] Not all Rajputs were patrons of this classical Rajasthani music. Amar Singh of Kanota, for example, says in his diary that he prefers his wife's singing to that of the 'public women' of the courts (Rudolph and Rudolph, forthcoming).

men of the family, or to please the royal patron to whom she might be married.

Professional dancers and singers, who were women, were not eligible for high social status outside of their artistic world of patrons and performers, which was in early twentieth century Jaipur confined to the palaces of their patrons, and occasional meetings for connoisseurs and artists at musical conferences. Thus the household of their patron, where they were regarded as artists, and the neighborhoods of their city, where they were regarded as prostitutes, had a common speech community, but differing linguistic communities. *Tawā'if*, a dancing girl, meant "artist" on the inside and "prostitute" on the outside. And Gohar Jan's petition to be exempted from dancing has further implications. She was raising her external status by appearing only in palace performances and limiting her presentations to singing. The attempt to exclude herself from the Gangore and Teej processions, in additon to ordinary services, is understandable if one knows what is involved in participation. On these two occasions processions are taken from the City Palace into the bazar avenues, and the *tawā'ifs* are asked to dance in the processions, making their dancing a public event, not restricted to the men's quarters or temples of the palace-household.[41]

In summary, there are two terms here which have been logically altered, though grammatically retained. "*Guṇījankhānā*" has been delimited to those who see the department as a place for respectable artists, and contrasted with another term for the same department, *Rundīkarkhānā*, which suggests that it houses prostitutes rather than artist-virtuosos. And *tawā'if*, which refers within the *Guṇījankhānā* to a dancing girl who performs dances and sings in the temples, court, and processions, as well as on daily duty in the palace, refers outside the palace to a public woman or prostitute, whose presence threatens the respectability of a neighborhood. *Guṇījankhānā* is the private and artistic preserve of the royal patron, whose morality with respect to women is an example of

[41] The women who occasionally are called upon to dance in the marriage processions in Rajasthan today, which bring the bridegroom to the doorway of his intended bride, are called *tawā'ifs*, and are regarded as prostitutes. They come from the prostitute's quarter of the city, there being no longer a *Guṇījankhānā* in the City Palace, now a family trust rather than a state residence.

their status in his state: as artists they are admired and honored. Sexual acts are arts in classical Indian conceptual domains, just as singing and dancing are arts.[42]

Yet, in society as represented by the Jaipur townspeople, sexual acts and arts are supposed to be private and hidden from public view. Propriety demands that respectable wives be maintained in secluded quarters, protected from the view and intrusion of strange men who are not part of their family. *Tawā'ifs* have become dancing girls who, despite their appropriateness for dancing in the sacred precincts of the temple, are, if publicly patronized, socially immoral. In extending access to the performing arts beyond the patron's household, as state functions in public view, the role of women in the arts is changed, as is the status of women artists in society.

## Cultural Substance and the Patron's Role

Embedded in the departmental structure of the princely household, and in a patronage tradition which was a continuation of the 19th century conceptual world, cultural performances were subject to both reevaluation by reformist rulers and recreation in a domain which had become the center of state administration. Substantial changes in the infrastructure for the performance traditions in Jaipur were integral to modifications in the complex patrimonial-bureaucratic functions of the household of the royal patron.

In the early twentieth century in Jaipur, Maharaja Madho Singh II (1880-1922) and his successor Maharaja Man Singh II were influenced by British efforts to create a Jaipur State which was a model for princely state behavior in the British Empire. Since in the early twentieth century Jaipur State was subject to treaties made with the British in the early nineteenth century, and since the two rulers of Jaipur State in the early twentieth century were both adopted

[42] See, for instance, the listing of the arts to be studied together with *Kāma Sūtra* in *The Kāma Sūtra of Vatsyāyanā*. "A public woman, endowed with a good disposition, beauty and other winning qualities, and also versed in the above arts, obtains the name of a Ganika, or public woman of high quality, and receives a seat of honour in the assemblage of men. She is, moreover, always respected by the king, and praised by learned men, and her favour being sought for by all, she becomes an object of universal regard" (p. 111).

and ruled under British advice, affirmation and guidance, the familial connections of servants and rulers were broken, and Jaipur State reforms, begun by Maharaja Sawai Ram Singh II during his long rule (1835-1880) were continued without the involved interest Ram Singh had in the performing arts. *Guṇījankhānā* artists, through patronage rather than affirmative action, had developed the concept of *paramparā*—traditions of family inheritance of artistic posts in their department. While it was acknowledged that not every son could succeed his father, nor daughter her mother, preference was given to those artists whose art was "in their blood", and who had been raised among artists, learning by apprenticeship and a *guru-shishya* or *ustād-ī-shaqirdī* pedagogy, the necessities of being an artist. As Sharon Lowen points out in her paper in this volume, traditional family ties continue as a method for artists to gain engagements, even in modern concert venues.

Lloyd Warner, in *The Living and the Dead*, pointed out that meaning flows from the past, to be again part of the present. A community's memory, he said, is selective, and their reconstitution of past events is a subjective interpretation of history, which plays a more important integrative function than the historian's objective account. The nostalgia of many contemporary Indian musicians and dancers for the princely patronage of the past, and blaming of present-day difficulties on its demise is, perhaps, just such a selective memory, which confuses and combines merit with duty, responsibility with servitude, and continuity with stability.

Patron-performer relationships were, in the early twentieth century in Jaipur, no longer a single system uniting specialists in the arts and rulers into a single household establishment. Support for *Guṇījankhānā* artists by the State continued, but for the artists their conception of inherited posts in an artistic tradition (*paramparā*) was posed against a criterion of excellence.[43] *Paramparā* was more important for these artists than the refinement, sophistication, and

[43] Erdman (1978) and Neuman (1978) discuss the organization of artists into "*gharānās*" in the same period. Neuman points out that *gharānās*, usually named for cities, indicate a style of music and denote the families of the musicians who are its exponents. The role of *paramparā* (inherited traditions) in the defining of *gharānās* deserves further exploration. While *gharānā* has come to refer to a musical style, *paramparā* denotes the succession of generations.

excellence characteristic of cultural achievement. The personal involvement of a connoisseur-prince in an art tradition was being replaced by the employment of performers to fulfill routine obligations of state functions. The objectives of "tradition"—continuing customs of the state, have been separated from the lines of performers who continue it. Performers, from the perspective of their twentieth century royal patrons, filled posts which were maintained to provide entertainment for the royal court and townspeople. The art was being separated from the artists, at the same time as it was given to the people.

From the perspective of the artists, on the other hand, the art continued to be embodied in their lines of generations, reaching from their ancestral past through the present embodiments into the future ones. Azim Bux wanted to carry on his father's and grandfather's line because he was born to it and, although as yet untrained, held the potential for musical arts. His father, now deceased, would have been his teacher in his arts, but his patron, still living, was expected to be his mentor, providing the conditions and circumstances for the cultivation of his potential abilities. Not fleeting moments of excellence but lines of artworks (performances) motivated these petitioners' efforts and expectations.

The patron, as a worldly maharaja, no longer found his pleasure in the music of his court, not did he require knowledge of excellent performances to substantiate his authority. His pleasures have been established elsewhere, and his authority was underwritten by the British Empire through treaties and affirmation at imperial ceremonies such as British durbars and royal treatment in England. Why did he maintain the *Guṇījankhānā*? Its traditional performances were religious, in temples and processions, and entertaining on special occasions and regularly in the *Hara Bangla* The British endorsed the maintenance of tradition in the princely states, supporting the continuance of custom while provoking social reform. But for the British, now "meta-patrons" for the princes, culture was material, and measured in values which were not customary, at least for the *Guṇījankhānā's* performing artists, for whom the process of performance was culture's substance.

For the artists, performances were personal, not art objects to be displayed and consumed. Since their art was embodied in their beings, it could not be bought and sold, but had to be tendered emotionally (albeit in highly disciplined forms) and communally to those who knew its potential beauties. Non-connoisseurs could listen and watch, but they could not hear or see the subtleties, nuances, and communications of the performance. For the artists, a narrow world which was the expansion of family into royal household was appropriate to the nurturance of their art. A patron was like a parent, supportive and protective. But patronage in early twentieth century Jaipur was turning from the personal involvement of a connoisseur-prince in an art tradition to the employment of performers to fulfill routine obligations of state functions, for a public untrained in these refined arts and their subtleties.[44]

Both the performers and the patrons argued for a tradition of cultural excellence in Jaipur, emphasizing its refined qualities. But the idea of tradition itself differed from patron to performer: it was no longer only a process of continuity but also—to the patron-rulers—a combination of items to be retained and performed. Social reform had brought about a change in culture's substance. The form of patronage was no longer primarily paternal but economic; the patron as *jajmān*[45] whose religious sacrifice required music and dance to reach the divine, produced entertainment for his guests and householders. Lavish gifts for special performances became rare, and regular payments were thrifty in a period when financial stringency was engendered by the building of social institutions such as hospitals and parks. A style of patronage in which the personal attentions of the patron to his servants' needs and livelihood was usual, was delegated to lower officials in the bureaucratic lines of order, and to budgetary decisions based not on needs of the serving artists, but on the needs of the state as a whole. Patronage of the performing arts continued in changed form, even within the princely state, when social progress gained priority over cultural process. The efforts to combine these two lines of change can be seen in every state, princely, democratic, or socialist. From the perspective of Jaipur's artists in the early twentieth century, the priority of social status and economic support was indicated in their petitions; competence in their art was required,

[44] See also Phillip Zarrilli's paper in this volume, for a similar situation.

[45] For discussions of patronage as *jajmānī*, see Wiser 1936, Beidelman 1959, and Wade and Pescatello 1977. The latter includes an elaborate bibliographical section on *jajmānī* literature.

but such competence no longer guaranteed a livelihood or even respect. Like the people of Rasta Kalyan ka Chowkri, the *Guṇījankhānā* artists were struggling to retain their status and maintain their honor in a context of social reform, when their particular place in a social scheme made up of domestic apprenticeship and inherited specialities was being turned into one of multiple opportunity through public education and new lines of specialization through technological innovations.

Jaipur's performers had to petition their patrons because they could no longer reach them in oral communications, and because they and their patron were no longer part of the same linguistic community. While the performers were trying to recreate the social ties which bound them to their patron-protectors, the patrons were, by virtue of their externally-affirmed authority, capable of breaking those bonds as personal ties. In their roles as reformist rulers, the patrons were creating new bonds with a more generalized and wider community. The household has grown into the state, and the privileged members of the royal households have become citizens of a state which includes non-household members as well. Their expectations of protection by their patron-ruler have not changed, but the context of their expectations has widened. And service, no longer personal but de-personalized to an impersonal status, was required but not honored.

The artists, seeing change through the concept of *paramparā*, continued to regard transitoriness as a permanent condition through both generations of artists and the passage of time. But the changes in early twentieth century Jaipur were not continuous; they were disruptive. So the *Guṇījankhānā* artists used their petitions to try to recall and retain the continuous change or transitoriness which they regarded as the way of the world.

Changes were, for these artists, based on *paramparā*—a tradition of continuity in this world, rather than an ideal to be achieved. They rejected changing their cultural structure of process and instead tried to maximize their ends in their social positions, roles and statuses. Analytically, we can establish the oppositions which their petitions attempted to reconcile and conjoin: employee/servant, employer/protector, state/household, justice/tradition, *mardānā-zenānā*/public-private. For *Guṇījankhānā* artists of the cultural tradition of *sangīt* (music, dance, and dance-drama), these were not oppositions but alternatives, routes to maintaining past ideals or roots for contemporary ones, as they saw them.

In recent years there have been discussions and publications which attribute problems in the support of the performing arts in India to the demise of princely patronage. Before independence, it is argued, when the princes ruled, the performing artists were able to maintain not only their livelihoods, but also their art. Now, since independence, according to the frequently encountered story, musicians and dancers and dramatists have had to struggle for their existence, for their audience, for their budgets, and their arts are no longer what they used to be. In the "good old days" of royal patronage artists were court treasures, and maharajas and nawabs were not only generous patrons but also connoisseurs of the arts of the *sangīt* tradition. "Gone were the days when art flourished under the patronage of kings and emperors or blossomed in places of worship," is the way a post-independence newspaper article began.[46] It went on to enlist the public as new patrons for *sangīt.*

Memories of past hard days for performers, mitigated by the flow of time and generations, have been superceded by an idealization of past excellence in the life of an artist supported by a connoisseur-patron, and by the extension of the success of a few excellent artists to the idea of a whole era of patronage. Just as it is the habit of enthusiastic travellers to remember the entertaining highlights of an adventure which may have threatened their lives, so also the artists remember their glorious past, forgeting selectively the hardships of the less-qualified and ordinary performers, and patrons no longer interested in their arts.

By evaluating the terms of the performers' petitions in early twentieth century Jaipur as signs in a system of concepts and values, we can understand the issues that motivated their actions. We find evidence that the patrons gave priority to the ideals of reform and state responsibility over continuing the cultural refinement and connoisseurship of their predecessors, while the performers subordinated the ideals of artistic excellence to a continuation of their rights under previous patrons. What patrons and performers had in common in this period was opposite as ideal and expectation; patrons placed change and its benefits over cultural continuities, and performers indicated an inverted priority

[46] "People Told to Patronise Artists," *Hindustan Times*, October 17, 1976.

in their petitions. The misunderstanding and confrontation in particular cases was systemic. The purposes were not entirely opposed but were differently valued, and the responsibilities as patrons of a state and performers of an art were distinctly different in a time characterized by purposeful social reform and cultural preservation.

The key to the differing perspectives of patrons and performers arises from different changes in the foci of their world views—the maharaja's expanding to Europe and British imperialist range, and the artists' reduction to individual and local needs and customs; and the distancing of their interests and relationships—through administrative mediators and differing time orientations. For the culture-bearer, the *gunījan*, the past was extended into the present, which was but another representation of the past. But for the princely patron, re-creating past glories meant reforming the present into an improved future, as determined by the modern world the princes were trying to enter. The formulation of patron-performer issues, exemplified in the *Guṇījankhānā* records, indicates changing form in a cultural structure, one which places the ideals of the past and future in opposition to each other. Semiotically one could speak of the irreducible triadic relationship of past-present-future as a logic of time, in which patrons were moving in one direction and performers in another, and the artists' petitions as a map of the times.

## References


Aries, Philippe. 1962. *Centuries of Childhood: A Social History of Family Life.* New York: Vintage Books.

Bahura, Gopal Narayan. 1987. *Literary Heritage of the Rulers of Amber and Jaipur.* Jaipur: Maharaja Sawai Man Singh II Museum, City Palace.

Beidelman, Thomas O. 1959. *A Comparative Analysis of the Jajmānī System.* Locust Valley, N.Y: Association for Asian Studies.

Bloch, Marc. 1963. *The Historian's Craft.* N.Y.: Alfred A. Knopf. (Tr. from French by Peeter Putnam)

Blochmann, H., trans 1965 [1871]. *The Ain-i Akbāri of Abu'l Fāzl Allāmi.* New Delhi: Naresh C. Jain for New Imperial Book Depot.

Cohn, Bernard S. 1987. *An Anthropologist Among the Historians and Other Essays.* New York: Oxford University Press.

Erdman, Joan L. 1978. "The Maharaja's Musicians: The Organization of Cultural

Performances at Jaipur in the 19th Century," *American Studies in the Anthropology of India*, ed. by Sylvia Vatuk, pp. 342-67, New Delhi: Manohar.

————. 1979. "Research Potential in the Archival Materials of Rajasthan," *American Institute of Indian Studies Newsletter*, New Delhi, Winter.

————. 1985. *Patrons and Performers in Rajasthan. The Subtle Tradition*. New Delhi: Chanakya Publications.

————. 1990. "Jaipur: City Planning in Eighteenth Century Jaipur," *The Śastric Tradition in the Indian Arts*, ed. by A.L. Dallapiccola (Heidelberg: University of Heidelberg).

Geertz Clifford. 1975. "Common Sense as a Cultural System," *Antioch Review* (Spring): 5-26.

————. 1973. *The Interpretation of Cultures*. N.Y.: Basic Books.

Neuman, Daniel M. 1978. "*Gharānās*: The Rise of Musical 'Houses' in Delhi and Neighboring Cities," *Eight Urban Musical Cultures: Tradition and Change*, edited by Bruno Nettl. Urbana. University of Illinois Press.

Rudolph, Lloyd I. and Susanne Hoeber Rudolph. Forthcoming. *Diary of a Rajput Nobleman: Amar Singh of Kanota* [tentative title]. Edited and introduced by Lloyd I. and Susanne Hoeber Rudolph and Mohan Singh.

Silverstein, Michael. 1976. "Shifters, Linguistic Categories and Cultural Description." *Meaning in Anthropology*, ed. by Keith H. Basso and Henry A. Selby. Albequerque: University of New Mexico Press.

Stocking, George. 1968. *Culture and Evolution: Essays in the History of Anthropology*. New York: Free Press.

Vatsyāyanā. (1963). *The Kāma Sūtra of Vatsyāyanā*. Tr. by Sir Richard Burton and F.F. Arbuthnot. Ed. by W.G. Archer. London: George Allen & Unwin, Ltd.

Wade, Bonnie C. and Ann M. Pescatello. 1977. "Music 'Patronage' in Indian Culture: The Jajmāni System," *Essays for a Humanist: An Offering to Klaus Wachsmann*. pp. 277-336, N.Y.: The Town House Press.

Warner, W. Lloyd. 1959. *The Living and the Dead*. Yankee City Series Vol. V. New Haven: Yale University Press.

Wiser, William H. 1936. *The Hindu Jajmānī System, a Socio-economic system interrelating members of a Hindu village community in service*. Lucknow: Lucknow Publishing House.

# PART THREE

# Motivations Markets and Logistics

# Patronage in India's Musical Culture

Bonnie C. Wade

This essay originated with a question about the history of Indian music: how did the North Indian vocal genre *Khyāl* come to be as it is? For nearly two decades I have been concentrating my research primarily on *Khyāl*, a genre of classical music developed in the 19th century and predominant in vocal performances in the twentieth century. While I have learned a great deal about the genre and about several styles of performing it (see Wade 1984), the explanation for why *Khyāl* is what it is musically remains unclear. It is considered to have developed with influences at different points in time from singers of three other genres of Hindustani vocal music: *Qawwālī, Dhrupad*, and *Thumrī*. Those three genres could hardly be more diverse in terms of cultural meaning and status, and in terms of the groups of musicians who cultivated them.

Seeking a fresh perspective on the question, I turned to another research interest and to a broader question: what can be learned about the history of Hindustani music from visual sources (primarily paintings) and from the chronicles, memoirs and other written sources contemporary with the paintings? My initial forays into such sources led me to focus on the contexts of music-making through time, and particularly on the people involved—the patrons and musicians who are depicted in the paintings, who are cited, praised, even just mentioned in passing by verbal sources. While the subject of *Khyāl* caused me to focus primarily on musicians, I have been led by the broader question to focus on the patrons as well, that is, on patronage of music in India and the role it has played in the development of particular types of music through time.

"Patronage of music" is a rubric under which diverse studies of many musical traditions have fallen. While social scientists (and dictionary definitions) consider patronage to be a social relation, extended to people rather than to things, we in music have usually subsumed discussion of patronage of musicians under the issue of patronage of a thing—music. In my work on Indian music, I have concluded that it is necessary to clarify with greater precision the relationships among patrons, musicians, and the music produced. By this means I hope eventually to understand a great deal more about why music in North India has developed the way it has.

Who are the patrons in the Indian musical scene? There are many types of persons. A fellow musician hosting a musical gathering might be the patron, or a group of students who have convened a private recital by their *guru* or *ustād*. In paintings from the Mughal period in North India, commissioned as they were by members of the social elite, the patrons shown were likely to be cloistered women in wealthy households, or some male member of the nobility. The patron, then, might be someone whose status is equal in some way—such as the fellow musician, or superior to the person patronized, or might even be of inferior status in some way—as a student is.

Who have been the musicians in the South Asian musical scene? There also are many types of persons, including singers and instrumentalists; soloists, accompanists, equal ensemble members; males, females, transvestites; amateurs and professionals. Musicians have been persons of high social status, such as members of the Hindu or Muslim nobility who learned music or Brahmins who have high caste status. Musicians have also been persons of low social status within the indigenous social ranking system, no matter how greatly respected as musicians.

The matter of different social status of different musicians is an important one in the patronage situation in India. One example of such a circumstance is recounted in a biography of the great Hindu musician Vishnu Digambar Paluskar (1872-1931). Paluskar was born into a family of high social status in the princely state of Kurundwad. He became a disciple of Balkrishna Buwa, a musician who was accorded high cultural status but was of lower social status than his disciple Paluskar, and was treated accordingly by their patron, the ruler of Kurundwad: while Paluskar would be an invited guest at state functions, neither Balkrishna Buwa nor his fellow disciples would be, due to their relatively low social status. This created an awkward and unpalatable situation for Paluskar who subsequently devoted his life to "trying to remove the miseries of the musicians as well as of the students" (Athavale 1967:7-8). Paluskar became a powerful force in the process of popularizing North Indian classical music, removing it from the cloistered circumstances of elite life and making it a vital aspect of North Indian cultural life in general. His activities were a major factor in preserving the classical music tradition past the period of court patronage. The social status of two different musicians *vis-à-vis* their patron, then, directly affected the court of Indian music history. Because of that possibility in other circumstances, as well, it is important to clarify the social status of musicians in studies of musical patronage in South Asia.

There is also the matter of cultural status to consider. In Indian culture, where high value is placed on cultivated musical knowledge and skill, accomplished musicians can be accorded high cultural status although they may rank low socially. This was the case with many Muslim musicians under Muslim rule during the period of the Mughal empire, and it was the case with Hindu musician Balkrishna Buwa, Paluskar's teacher, whose cultural status was higher than his social status.

In India where there are many types of music, the different types are accorded differential value as items of culture. That is to say, they are accorded different cultural status. Classical music (*śastrīya sangīt*) has a higher cultural status than light classical, and light classical higher than film music. Until recently in North India classical vocal music had a much higher cultural status than classical instrumental music, and in South India it still does. Among the types of classical vocal music in North India, *Dhrupad* holds the highest cultural value and study of the development of its successor *Khyāl* must take cognizance of that. Reasons for the different cultural status for these types of music are both musical and contextual, having to do in part with the nature of the patronage under which they developed.

Focus on the motivations of patrons offers a piece of the explanation for why Indian music have developed the ways it has. A patron is motivated for some reason to foster (i.e. patronize) either a musician or music itself. Taking the musicological perspective, the discussion below is couched in terms of the "patronage of music," but with the intention of clarifying the personal and social factors involved. In the type of patronage I shall call "direct patronage of music," the patron is motivated to foster music; the primary motive is presumed to be love of music. If patronage of music is a result rather than a purpose of patronage, I shall call that "indirect patronage of music." Of the numerous possible motivations of a patron which result in the indirect patronage of music, I shall discuss 1) the seeking of entertainment, 2) the accruing and display of cultural status, 3) of political rank/status, 4) of social status; and 5) the practice of religion.

For the sake of discussion, I have put this in chart form. The chart is obviously a simplification of complex processes and sets of factors. While it might seem to imply, for example, that a patron has only one intention and that intention is absolutely clear, that is not always the case. It is helpful, however, for organizing the discussion of the typology and motivations for patronage.

CHART I

| | Motivation of Patron | Action | Result |
|---|---|---|---|
| Direct Process | Fostering of music | Patronage of music | Patronage of musician |
| Indirect Process | Entertainment | Patronage of musician | Patronage of music |
| | Social status | Patronage of musician | Patronage of music |
| | Cultural status | Patronage of music | Patronage of musician |
| | Political rank/ status | Patronage of musician | Patronage of music |
| | Practice of religion | Patronage of musician | Patronage of music |

## Direct Patronage

Evidence for direct patronage of music—the motivation being to foster music itself—is not always clear, but there have been striking instances in the history of Indian music when a patron became so intimately involved with the music that was being made under his or her control that it appears that direct patronage is in effect. An instance of that in the history of *Khyāl* is the case of Muhammad Shah, the last sovereign in the Mughal dynasty (ruled 1720-48) who could afford to patronize the performing arts and did so with more apparent personal relish than any of his predecessors. Elite ıore maintains that Muhammad Shah loved music so much that he neglected his duties to the point of ignoring a warning that the Persian armies of Nadir Shah were threatening not only the waning empire, but Delhi itself. History records that due to Muhammad Shah's failure and inability to prepare for the onslaught, Delhi was easily taken, the treasury looted, and the city and its population devastated. For the history of Hindustani music, however, Muhammad Shah was a significant figure: he patronized musicians who apparently began to make the genre of *Khyāl* a tangible type of musical style. It seems irrefutable that Muhammad Shah's direct patronage of music influenced the direction of classical vocal music in the northern sections of the subcontinent from his time to the present.

A second example is Wajid Ali Shah, ruler of the princely state of Oudh at the time when the British were beginning to control the political situation in North India. Wajid Ali Shah's personal involvement in music and dance and as a patron of musicians and dancers was clearly a great influence on the history of Hindustani music, fostering as he did Kathak dance and the vocal genre *Thumrī*.

A third example of direct patronage in North India is the ruling family of the princely state of Rampur in the second half of the nineteenth century and the first half of the twentieth century. In Rampur a succession of *nawāb*s patronized musicians very generously, including illustrious members of the instrumental Seni tradition. Nawab Hamid Ali Khan particularly involved himself in a personal way in the musical life in his court. His own musical expertise is reported to have been thorough—systematic and theoretical, and he patronized and directed musicians of the Sahaswan *gharānā* who developed a style of performing the genre *Khyāl* distinctive to that group and his court. Regional and group (*gharānā*) styles have been extremely important to the vitality of Hindustani music, both instrumental and vocal, and Nawab Hamid Ali Khan contributed tangibly to that vitality by his direct patronage. Under the influence of musicologist V.N. Bhatkhande, Nawab Hamid Ali Khan caused his musicians to sing their coveted orally-contributed repertoire of songs for rendering in notation. Bhatkhande's publications of songs, among others, have been powerful forces in the change in North Indian art music from relatively secret, personal and localized styles to a much more generalized tradition in terms of musical materials widely available to music makers. Thus, Nawab Hamid Ali Khan, whose patronage of music was direct and involved, played two consecutive and different roles in recent Hindustani music history.

The illustrious Maharaja Swati Tirunal (1813-1846), ruler of Trivandrum (Travancore), is an example of a patron in South India who clearly loved music. His biographers picture him as the cultural epitome of a South Indian artist who believed the purpose of music was to sing the glories of God and to express devotion. Swati Tirunal was not only an accomplished performing musician, but a prolific and good composer as well. The significance of Swati Tirunal here, however, is his patronage of other musicians. For the history of South Indian classical music, four significant results of his direct patronage of music can be pointed out.

First: in Swati Tirunal's court the *vīnā* was raised from its role of accompanying stringed instrument for concerts to the position of principal concert instrument. A second result of Swati Tirunal's direct patronage of music was the development of music for dance in South India from the Maharaja's interest in composing *pada*, songs for interpretive dance (*nātyābhinaya*) in Bharata Natyam style. Swati Tirunal's biographer, S. Vankita Subramonia Iyer. recorded the prince's involvement with this form.

> " . . . It was with a view to encouraging *nātyābhinaya* that Swati Tirunal composed these *padas*. And for giving them musical perfection and popularity, he got the services of the renowned Vadivelu, the best *nātyācharya* of the time, and through him got down from Tanjore and other places a troupe of Devadasis who performed Bharata Natya in the royal court.
>
> During the days of His Highness it was the practice for the court musicians to sing the *padas* and *varnas* after the royal supper, and this helped in their further popularization (Iyer 1975:135).

Vadivelu, patronized by Swati Tirunal from 1835, is said to have created almost all the *padavarna* which are used in Bharata Natya dance today. He and his three brothers are recognized as the moving force behind the development of the dance concert form of Bharata Natyam.

Swati Tirunal's direct patronage of music, which resulted in patronage of Vadivelu, had a third result significant for the history of Karnatak music. With one other musician (Baluswami Dikshitar, brother of the famous composer Muthuswami Dikshitar), Vadivelu was responsible for introducing the violin in South Indian music.

The fourth significant result of direct patronage by Swati Tirunal was the role he played in the dissemination of knowledge of compositions of the saint-singer Tyagaraja to Trivandrum. Of the great trinity of composers in South India at that time, the songs of Dikshitar were more known in Trivandrum than those of Syama Sastri or Tyagaraja. There was little communication between Trivandrum and Tyagaraja's home place Tiruvaiyar due to some political tension (and lack of railway connection) at the time. Swati Tirunal offered patronage to Kanniah Bhagavatar, a prominent disciple of Tyagaraja. Thus, Swati Tirunal facilitated the significant spread of Tyagaraja's music throughout the south. Swati Tirnual's direct patronage of music can be said to have been the most powerful force in the shaping of South Indian classical music in the last 150 years.

One further example of direct patronage provides a bridge to discussion of indirect patronage of music. The patron Baz Bahadur was sovereign of Malwa in the time of the Mughal emperor Akbar (ruled 1556-1605). The chronicler of Akbar's reign criticized Baz Bahadur for his great love of music: "Music and melody which the wise and farsighted have employed at times of lassitude and depression, such as arise from the press of business and the burden of humanity, as a means of lightening the mind and of cheerfulness, were regarded by this scoundrel as a serious business, and he spent upon them all his precious hours . . ." (Beveridge 1977:211). Apparently Baz Bahadur patronized music as a primary interest, rather than an approved distraction.

## Indirect Patronage

In the indirect patronage of music, motivations of patrons led them to employ musicians and therefore indirectly to foster music itself (see Chart I). In his criticism of Baz Bahadur, Abu-l-Fazl provided a clear statement of one motivation of patrons which results in indirect patronage of music: finding "a means of lightening the mind and of cheerfulness." On Chart I, I call that "seeking of entertainment."

While seeking entertainment is rarely accorded high "status" among motivations (and in India the entertainment value of music rarely accords that music high cultural status), the desire for entertainment is nevertheless a real motivation for causing music to be made or heard. North Indian paintings depict numerous instances where patrons appear to seek pleasure through music (and dance)—which results in the patronage of musicians (and dancers) and of music. Particularly in regional (non-Mughal) styles of painting, the theme of a nobleman or lady seated on a terrace with one or more musicians seated or standing before him or her occurs frequently. Even if there are multiple listeners and therefore social considerations involved in the context of the music-making, the prime motivation of the patron can be the seeking of entertainment.

A second motivation for indirect patronage of music is to accrue social status. A musical establishment was a form of manifestating social status for centuries in the courts of India (for a discussion of this, see Erdman 1978 and 1985). Thus, the system of patronage was embedded in the general system of household retinues. In Mughal courts of North India, for example, each "lady of quality" in the sovereign's household had her own quarters and private establishment, including her own group of musicians. Other musicians entertained in the male sphere of court life, in formal court contexts and informal contexts. Showing off one's musical retinue at festive times was a part of court life that is documented in paintings—in scenes of marriages, births of princes, royal birthdays, the New Year and the like. Indeed, the high percentage of paintings from courts throughout central and north India from the 16th through the 18th centuries which display retinues of musicians and dancers testifies to the social significance of having such an establishment.

While having the economic wherewithal and hiring musicians and dancers display a patron's social status, the decision to hire performing artists—and further, which performing artists—determines a patron's cultural status. A third motivation for indirect patronage of music, then, is attaining cultural status. In India music which manifests an accumulation of knowledge and cultivation of skill has high cultural status, as does music which is a vehicle for a "higher purpose" such as expression of religious devotion. Music has a higher cultural status than dance in North India, for example. Therefore, to accrue high cultural status in courtly North India, one would patronize music. To do that, one had to patronize musicians. In any case, the patronage of music itself is indirect.

Within the category of cultural status there is a ranking system and the type of music you patronize will affect the level of cultural status you attain. While the Mughal Muhammad Shah is credited with his contribution to the development of *Khyāl*, he is more frequently scorned for having loved the wrong kind of music. He apparently preferred "light music" to serious music, and *Khyāl* belonged in that category for a long span of its history. Serious music was *Dhrupad*. To this day, the vocal genre *Dhrupad* holds the highest cultural status among genres of classical vocal music and the route to high cultural status through the patronage of musicians of classical vocal styles in North India is having *Dhrupad* singers in one's home for a private performance.

The quest for cultural status comes into play in another way—in the frequent occurrence of musical competitions. The anecdotal lore of Indian music is rich with stories of contests in which musicians vied to win, to be considered the best, to achieve the highest status among the musicians involved. A number of such stories are set in courts, with the rulers involved in some way, providing other examples of indirect patronage of music resulting from the motivation of accruing cultural status. In his book *Great Composers* (1962:95-101), Sambamoorthy cites an instance which I paraphrase here. During the reign of Sarabhoji (1797-1832) in Tanjore, a vain musician from Bobbili in Andhra whose name was Kesavayya was making the rounds of musical establishments in the South, challenging the learned musicians to contests which he consistently won. He would then insist that the musicians surrender to him their *tamburās* (their personal drone stringed instrument) and also the rich gifts which they had received from their patrons. Eventually Kesavayya reached Tanjore and proceeded to challenge the musicians in the court there. "To save the reputation of Tanjore," the palace musicians were obliged to accept the challenge. All of them were unnerved by the pompous bearing of Kesavayya, however, so they went in a body to ask the great musician Syama Sastri to come perform on their behalf. Sastri ordinarily disdained royal patronage, but he agreed to sing in the contest to "save musical the reputation of Tanjore." "The Maharaja was hopeful that the reputation of Tanjore would be saved by Syama Sastri" and on the occasion of the contest, the "Maharaja had ready before him all the costly presents on a big silver plate to be given to the person emerging victorious" (1962:97-98). Not surprisingly, Syama Sastri did save the cultural status of Tanjore.

The fourth motivation for indirect patronage of music discussed here arises with the patron who wishes to assert political rank and status. Two examples are from the period of the Mughal dynasty in North India. The *naubat*, the "orchestra of world dominion," was so closely associated with the function of wielding power by the Mughals that it even symbolized that power. Only the Mughal sovereign himself had the right to own this ensemble of trumpets and horns, double-reed instruments, cymbals, and drums. Sitting high in the gates of fortress or palace, the *naubat* musicians would announce the beginning of day with a concert and mark successive periods through the day, would herald the arrival of important guests, and would sound in glorious blasts to announce widely the ascendance of the sovereign to his throne for daily court sessions. So important was the *naubat* as a resounding symbol of power that during the New Year's festivities in 1619 the young prince Shah Jahan made a gift to his father, the sovereign Jehangir: a magnificent set of instruments—a drum pair made of gold, and other instruments of silver. In his memoirs, Jehangir recounted: "At the auspicious hour at which I had seated myself on the throne of success these were all sounded" (Rogers 1968:2, 78-9). The *naubat* has continued to exist in India for eight centuries, although remnants of the grand imperial *naubat* ensemble are meager. A huge kettle-drum is brought out on a few grand official occasions to herald the highest officers of the Republic. Likewise, in the Rajasthani cities of Jaipur and Jodhpur tourists are treated to a hearing daily. Although the patronage of the musical tradition of the *naubat* during the Mughal period was only an indirect type of patronage, the nature of the patronage as symbolizing power, undoubtedly contributed greatly to the continuing existence of the tradition in any form today (see Wade:1986a and 1986b).

A second example of patronage with the intention to accrue (or assert) political rank and status concerns the legendary North Indian singer Tansen. Abu-l-Fazl, the chronicler of the reign of the great Mughal Akbar, made it quite clear that the patronage of Tansen by Akbar came about as a facet of power-play with Ram Chand, the third generation of *raja*s of the small princely state of

Pannah, who had refused to "doff his cap of pride and place the ring of submission in his ear, and come into the list of tributaries" (Beveridge 1977:II, 282). As told in the *Akbar Nāmā*, upon hearing of the fame of Tansen and that the musician "was spending his days in attendance on Ram Chand," Akbar "ordered that he should be enrolled among [his] court musicians. Jalal Khan Qurci, who was a favorite servant, was sent with a gracious order to the Raja for the purpose of bringing Tansen" (Beveridge 1977:II, 279-80). Ram Chand apparently felt powerless to refuse Akbar's order and sent Tansen along to Akbar with (other) numerous gifts. Here is the interplay of different types of status in the process of patronizing music indirectly: Akbar accrued political status, but would not have chosen that method if Tansen had not been a musician of such high cultural status.

If the rulers in the regional courts of the Mughal empire became patrons of musicians because they considered it necessary to manifest their political status by emulating the musical establishments of the central Mughal court, then the types of music, specializations fostered by musicians and the sorts of musical expertise developed in families of musicians hired were likely to reflect that. Patronage for the sake of political status, then, would not only influence which genres of music were developed, but would influence as well the very nature of the genres themselves.

One example bridges indirect patronage of music to accrue political status and the motivation of religious practice. There might have been some interest in gaining political status when Swati Tirunal and his regional contemporaries patronized North Indian musicians and cultivated Hindustani musical forms and modes at the time Tanjore had been taken over by the northern Marathas. Characteristically, however, a patron of the integrity of Swati Tirunal would have personal preferences for those particular elements of Hindustani music and culture which he favored. Being a deeply religious man, he found delight in *Harikatha*, the musical discourse of religious themes which had developed in Maharashtra in the *bhakti* movement. To an exceptional *Harikatha* singer Swati Tirunal extended the sort of patronage to which he treated his court musicians: "Meruswami performed *Harikatha* in the royal presence . . . and the delighted Maharaja presented him with a pair of gold bangles, a golden necklace, a pair of shawls and Rs. 500" (Iyer 1975:95).

The patronage of musicians—and indirectly of music—motivated by the practice of religion is basic in Indian culture, no matter what religion or what part of the country or what level of society. Temples hire musicians on a regular basis or as needed for festivities. Royal or other wealthy patrons supported and still support musicians for a temple. The Mughals listened regularly to *qawwāli* and must have supported the musical establishments at Sufi centers. Other examples of patrons are participants in a present-day Sufi assembly, the audience for Baul singers, the housewife who gives food or coins to the mendicant yogi. In South India particularly, where the repertoire of songs which is the basis of the classical musical tradition is clearly devotional in nature (unlike the songs of North Indian *Khyal*, for instance), the patronage of musicians and indirectly of their music has undoubtedly been motivated to some extent by considering such patronage an element in the practice of religion.

The motivations for the patronage of music have been significant contributing factors in the history of music in India. Particular reasons for patrons to support musicians and music have contributed tangibly to determining what music has been developed in India through time, by whom, and with what musical result. The patronage of music is not only of music itself, but of musicians and even of the patrons themselves.

## References

Athavale, V.R. 1967. *Pandit Vishnu Digambar*. New Delhi: National Book Trust.

Beveridge, H., translator. 1977. *The Akbar Nāmā*. By Abu-l-Fazl. Translated 1921. Volume II. Delhi: Ess Ess Publications (2nd Indian Reprint).

Blank, Judith. 1973. *The Story of the Chou Dance of the Former Mayurbhanj State, Orissa*. Ph.D. thesis, Department of Anthropology, University of Chicago.

Erdman, Joan. 1978. "The Maharaja's Musicians: The Organization of Cultural Performance at Jaipur in the 19th Century," *American Studies in the Anthropology of India*, ed. by Sylvia Vatuk. New Delhi: Manohar.

————. 1985. *Patrons and Performers in Rajasthan: The Subtle Tradition*. New Delhi: Chanakya Publications.

Iyer, S. Venkita Subramonia. 1975. *Swati Tirunal and His Music*. Trivandrum: College Book House.

Patnaik, Naveen. 1985. *A Second Paradise: Indian Courtly Life: 1590-1947*. New York: Doubleday Books.

Rogers, Alexander, translator. 1968. *Tuzuk-i-Jahangir (or Memoirs of Jahangir)*.

Henry Beveridge, ed. Delhi: Junshiram Manoharlal, 2nd ed. (First published 1909-1914).

Sambamoorthy, P. 1962. *Great Composers*. Book I. Madras: The Indian Music Publishing House.

Wade, Bonnie C. 1984. *Khyāl: Creativity within North India's Classical Music Tradition*. With audio cassette. Cambridge: Cambridge University Press.

———. 1986a. "Music as Symbol of Power and Status: The Courts of Mughal India," *Explorations in Ethnomusicology: Essays in Honor of David P. McAllester*, ed. by Charlotte, J Frisbie. Detroit: Information Coordinators.

———. 1986b. "Playing for Power: Drum and *Naubat*, the Symbols of Might," *Proceedings of the Thirteenth Congress, 1982* (International Musicological Society). Strasbourg.

# Market Structure and State Patronage in Karnataka's Feature Film Industry: Implications for the New Cinema

Manjunath Pendakur

> What really distinguishes the New Indian Cinema is a definitive set of liberal-humanitarian values, embracing progressive solutions to urgent problems, a sensitivity to the plight of the poor and oppressed, a faith in the ultimate movement of man towards change. Drawing its inspiration largely from the neo-realists, it is a cinema of social significance and artistic sincerity, presenting a modern, humanist perspective, more durable than the fantasy world of the popular film.
>
> Raghunath Raina, Director,
> Directorate of Film Festivals
> New Delhi.[1]

Raina's comment captures the contribution made by the New Cinema in India which emerged as a national phenomenon in the late sixties. Foundations for this interesting development were laid much earlier, however, by three prominent film-makers in Bengal: Satyajit Ray, Ritwik Ghatak, and Mrinal Sen. Their critically acclaimed work had shattered a Government Tourist Bureau vision of India as a tranquil, peace-loving society with traditional gaiety and color. Buttressed by policies of the state, the New Cinema spread to different regions of India in the late sixties with the release of Mrinal Sen's *Bhuvan Shome*, Basu Chatterji's *Sara*

[1] *Film India. The New Generation*, (New Delhi: Directorate of Film Festivals, 1980).

*Akash*, and Mani Kaul's *Uski Roti*. New-comers all over India, working outside the commercial system, generated great enthusiasm in film circles.

Karnataka became the locus of the New Cinema for some time in the seventies. For various reasons, explained below, the state government in Karnataka played an interventionist role attempting to develop a regional film culture. While state patronage may have resulted in sustaining film production for a while, one can, in the mid-1980s, observe a certain sense of failure and disillusionment among these film makers. Their audiences have lost interest as well. The popular press in Karnataka, which had supported the development of the New Cinema as an alternative to the formulaic "commercial" cinema, has started to dub it as the 'death of the New Cinema' in the state of Karnataka.

This paper analyzes various reasons that may have led to the lack of success of Karnataka's New Cinema. It argues that three important structural characteristics—financing/production, distribution, and exhibition as well as policies of the state government need to be reformed to assist further development of Karnataka's New Cinema.

## The Setting: Kannada Films in the Great Indian Film Bazaar

Cinema in India is a capitalist enterprise. Films are financed, produced, distributed, and exhibited primarily to generate a profit. Exceptions to this general rule are government sponsored and distributed feature films, documentaries, and news reels. Occasionally certain political parties and cooperative societies have financed films for ideological reasons but those films are rare.[2] Since 1971, India has ranked as the world's largest producer of feature films with Japan and the United States being the second and third major producers respectively.[3] With an annual output of

[2] The Shyam Benegal-directed Hindi film, *Manthan* (1974), was financed by one rupee donations by the 50,000 members of the Gujarat Milk Cooperative Society. It tells of problems in inducing change in India's caste and class ridden village society by urban interests and government agents. A Communist Party (Marxist) group called Navashakti Films produced *Ellindalo Bandavaru* (1979) in Kannada, which was the story of a landless laborer and his position in a village.

[3] B.V. Dharap, *Indian Films*, (Pune: Motion Picture Enterprises, 1979)

742 feature films in 1980, and an estimated gross box office revenue of 720 million rupees, the film industry in India holds the position of tenth largest industry in the country.[4]

The Southern region where Karnataka is located has become increasingly important to India's film economy in recent years. In 1980, the south as a whole produced 486 features in five different languages or 63 per cent of the year's total film output. Nearly seven million of the estimated 12.5 million daily movie-goers flocked to 51 per cent of the country's cinemas located in the south. Those theatres grossed well over half of India's box office take in 1980.[5]

Although films made in Karnataka do not constitute the bulk of the films made in the Southern region, they have grown steadily in number and importance since the seventies. Systematic analysis of Karnataka's film industry is difficult as there is no ready data base and independent researchers have limited access to industry data. What has become available to me, however, suggests some interesting patterns of relationships. About 600 feature films have been made during the 50 year history of Kannada cinema, and half were produced between 1972-1980.[6] Until the 1960s, production was sporadic. One account estimated that only 40 silent films were made in the state.[7] The advent of sound in the early 1930s seems to have brought much enthusiasm in the film industry as it created a natural barrier to other language films in the state, but the output was too low to provide a steady supply of films to theatres. Between 1934 and 1952, 21 films were made in Kannada, most of which were produced outside the state in Madras, the most important film production centre in the South.[8]

Lacking the necessary industrial infrastructure (studios, laboratories, outdoor film equipment, etc.) and enthusiasm on the part of the audiences who were receptive to other language films, and faced with a small market, Kannada cinema remained underdeveloped until the state government intervened in the mid sixties.

[4] *India Today*, July 16-31, 1981.

[5] *Ibid.*

[6] Santosh Kumar Gulvadi, "What happened to Karnataka's New Cinema?" *Filmfare*, January 16-31, 1980.

[7] M.B. Singh, "Kannada Films in Retrospect", *March of Karnataka. Kannada Films Supplement*, (Bangalore: The Director of Information and Publicity, August-September 1977), p. 4.

[8] *Ibid.*

Two important reasons which contributed to involvement of the state were linguistic reorganization of the states which occurred in the early fifties and pressure brought on by various industry and public groups to assist development of a Kannada cinema.[9] The results were a state subsidy scheme for film production and studio construction which laid the foundations for Kannada cinema in general and later on the New Cinema in particular. Those policies addressed issues of financing and production only but not the issue of marketing, which would have an adverse impact on the New Cinema in the seventies.

### The New Cinema and the Market Structure

The New Cinema in Karnataka was launched by three important film makers. In 1970, Pattabhi Rama Reddy made *Samskara*, a satire on the caste-ridden Indian village, adapted from U.R. Anantha Murthy's popular novel of the same name. Following that in 1971 came *Vamsya Vruksha*, the combined effort of Girish Karnad and B.V. Karanth, both talented writers and dramatists. They adapted a novel of the same name written by S.L. Bhairappa, who was well read in Karnataka at the time. Their film analyzed the psychological trauma of a Brahmin priest in a village who finds out that he was actually born out of wedlock to an untouchable woman. Karnad contributed another important film, *Kaadu* (1973), which explored the origins of growing violence in Indian villages and graphically described how the feudal power structure was cracking with the onslaught of forces of change. Karanth made *Chomana Dudi* (1975) which won the President's Gold Medal for the year and placed Kannada cinema firmly on the nation's film map. That film portrayed the utter poverty and degradation to which untouchable people are subjected in the state of Karnataka. Many others joined the ranks of these film makers, noteworthy among them P. Lankesh and Girish Kasaravalli.

What these film makers faced however was a film market predominantly occupied by the better-looking Telugu, Tamil, and

[9] For a more detailed analysis of the evolution and growth of Kannada cinema see Manjunath Pendakur, "Kannada Cinema As A Cultural Force," paper presented at the University Film & Video Association Annual Conference, Southern Illinois University, Carbondale, Illinois, July, 1980.

Hindi films as well as commercial Kannada films. Earlier, off-beat films such as *Naandi* (1964), a sensitive portrayal of a deaf-mute woman attempting to live a normal family life, had succeeded in breaking into the market mainly because they had recognizable star commodities. *Samskara* and others of the kind had no stars, were shot on shoe-string budgets, and broke significantly from the "commercial" film paradigm of song, dances, fights, predictable characters and endings. Such New Wave Films were to face immense problems in the market place.

The film market in Karnataka is characterized by a relatively small population of 40 million persons, most of whom speak a language called Kannada. Only about 30 percent of them are regular movie-goers, which is too small to support a film industry based on a profit motive.[10]

The average cost of production of a color film in 1970 without a major star such as Raj Kumar was about 400,000 rupees and in black and white about 150,000 rupees.[11] In 1980, those costs more than doubled. It is generally believed that to recover the principal invested in a film, it would have to gross 5.5 times of the amount at the box office.[12]

Karnataka's market consists of only about 1,000 theatres out of which nearly half are touring cinemas, operating only in the non-monsoon seasons.[13] Nearly ten per cent of the permanent houses are located in Bangalore, which is the state's capital with a little over two million inhabitants. That high degree of concentration of theatres in one single market essentially means that access to the Bangalore theatres is crucial for a Kannada film to recover costs and make a profit.

The release and the ensuing publicity of a film's appeal to Bangalore audiences often determines a film's market ability in other areas of the state and its growing potential there. The remaining 900 theatres are spread out in 'B' centres (big towns) and 'C' centres (small towns and rural locations).

For distribution and exhibition purposes the state is divided into

[10] C.H. Nagaraj, Partner, Nagaraj Film Distributors, Interview, Chitradurga, August 4, 1980.

[11] *Ibid.*

[12] *Ibid.*

[13] Official of the Karnataka Film Chamber of Commerce, Interview, Bangalore, July 20, 1980.

three territories—Bangalore and suburbs, Chitradurga, and Hubli. Except for Bangalore, all others are considered a mixture of 'B' and 'C' centres by the distributors, thereby suggesting the marginality of those markets for a film's financial success or failure in the state. Although marginal, 'B' and 'C' centres yield often considerable amounts of revenue as exhibitors in those areas demand pictures that do well in the 'A' centres and are willing to pay the price. All of this suggests that access to the Bangalore market is the key factor in a film's overall market success.[14]

Since theatre construction is a costly but lucrative enterprise, big industrial capital and banking capital are involved.[15] No doubt the same interests would be less keen on involvement in film production where costs are seldom in control. Because investors' confidence in a film rests on the dubious possibility of making a profit, investment monies would be scarce if it were known that marketability is a problem.

Data on vertically integrated structures of production, distribution, and exhibition are sketchy. There are many integrated production and distribution firms but none own any theatres. Major firms such as B.R. Pantulu Films and R.N.R. Pictures did not integrate their operations with theatres in Bangalore. However, some Hindi film production firms do own theatres in that city. Prominent among them are Rajshree Pictures and Mandra Brothers which have nation-wide distribution offices and produce their own films. Owning and/or leasing important theatres in Bangalore gives them guaranteed access for their films.

A high degree of economic power in the Kannada film industry rests in the hands of theatre owners, particularly those who own theatres in 'A' and 'B' centres. All pictures in the state are released on a fixed-share basis. This means that the distributor agrees to pay a fixed rent to the exhibitor on a weekly basis irrespective of box office performance of the film. The contract contrasts with the American film industry where the major distributors have significant economic power and demand advances and often a minimum guarantee irrespective of a film's box office take. What Karnataka

[14] C.H. Nagaraj, *Op. Cit.*

[15] An average theatre in a 'B' or 'C' centre with a 1,000 seat capacity cost about 200,000 rupees and 800,000 rupees in an 'A' centre in the fifties. Today, the costs have so escalated that one would need 5-10 times those amounts to build new theatres. No small capitalist could afford to invest such sums in theatre construction.

theatre owners are doing is minimizing their risks, thereby having a guaranteed return on their investment in the theatre. State policies in the 1960s did not address these important issues at all, which has had adverse effects on the financial viability of the New Cinema.

A vertically integrated structure emerged in the late seventies which, some in the industry claim, has further affected the New Cinema negatively. C.H. Nagaraj Film Distributors, once a small sub distributing company mainly functioning in the Chitradurga territory, aligned itself with Raj Kumar, the matinee idol of Kannada commercial cinema. All of Raj Kumar's pictures were to be jointly financed by the distributor and the star himself, and would be monopolized by that one company. Additionally, that company started leasing key theatres in big towns such as Davanagere and Hospet, and expanded its distribution network state-wide, shaping a fully integrated firm.[16] Thus only a certain number of Raj Kumar films would be produced and all profits in distribution, exhibition and production would accrue to the star and his partners.

This vertical monopoly caused controversy in the state. Some film makers have alleged that Nagaraj Film Distributors has employed predatory practices which have hurt a competitor's release.[17] One exhibitor indicated that Nagaraj Film Distributors indulges in monopolistic trade practices such as block booking whereby a distributor sells a package of films consisting of one or two commercial hits with the rest marginal films. While this practice allows a distributor to gain market access for marginal films, it has the effect of reducing the number of play dates for other films waiting to be released. In the case of Karnataka, such monopolistic schemes can be practiced only in 'B' and 'C' centres, as Bangalore theatre owners are too powerful to give in to such tactics.

As theatres in Karnataka are pre-empted by star-studded commercial films in Kannada and other languages, New Wave films' makers have often had to wait nearly two years to find play-dates for their films. It appears that the state government has not shown

[16] C.H. Nagaraj, *Op. Cit.*

[17] For example, when a New Wave film is released in Davanagere, a 'B' centre, Nagaraj would reissue an old but popular Raj Kumar film which would draw most of the audiences away from the new film. When confronted with that allegation, Mr. Nagaraj said that he was just being a competitive businessman.

any interest in utilizing its regulatory powers to correct such market abuses. *Grahana* directed by Nagabharana, *Akramana* by Girish Kasaravalli, and *Savithri* by T.S. Ranga, all completed in 1978, had not been released by 1980.[18]

Another monopolistic practice with adverse consequences to New Cinema in Karnataka is what is known as 'padding' This means that a distributor augments inadequate box office collections thereby sustaining a film for a longer run. The assumption is that if a film appears to run for a certain number of weeks in Bangalore, more revenues could be extracted from other markets. A film celebrating, for instance, its silver jubilee in a major city has publicity value as well. However this practice effectively reduces the availability of play-dates for other films waiting in line. P. Lankesh, who has made four New Wave films, claimed that Rajshree Pictures padded the release of a Hindi film, *Tarana*, and consequently pre-empted play-dates that would have become available to one of his films waiting for that theatre in Bangalore. He went on to say the following which summarizes the feelings of many Kannada film makers.

> . . . Due to such monopolistic practices, we have to go for morning shows. Not only are Hindi films destroying the taste, they are destroying the regional cinema. Raj Kapoor and others should be immediately sent to the Andamans.[19]

Many film makers lobbied the state government to intervene in the industry to correct such abuses. Nagabharana, a New Wave director, went on hunger strike before the state legislature in July 1980 demanding that a screen quota be legislated to guarantee a certain number of play-dates for Kannada films. But the state paid no attention to such demands.

Disillusioned by bottlenecks in distribution and exhibition, many New Wave film makers have turned to making commercial films. Girish Karnad, who had contributed significantly to the New Wave Cinema in Karnataka, went to Bombay to make big budget, multi-star feature films. Nagabharana, whose *Grahana* won the State Award for the Best Picture of the Year, changed tracks and made

[18] Santosh Kumar Gulvadi, *Op. Cit.*
[19] P. Lankesh, *Op. Cit.*

*Anveshana*, an action-adventure film. V.R.K. Prasad, whose *Rishyashrunga* had won two National Awards, announced that he would make a commercial film in 1980.

## The State as Patron

In a historical sense, the government of Karnataka has played a decisive role in aiding the state's film industry. The mechanisms used by the state are financial subsidy, state awards, and assistance for infrastructural development. Due to the pressure from industry organizations, the press and the general public, the state government established a subsidy scheme in 1967 which guaranteed a return of 50,000 rupees for every film made in Karnataka. Film output steadily grew, as indicated in Table 1.

TABLE 1 NUMBER OF FILMS TO WHICH STATE SUBSIDY WAS PAID FROM 1967-1980

| Year | Number of Films | Amount |
|---|---|---|
| 1967-68 | 5 | Rs. 250,000 |
| 1968-69 | 16 | Rs. 800,000 |
| 1969-70 | 20 | Rs. 1,000,000 |
| 1970-71 | 32 | Rs. 1,600,000 |
| 1971-72 | 33 | Rs. 1,650,000 |
| 1972-73 | 23 | Rs. 1,150,000 |
| 1973-74 | 24 | Rs. 1,200,000 |
| 1974-75 | 28 | Rs. 1,400,000 |
| 1975-76 | 19 | Rs. 950,000 |
| 1976-77 | 43 | Rs. 4,200,000 |
| 1977-78 | 55 | Rs. 5,975,000 |
| 1978-79 | 32 | Rs. 3,995,000 |
| 1979-80 | 51 | Rs. 5,975,000 |
| Total | 381 | Rs. 30,145,000 |

**Source:** Government of Karnataka Department of Information and Publicity (Film Unit)

In 1966, a year before the scheme was introduced, 21 Kannada films were made, out of which only one was produced in the state. Between 1967 and 1977, a total of 375 films were produced in Kannada out of which 67 per cent were produced in the state.[20] As

[20] K.C. Chowdappa Reddy, "Awards and Subsidy", *March of Karnataka. Kannada Film Supplement*, p. 68.

the subsidy was not restricted by language, other language films could take advantage of it by making films in the state. In the 1967-1977 period, a total of 57 other language films were made in Karnataka thus bringing jobs and other investment to the state.[21]

When the subsidy was introduced in 1967, the average cost of a Kannada film in black and white was around 100,000 rupees. Color films cost 3-4 times as much and they were seldom made. However, by the mid-1970s, costs had soared steeply. A black and white film on the average cost about 400,000 rupees and a color film about 800,000 rupees.[22] This meant that the subsidy was inadequate. Through various lobby organizations the film industry mounted considerable pressure on the government to increase the subsidy.[23] Yielding to industry pressure, the government increased the subsidy in 1975 to 100,000 rupees for black and white films and 150,000 rupees for color films made in the state. However, it stipulated that only Kannada, Tulu, Konkani, and Coorgi language films were eligible for that level of support. Other language films produced entirely in the state would continue to get 50,000 rupees aid.[24]

A subsidy minimized investor risk and the uncertainty of even minimal returns if Kannada films were left to the market forces. As soon as a producer got a censorship certificate, which is issued by the federal government, s/he could apply for the subsidy. After ensuring that certain eligibility requirements were met, the state government issued a check.

The state government also enticed potential investors to build studios in the state by offering them water and electricity free of charge. Premier studies in Mysore, which had been closed for some time, began operating again. Preparations began to build two more studios in Bangalore. As the subsidy scheme required all shooting be done in the state, aspirants to the scheme made use of the studios and also began location filming in the state. These studios were, however, not as well equipped as those in Madras. Other facilities such as processing, recording/mixing and outdoor equipment did not exist in the state. Consequently, some major

[21] *Ibid.*

[22] Girish Kasaravalli, producer/director, Interview, Bangalore, July 21, 1980.

[23] Government of Karnataka, Department of Information and Publicity, *Guidelines for the Film Subsidy*, no date.

[24] *Ibid.*

commercial film directors—B.R. Pantulu, S.R. Puttanna, and R. Nagendra Rao—did not shoot films in the state.

Another mechanism employed by the state to encourage Kannada film industry development was state awards, introduced in 1966. A novel approach, in that cash awards were given, it was appropriate in a financially unstable industry. Initially, awards were given in two categories—best film of the year which came with a purse of 25,000 rupees, and best director of the year with an award of 10,000 rupees. These amounts have been increased to 55,000 and 25,000 rupees respectively (See Appendix).

The awards served at least three essential purposes. One, they recognized home-grown talent in production and direction of films; two, they created a certain degree of enthusiasm for these films in the market place; three, as cash awards they provided an additional source of support to many film makers who may not have made their second film in the absence of such an award.

Continued support for new directors in the Kannada film industry created by the awards is best illustrated in the case of *Pallavi*, which won the best film award for 1977. It was the first directorial enterprise by P. Lankesh, a controversial novelist and poet. According to him, the black and white film cost approximately 40,000 rupees to produce. The Best Film of the Year award brought him 55,000 rupees and the subsidy brought another 100,000 rupees. The Government of India awarded Lankesh the best director award for that film which yielded another 20,000 rupees. Even before the film was distributed, it had earned a profit of 135,000 rupees.[25] Lankesh has gone on to make three more films to date. Although the *Pallavi* case may be exceptional as costs of production have gone up and awards are based on chance, the fact that the film won these cash awards made it posible for Lankesh to continue to produce films. Undoubtedly awards and subsidy schemes have a stabilizing influence on the Karnataka film industry.

Despite its overall success, the subsidy scheme is riddled with problems of bureaucratic red tape and mismanagement. Some film makers pointed out that it took too long for the producer to receive the subsidy check. Waiting time often can be as long as a year.[26] For instance from March 1980, 85 applications were pending a

[25] P. Lankesh, producer/director, Interview.

[26] Girish Kasaravalli, producer/director, Interview.

decision in August of that year at the Government Film Unit, which processes subsidy applications.[27] The primary reason for delay according to the officials was that the legislature had to make annual appropriations from the general treasury and often there were no funds to do so.[28] This problem arose because the entertainment tax collected from ticket sales went directly to the general treasury and not into a separate fund. The government had been unwilling to change this pattern of organization despite repeated industry representations.

According to some film makers, delays in receiving the check invalidated the intended benefits of the scheme. Such delays made it difficult for New Wave film producers as they operate on a fragile financial infrastructure. If one takes a close look at the way commercial films and New Wave films are financed in Karnataka, it will be evident that they follow distinctly different patterns. A commercial film maker utilizes a method called 'forward selling' whereby s/he shoots a song, a dance, a fight scene, or some melodramatic scene with the principal stars, and screens that package to potential distributors. When a willing distributor is found, the film maker receives all necessary finances from that company to complete the film and to release it. The pattern of financing for New Wave films is radically different. Often a film maker promotes an idea among his friends who put up the initial investment. S/he then may borrow the rest of the capital from money lenders at usurious interest rates often as high as 60 per cent and beyond to complete the film as no distributor is interested in risking capital on a film without the necessary box office ingredients. Nationalized banks have become involved in financing films recently. Although the interest they charge is regulated, their level of investment is a maximum of two thirds of the film's budget and they require that they be paid first when the subsidy check is issued. More often than not, New Wave films have been made because crew, actors, and others worked for the film with a small advance and waited to receive salaries until the film was marketed.

The government's taxation policy with respect to film exhibition is at best impractical and inconsistent. The state collects about 40

[27] Official, Department of Information and Publicity, Interview, Bangalore. July 22, 1980.

[28] *Ibid.*

per cent of the ticket price in the form of an entertainment tax which in 1975-1976 amounted to about seven million rupees.[29] A small part of that is spent on the Karnataka Film Development Corporation (KFDC), awards and subsidy, and the rest is allocated for people's welfare programs. The state has exempted certain New Wave and other films from that tax but the exemption is not consistently applied to all New Wave Films. Moreover, this policy is susceptible to political influence. The state has also for some time penalized films that received an 'A' certificate from the Censor Board by doubling the entertainment tax. Such penalties had a direct impact on films such as *Ghatashraddha* and *Kadu Kudure*, both award winning films which were given an 'A' certificate.[30] In the same year, two commercial films, *Muttu Ondu Muttu* and *Putani Agents* were exempted from the tax because they were billed as children's films, while *Arivu* was denied this classification. As *Arivu* had won the Best Regional Film Award from the Central Government, it should have been exempted from entertainment tax. A press battle ensued and two days after its release, the state approved the tax relief application.[31]

The KFDC has been a fiasco according to many film makers and the press. It has not only not met its mandate of assisting the development of 'good cinema' in Karnataka but has been a den of corruption and misused state funds. Established in 1968, KFDC remained dormant until 1975 when the then Chief Minister of the state appointed his own brother Kemparaj Urs, earlier an actor, to head the KFDC. Urs launched four expensive films which cost around a total of 4 million rupees. Only two were released and they brought no returns to the corporation.[32] The Corporation claimed it had partly or fully financed eight mini theatres since Urs came to power but none of the film makers interviewed seemed to know about them.

P. Lankesh summarized the conditions in Karnataka's film industry in an interesting manner:

In Karnataka, we don't have money to make films; secondly we

[29] K.M. Shankarappa. *March of Karnataka. Kannada Film Supplement.*

[30] Girish Kasaravalli, film's director, Interview. Also see, Santosh Kumar Gulvadi, *Op. Cit.*

[31] Ibid.

[32] Official, Karnataka Film Development Corporation, Interview, Bangalore, July 22, 1980.

don't have theatres to screen them; and thirdly, we don't have the money to influence the Censor Board.

Censorship is an important problem facing New Wave Film makers because it imposes boundaries on subjects to be explored as well as the extent they can be dealt with in a film. Although the issue of censorship is not treated here fully, suffice it to say that New Wave film makers in Karnataka see it as a major problem. One film maker, whose *Khandavideko Mamsavideko* (1979), dealing with prostitution, was cut by 2,000 feet by the Censor Board, made the following observation:

> To have the Censor Board in your mind when you make a film is a terrible thing for an artist. It is convenient to the Hindi people because they can buy the Censor Board. Once they buy the Censor Board, they can have a better market than the people who can't afford to do so. . . . Your film will be as innocent as mother's milk, whereas a Hindi film can be as uninnocent as a brothel. Such disparity in India has its influence everywhere.[33]

### Public as Patrons

Besides these formidable problems, many New Wave film makers conceded that they have not been able to create a big enough audience for their films. Initial enthusiasm among city audiences had dissipated by 1980. As most New Wave films are produced with budgets that are a small fraction of a Kannada commercial film, they are hastily shot and end up looking poor technically. For instance *Shankaraguru* (1979), a Raj Kumar picture, was produced at a cost of 2.5 million rupees. When released it grossed a total of seven million rupees and was expected to hit the ten million rupee mark.[34] Whereas The New Wave film *Ellindalo Bandavaru* (1978) completed with 250,000 rupees, could not secure a distributor and was waiting to be released in August 1980.[35]

[33] P. Lankesh, Interview.
[34] C.H. Nagaraj, film's distributor, Interview.
[35] Shanker Kondajji, film's producer, Interview, Bangalore, July 23, 1980.

Not only are there technical/production, and marketing problems impeding the viability of New Wave Cinema, problems of style and censorship further restrict its appeal. New Wave cinema shuns the commercial film formula, but it has not been able to devise its own formula yet that would be acceptable to the mass audience. As indicated by Table 2, many New Wave films released in the 'C' centres do not run for even a week. If the film does not generate a repeat audience, in Karnataka it is practically impossible to recoup costs let along make a profit.

TABLE 2 GROSS BOX OFFICE REVENUE FOR SELECTED NEW WAVE FILMS IN A 'C' CENTRE, 1975-80

| Film Title | Director | No. of days Run | Gross Box Office Revenue (Rupees) | Profit/ Loss to Theatre |
|---|---|---|---|---|
| Samskara | P.R. Reddy | 1 | 100.00 | Loss |
| Kadu | Girish Karnad | 3 | 450.00 | Profit |
| Chomana Dudi | B.V. Karanth | 3 | 300.00 | Profit |
| Kakana Kote | S.N. Simha | 3 | 400.00 | Profit |
| Madi Madidavaru | Shankarappa | 1 | 250.00 | Loss |
| Kokila | Balumahendra | 3 | 500.00 | Profit |
| Tabbaliyu Ninade Magane | Girish Karnad | 3 | 350.00 | Profit |
| Gende Timma | Maruthi Shivaram | 5 | 2000.00 | Profit |
| Kankana | P. Lankesh | 1 | 125.00 | Loss |
| Ondanondu Kaaladalli | Girish Karnad | 3 | 500.00 | Profit |
| Aparichita | Kashinath | 3 | 450.00 | Profit |
| Sangharsha | Basavaraj Kesthur | 2 | 400.00 | Profit |
| Tappida Tala | K. Balachander | 3 | 400.00 | Loss |
| Huli Bantu Huli | Not Known | 1 | 100.00 | Loss |

**Source:** Manager, Sri Krishna Picture Palace, Hagaribommanahalli, Karnataka Population: Approx. 20,000.

Audiences and businesses expect a certain type of formulaic entertainment from Kannada films; New Wave cinema would have to overcome that obstacle in order to become viable. Film makers would have to devise a new idiom for their films to reach a wider population base. Shyam Benegal appears to have struck such a compromise in many of his films which are produced in Hindi. The recent successes of some New Wave Hindi films in securing play dates in key cities of India indicate a glimmer of hope for the New Cinema.[36] Whether Hindi film successes can set a model for Kannada film makers is hard to tell because of differences in market size and elements of competition and monopoly specific to Karnataka.

**Conclusions**

Troublesome conditions of financing, production, distribution and exhibition characterize capitalist cinema everywhere. Film makers working outside the major integrated production-distribution corporations are in the U.S. relegated to the same obscure status in the film industry as many Kannada New Wave film makers. However, what is different and interesting about cinema in India is that the State plays a major role of patron, regulator, and disciplinarian. It speaks of assisting the development of a "good cinema" to uplift the masses, but given the market structure and uncompetitive position those films are faced with, they have little contact with those masses.

The state has many regulatory mechanisms at its disposal if it intends to ensure market access to New Wave films in Karnataka. A "good cinema" cannot be nurtured if left only to the market forces. It can come about by making the works of innovative film makers widely available to all audiences so that existing consumption patterns of audiences may change.

[36] Two Hindi films, *Chakra* and *What Makes Albert Pinto Angry*? have been reported to have successful commercial runs recently.

APPENDIX

FILMS THAT HAVE WON KARNATAK STATE AWARDS, 1966-1978

| Year | Award | Name of the Film | Director |
|---|---|---|---|
| 1966-67 | I Prize | None | |
| | II Prize | Nakkarade Swarga | M. R. Vittal |
| | III Prize | Sandhyaraga | A. C. Narasimha Murthy |
| 1967-68 | I Prize | None | |
| | II Prize | Belli Moda | S. R. Puttanna Kanagal |
| | III Prize | Sarvamanagala | Chaduranga |
| | III Prize | Bangarada Hoovu | B. A. Arasukumar |
| 1968-69 | I Prize | Hannele Chiguridaga | M. R. Vittal |
| | II Prize | Namma Makkalu | R. Nagendra Rao |
| | III Prize | Mannina Maga | Geethapriya |
| 1969-70 | I Prize | Gejje Pooje | S. R. Puttanna Kanagal |
| | II Prize | Uyyale | N. Lakshminarayan |
| | II Prize | Mukti | N. Lakshminarayan |
| | III Prize | Eradu Mukha | M. R. Vittal |
| 1970-71 | I Prize | Sharapanjara | S. R. Puttanna Kanagal |
| | II Prize | Samskara | Pattabhirama Reddy |
| | III Prize | Kula Gaurava | Peketi Shivaram |
| 1971-72 | I Prize | Vamsha Vriksha | Girish Karnad and B. V. Karanth |
| | II Prize | Bangarada Manushya | Siddalingaiah |
| | III Prize | Sipayi Ramu | Y. R. Swamy |
| | III Prize | Yava Janmada Maitri | Geethapriya |
| 1972-73 | I Prize | Sankalpa | P. V. Nanja Raj Urs |
| | II Prize | Nagarahavu | S. R. Puttanna Kanagal |
| | III Prize | Bisathi Babu (Tulu) | Arur Pattabhi |
| | IV Prize | Hridaya Sangama | Rasi Brothers |
| 1973-74 | I Prize | Boothayyana Maga Ayyu | Siddalingaiah |
| | II Prize | Kaadu | Girish Karnad |
| | II Prize | Maadi Madidavaru | K. M. Shankarappa |
| | III Prize | Abachurina Post Office | N. Lakshminarayan |
| | IV Prize | Koti Channaya (Tulu) | Vishukumar |
| 1974-75 | I Prize | Upasane | S. R. Puttana Kanagal |
| | II Prize | Kankana | M. B. S. Prasad |
| | III Prize | Bhakta Kumbara | Hunsur Krishnamurthy |
| | IV Prize | Jagruthi | B. Sridhar |
| 1975-76 | I Prize | Chomana Dudi | B. V. Karanth |
| | II Prize | Hamsageethe | G. V. Iyer |
| | III Prize | Premada Kanike | V. Somasekhar |
| | IV Prize | Kahtha Sangama | S. R. Puttanna Kanagal |

| | | | |
|---|---|---|---|
| 1976-76 | I Prize | Pallavi | P. Lankesh |
| | II Prize | Riṣhyashrunga | V. R. K. Prasad |
| | III Prize | Kakanakote | C. R. Simha |
| | IV Prize | Ritugana | Vijayakumar |
| 1977-78 | I Prize | Ghatashraddha | Girish Kasaravalli |
| | II Prize | Spandana | P. N. Srinivas |
| | III Prize | Anuroopa | P. Lankesh |

**Source**: Karnataka Film Chamber of Commerce, Bangalore, India.

# A Performance Model from South India*

Norman Cutler

Reading Bonnie Wade's paper on the patronage of music at the Mughal court in tandem with Manjunath Pendakur's paper on the fortunes of the "New Cinema" in Karnataka, one cannot help but conclude that the patronage/performance paradigms invoked by these two authors are worlds apart. One may rightfully wonder if any plasisble connections can be made between a courtly musical performance and the screening of a film in a movie house or between the motives of Mughal emperor and those of the elected members of modern political body such as the Karnataka state government. While apparent dissimilarities do sometimes mask deeper similarity, in these comments I will not attempt to undermine first impressions; instead I will offer a model which, in my view, substantiates the initial impression of disparity and provides theoretical depth to the assertion that the situations described in these two papers are "worlds apart".

For the past several years I have been translating and thinking critically about the poetry of the Tamil Vaiṣṇava and Śaiva saints. The *āḻvārs*, as the Vaiṣṇava saints are known, and their Śaiva counterparts, known as *nāyaṉmārs*, lived and composed hymns of devotion to the god they viewed as supreme between the sixth and

* This paper was written for the Conference on Patronage and Performance in India, University of Chicago, September 30-October 2, 1982, session on "Tradition, Politics and Cultural Media" as a response to the following two papers: "Patronage: Of the Art, of the Artist, or of the Patron Himself?" by Bonnie Wade, and "Structures and Policies in Karnataka's Feature Film Industry: Implications for the New Cinema" by Manjunath Pendakur.

ninth centuries A.D. About a century or two later, these hymns were codified, given sacred status, and integrated into the ritual of Vaiṣṇava and Śaiva temples in Tamil Nadu, a position they enjoy to this day. In the following pages I will construct a model of patronage and performance with reference to the culture of the sacred Tamil hymns, particularly with reference to a text called *Kōyil Oḻuku*, the official chronicle of the temple of Raṅkanātaṉ (a form of Viṣṇu) at Śrīraṅkam.[1] Historically, this temple is one of the most important, if not the most important center of Tamil Vaiṣṇava culture. As different as the world of the *Kōyil Oḻuku* is from both the Mughal court and the modern movie house, I think the model I will develop on the basis of material from the *Kōyil Oḻuku* can throw light upon the underlying differences between the performance situations described in Wade's and in Pendakar's papers.

*Kōyil Oḻuku*, which by the standards of Western scholarship would be considered a mythologized history, relates many of the events which Tamil Vaiṣṇavas consider to be most important in the evolution of their sectarian identity. Among the events narrated in the temple chronicle is one which provides a paradigm for a certain kind of patronage/performance situation which, as I hope to demonstrate, is not confined solely to the Tamil Vaiṣṇava context. The principal actors in this event are Viṣṇu, the deity enshrined in the Śrīraṇkam temple, and the poet-saint Nammāḻvār who, in Tamil Vaiṣṇava tradition, is considered to be the most important *āḻvār*.

The chronicle describes how Nammāḻvār came to Śrīraṇkam (in the form of an iconic image or *vigraha*) to recite his hymns of praise for Viṣṇu in the presence of the deity. In the model I will subsequently describe, Viṣṇu assumes the role of patron and Nammāḻvār of performer. However, they should not be regarded as mere individuals who assume these roles as anyone else might. Becasue both Viṣṇu and Nammāḻvār "live" eternally in the temple in the form of icons, and because Nammāḻvār's recitation of his hymns for the deity is ritually reenacted annually at Śrīraṇkam and other temples, Viṣṇu and Nammāḻvār may be interpreted as supra-real archetypes of "the patron" and "the performer." One might say that they are not so much individuals filling roles as the roles

[1] V.N. Hari Rao, ed. and trans., *Kōil Oḻugu: The Chronicle of the Śrīraṅgam Temple with Historical Notes* (Madras: Rochouse and Sons, 1961).

themselves. The chronicle depicts an "ur-performance" in which the saint sings and acts out with gestures (*abhinaya*) his hymns in the presence of the deity. According to sectarian tradition, the original performance related in the text was subsequently fixed and enacted ritually in the temple. Following is a more detailed description of this paradigmatic performance.

The scene opens at Śrīraṇkam where the saint Tirumaṇkaiyāḻvār is reciting his own compositions for Viṣṇu. The chronicle relates that Viṣṇu was delighted with the *āḻvār's* performance and asked him what boon he would like to receive in recognition of the service he had performed. In reply, Tirumaṅkai petitioned the god to listen to the recitation of Nammāḻvār's collection of devotional hymns, called *Tiruvāymoḻi* ("holy word of mouth") and to grant this great work a position equal to that of the Vedas. Viṣṇu agreed to listen to *Tiruvāymoḻi* during the Adhyayanotsava ("recitation festival") celebrated during the month of Mārkaḻi (December-January) and gave orders to the temple servants to summon Nammāḻvār. At this time Nammāḻvār's disciple Madurakavi was tending his master's image in a shrine located at Kurukūr, the saint's birthplace. (Nammāḻvār had already left his corporeal frame and achieved union with Viṣṇu.) Thus, when Viṣṇu's invitation reached Kurukūr, Madurakavi set out for Śrīraṇkam with the image of Nammāḻvār.[2] For ten days during the Adhyayanotsava the Vedas were recited in the morning, and in the evening Madurakavi, representing Nammāḻvār, recited verses from *Tiruvāymoḻi* and acted out the meaning of the verses with gestures. After the recitation was completed, Viṣṇu honored Nammāḻvār by sharing his seat with him and by bestowing gifts in the form of garlands, *prasāda* (food offerings returned by the god to his devotees), *kasturi* (fragrance), and *tiruman̲* (the paste used by Tamil Vaiṣṇavas to draw a characteristic sectarian mark on their foreheads). Taking his gifts with him, Nammāḻvār (that is, his image), accompanied by Madurakavi, returned to Kurukūr.

This then is the paradigmatic performance referred to above. The chronicle relates that Nāthamuni, a later figure in the *guruparamparai* (lineage of teachers) of Tamil Vaiṣṇavism revived the Adhyayanotsava after a period of neglect and recited *Tiruvāymoḻi*

[2] Note that in the eyes of the *Oluku's* author, the saint's image, in essence, *is* the saint.

for Viṣṇu as a representative of Nammāḻvār, just as Madurakavi had done. He also ensured that the original performance would periodically be reenacted by assigning the duty of recitation to a temple functionary known as *araiyar* ("king"). In theological terms the *araiyar* represents Nammāḻvār when he recites *Tiruvāymoḻi* during the Adhyayanotsava. Thus the performance recounted in the *Oḻuku* has become a periodic ritual—a ritual which is still performed in certain Tamil Vaiṣṇava temples.

What are the major characteristics of this model patronage/performance situation? First of all, Nammāḻvār (the performer) serves his patron (Viṣṇu) by causing him to experience enjoyment. Nammāḻvār does this by artfully reciting hymns of praise for Viṣṇu. Not insignificantly, the notion of "enjoyment" has far-reaching resonances in Tamil Vaiṣṇava tradition. Traditional scholars have written a great deal about "enjoyment," for in a sense it is the glue that binds together the members of the Tamil Vaiṣṇava community. For instance, the sectarian commentaries on *Tiruvāymoḻi* are said to document the Vaiṣṇava gurus' enjoyment of the saints' hymns.[3]

In light of these considerations, service to the patron is an underlying purpose for a performance. A second purpose is to establish contact or communion between performer and patron. The *āḻvār* does not really tell Viṣṇu anything about himself that the god does not already know. It is the *fact* of performance whereby contact between the two is established that really matters. Finally, the ritual context for the recitation of the saint's hymns in the temple points to a third purpose. When the *araiyar* recites *Tiruvāymoḻi* during the Adhyayanotsava he is "backed up" by a group of sectarian members, collectively known as the *goṣṭi*, who join him in reciting certain verses. This indicates that the *araiyar* represents not only Nammāḻvār, but also a whole community of devotees. From this perspective it may be said that the purpose of the performance is to establish and/or affirm the patron's status in a community. Secondarily, this community, as an audience for the performance, receives enjoyment when it "overhears" a performance that is offered directly to the patron.

The performance model, presented thus far, can be visualized as a kind of flow from performer to patron, and secondarily, to an

[3] K.K.A. Venkatachari, *The Maṇipravāḷa Literature of the Śrīvaiṣṇava Acāryas* (Bombay: Anantacharya Research Institute, 1978).

audience "listening from the wings." From this point of view the content of the performance—the *āḻvār*'s recitation of hymns in praise of Viṣṇu, in the example taken from *Kōyil Oḻuku*—is a medium whereby the performer (Nammāḻvār) serves his patron (Viṣṇu). But the model thus construed is not complete. The chronicle further relates that after Nammāḻvār completed his recitation of *Tiruvāymoḻi*, Viṣṇu honored him with gifts. In like manner the temple functionary who ritually recites the verses of *Tiruvāymoḻi* (*araiyar*) receives honors which are understood to come from the god. The flow, in the form of service, from the performer to the patron, is matched by a return flow, in the form of honors, from the patron to the performer. In overview this performance/patronage model describes a situation in which the performance and reciprocated honors mutually create a bond between patron and performer.

This model suggests that a performance can be viewed in at least two ways. If one focusses on the content of the performance, the relevant question is "what message (verbal or otherwise) is communicated by the performance and how do the patron and other audience members react to that message?" In the example under discussion, this question calls attention to the following points: (1) the *āḻvār*'s performance consists of hymns of praise for his patron; (2) these hymns bring enjoyment to Viṣṇu and affirm his status as an object of reverence in a community of devotees. If, on the other hand, one views the performance primarily as a medium of exchange between patron and performer (as well as the community he represents) the most salient feature of the performance situation is contact: the performance creates a community and articulates its structure through the idiom of service and honors. From this point of view the very fact of performance overshadows its specific content as long as the content does not undermine the patron's status or prove counterproductive to community formation.

The *Kōyil Oḻuku*'s account of the institution of the Adhyayanotsava documents how an initial performance can become the basis for a periodic ritual. In the initial performance the content of Nammāḻvār's performance is by no means insignificant. The aesthetic value of the saint's hymns, that is, their ability to induce enjoyment, is a kind of trigger which activates the model. But as a recurrent ritual the aesthetic dimension of performance is automatized; the content of the performance is rarely scrutinized for aesthetic success or failure. What matters most is the fact of performance and the intracommunal contact it establishes. Content cannot be eliminated, but it is a given of the situation. In this light, any distinctive difference between performance and ritual follows from the participants' point of view. When content predominates, the performance is valued for what it *is*. When content becomes automatic and the very fact of performance is of foremost concern, the performance is valued for what it *does*. It is the latter, I think, which we often describe as ritualized performance.

Turning now to the performance situations described in Wade's and Pendakur's papers, I think that the performance model I have described casts in high relief the fundamental differences between the two. I will apply the model first to Wade's material and then to Pendakur's.

There is no question that the Adhyayanotsava has become institutionalized as a ritual, and while the role of music at the Mughal court cannot so unequivocally be described as ritualized performance, I think it is fair to say that Wade's sources and her analysis of them suggests a number of points of congruence with the performance model outlined above. Surely, it would be far-fetched to claim that the content of musical performance in the context of the court was completely overshadowed by its occasion. Wade's sources make it clear that Tansen was recognised as an extraordinary musician; a performance by Tansen was a special occasion that was not just like that of any other musician. But at the same time Wade had suggested that in some contexts, at least, the content of musical performance is taken for granted; what matters most is that appropriate music be performed at the appropriate place and time by appropriate performers. Does it not appear that the dominant motive for musical performance by an ensemble like the *naubat* was to affirm the status of the Mughal emperor at court and in the empire? Wade has shown that during the reign of Aurangzeb, when almost all music and occasions for aesthetic enjoyment were suspect, the *naubat* survived unscathed. I think Wade's material strongly suggests that under the Mughals the music of the *naubat*, at least, was perceived in ritual terms. Of course the *naubat*'s blaring trumpets and thundering drums were perfectly suited to announce the emperor's presence. One might even claim that the music of the *naubat* was an auditory medium whereby the emperor's status was established in the minds (and through the ears) of all listeners. But given the suitability of the content of a *naubat* performance to the purpose it was designed to serve, differences between one particular performance and another—from an aesthetic point of view—do not appear to have mattered very much. What did matter very much was that the performance take place. Apparently, under Aurangzeb, the music of the *naubat* was valued for what it *did*, and certain other kinds of music were disvalued for what they *were*.

Perhaps the same principle applies in the many pictorial representations of musical performance Wade has discovered in which people do not seem to be paying much attention to the music-making going on around them. Here again, is it not possible that the fact that music was being performed, perhaps as a statement about the patron's status, mattered more than the specific content of the performance?

Wade has provided an analytic summary of the dynamics of music patronage under the Mughals. She has, first of all, distinguished cases where the patron's intention is something other than the patronage of music for its own sake ("indirect processes") from direct fostering of music. She shows that a patron may support musical activity not only for love of music, but also to achieve cultural, political, or social status; to show favor to a particular musician; or in the interest of religion. She has further broken down the patronage process into a systematic representation of the patron's intention (as detailed above), the action the patron takes to realize that intention (patronage of music or patronage of a musician), and the result of that action (patronage of a musician, patronage of music, and/or status).

I think that the model I have offered in response to the Tamil Vaiṣṇava data adds a helpful perspective to Wade's analysis. All the examples Wade gives of patronage of music as an indirect process are consistent with the notion of performance as a medium—a medium whereby the patron attains cultural, political and/or social status which may or may not be tied to the practice of religion. Wade has also listed "favoring of a particular musician" as one of the intentions a patron may harbor. I find it helpful to think of the rewards a patron bestows upon a performer not so much as an intention on par with attaining status, but rather as a return for services rendered. I think that the various indirect processes Wade speaks of can be profitably thought of as dimensions of a larger process in which patron and performer reciprocally exchange service and recognition for service. The media of this process is the performance itself and the honor bestowed upon the performer. The result which motivates the whole process is the bonding of patron and performer in a relationship which confirms the patron's status. From this perspective there is really no need to distinguish patronage of the performance (here, music) from patronage of the performer (here, musician). The performance as well as reciprocated honors are the media of a process in which both performer and patron are actors. All four elements are indispensible components of a patronage/performance situation.

The emphasis is entirely different, however, in Wade's example of "direct process," the fostering of music for its own sake. Undoubtedly Mughal rulers who patronized music were sometimes motivated by aesthetic concerns; they listened to music because they enjoyed it. In such instances music ceases to be a means to what Wade has described as "nonmusical" ends. In such circumstances it is the content of a particular performance that most matters; music, under these conditions, is deritualized.

I wish to emphasize that during any performance occasion, different models may be operative for different participants. For some the content of the performance predominates. For others the fact that a performance takes place under certain conditions is the most important consideration. Hence, what distinguishes ritualized from nonritualized performance is the mind set of the participants, not any "objective" features of the performance. In her conclusion Wade speaks of the simultaneous patronage of art, the artist, and the patrons themselves. I think that this is especially true when it is the fact of performance *per se* that is uppermost in the minds of participants.

That a model of patronage and performance, developed in response to Tamil Vaiṣṇava materials, should prove relevant to the situation of music in Mughal India may be unexpected, but if one considers that in both cases a direct personal relationship between patron and performer is involved, the connection becomes plausible. The film industry in today's India, on the other hand, inhabits a very different kind of world. In this world personal relationships have been largely superceded by the law of supply and demand. Viṣṇu's "court" and the court of the Mughal emperor have a great deal more in common with one another than either have with the capitalist marketplace. This being the case, it would be foolish to attempt to directly apply my model to Pendakur's observations concerning the production, distribution and marketing of Kannada films. However, by attending to the important ways in which Pendakur's material does *not* exemplify this model, the fundamental differences in the situations described by Wade and Pendakur are clarified.

I have attempted to show how, in situations where performance is valued as a medium, the very fact of performance tends to overshadow its specific content. Obviously this principle does not obtain to any significant degree when a film is offered for public consumption. There are very few people for whom attendance at a film showing in and of itself carries intrinsic value. In this world it is the content, not the mere fact of performance that matters most. Performances such as the Adhyayanotsava or musical performances at the Mughal court can be read as an index of a structure of relationships within a community. While a film may address social issues—this, in fact, is a prominent motif in the New Cinema—the showing of a film in itself does not articulate a structure of community relations. Apparently a different model is involved here.

When speaking of a film it is not even clear who should be regarded as patron and who as performer. Is the patron the producer, private donors who offer financial support, or the state government, if state subsidy is involved? Who is performer: actor or director? Pendakur's perspective includes all of the above. The very fact that roles and participants cannot be neatly matched is a forceful demonstration that the model described above does not apply.

Pendakur has shown that an important "patron-like" participant in the making of a Kannada film is the Karnataka state government. He has enumerated three mechanisms whereby the Karnataka government has promoted the state's film industry. These are: (1) direct financial subsidy of film production, (2) granting of cash awards to the directors of films deemed to be outstanding, and (3) assistance for infrastructural development, such as providing free water and electricity for film studios. While one may speak loosely of all three activities as "patronage," only the second relates in a direct way to the model exemplified by the Adhyayanotsava. The cash award by which the government recognizes a director's outstanding achievement in a sense is an "honor" bestowed in return for "service" rendered by the director to the people of the state.

The other forms of assistance, on the other hand, are most appropriately regarded as investment designed to attract capital to the state.

There are two other considerations that should be accounted for when considering state support for the arts. One would expect the state to take on the role of "model patron" of the arts insofar as support for the arts is viewed as "a good thing" by the public—*dharmic*, to use a traditional idiom—and hence contributory to the patron's (here, the government's) status. In the case of film I wonder if this is the case among a sufficiently large proportion of the public to motivate state patronage of film in the traditional sense.

The next point pertains particularly to state support for the "new" cinema. In the model I have described, the fact of performance tends to overshadow content as long as content does not undermine the purpose inherent in the whole patronage/performance process, namely, to articulate a structure of community relations in which hierarchy is a primary structural principle. Performance in this context is a conservative force; it expresses an "establishment" point of view. The content of many films of the New Cinema movement forcefully and deliberately undermines this kind of built-in conservative imperative. The message of many of these films is anti-establishment in nature; such films attack hierarchically-defined social relations. To the extent that the government is identified with "the establishment," these films discourage a traditional kind of patronage.

By and large I think it is fair to say that the New Cinema inhabits a world where the fact of performance *per se* is not perceived as sufficient cause for support—certainly not by the film-viewing public, and only to a limited degree, if at all, by the government. The fortunes of a film rise and fall on the basis of its content and its ability to attract approving attention to that content. It will succeed at the box office if the public approves. It may receive official recognition if the government approves. This world, in a sense, is the world inhabited by the *naubat* musicians turned inside out.

These considerations may lead one to question whether my model patronage/performance situation is an artifact of the past. Its applicability to modern-day situations may be fading, but I can think of at least one event of the recent past where a state government, in this case the government of Tamil Nadu, assumed the role of "model patron." The event in question is the Fifth International Conference-Seminar of Tamil Studies, held in Madurai in January 1981.[1] Here is a case where the fact of performance, by and large, overshadowed its specific content. Wherever possible, content was selected to favorably reflect upon the patron's (that is, the state government's and particularly its Chief Minister's) status and upon values favored by the patron—here, notions of Tamil cultural pride. The government invested an enormous sum—the newspapers reported 1,200,000 rupees—not to attract capital to the state, but to affirm its protective relation to the "performers" and to the public at large. In this the performers consisted of Tamil scholars and artists working in traditional "Tamil" art forms. The "conference" was an extravagant week-long affair that included scholarly sessions conducted at Madurai Kamaraj University; displays of traditional Tamil scholarship for the "man in the street" through debates and other traditional rhetorical performances; dance, music and drama; a fair-ground exhibition; and, as a grand finale, a parade of floats attended by so exalted a personage as the Prime Minister of India. Many critics of the Conference, critics who perhaps were out of touch with traditional values, considered the government's expenditure wasteful, misguided extravagance. But in terms of the model I have developed, the government was playing the role of classic patron to the hilt. We have now come full circle from traditional Tamil Vaiṣṇavism to public life in modern Tamil Nadu, and apparently there is very little new under the Tamil sun.

[1] See my account, "The Fish-eyed Goddess Meets the Movie Star: An Eyewitness Account of the Fifth International Tamil Conference," in *Cultural Policy in India*, ed. by Lloyd I. Rudolph (New Delhi: Chanakya Publications, 1984), pp. 105-25.

# Patronage and Dance in India Or, "You Think Learning to Dance Was Hard!"

Sharon Lowen

The logistics of performance begin while still a student. In addition to whatever ability, talent and motivation the student has, the choice of a teacher is an essential component in the future success of an artist. Given the importance of *guru-shishya paramparā* (the master-disciple line), in the Indian context a rather intense, multi-faceted teacher-student relationship which precludes the relatively easy shifts from instructor to instructor possible in the West when one's abilities or desires demand, a student of classical Indian dance or music is unlikely to surpass the level of his or her teacher. A novice will find it difficult to shift through popular opinions in order to understand which teacher is truly most outstanding, particularly a foreign student with a limited frame of reference, but this decision is crucial to the student's potential for artistic and professional success.

The stature of the guru not only determines the quality of training, but is also a significant reflection on a budding artist's reputation. Being a disciple of Padmashri Guru Kelucharan Mohapatra does not guarantee that one is a good dancer, but it increases the likelihood as virtually every Odissi artist of note is his student. In America or Europe, a dancer strives to get into the best dance company possible and his or her reputation depends on that of the company. One can then work up to soloist standing and perhaps even a name recognized independently of the ensemble. For example, Judith Jameson will draw crowds today, but for many years she could count on audiences and sponsorship because she was in the Alvin Ailey Modern Dance company. In India, the dancer in most classical styles is a soloist from the beginning. There is no company name to draw the interest of sponsors and audiences. The dancer must not only offer a performance good enough to hold an audience for two and a half hours, but must also garner personal patronage for any opportunity to perform at all. Therefore, getting patrons and the audiences they bring to a program depends a great deal on the efforts of an individual artist. Sometimes the patrons of a new artist's teacher will extend their support to his or her students.

As Indian independence brought an end to royal patronage, support for art and artists has devolved onto the government and wealthy individuals and business families such as the Tatas, Birlas, Bharat Rams and Charat Rams. The agent-manager-impresario infrastructure that we have in the West to promote classical arts is virtually non-existent in India. Contacts are personal, very often familial, but never just business. The practice, common in the West, of an agent contracting a performance for an artist who has never even met the sponsor will not happen in India unless the artist has a stellar reputation.

When I first arrived in India to continue my study of Manipuri dance (Odissi and Chhau were added in later years), my total focus was on learning and seeing as much dance as possible. After a few years of study in India, preceded by over fifteen years training in modern dance and ballet in the United States, I wanted performance opportunities in India appropriate for my new artist status. I then realized that I did not understand the mechanics of arts sponsorship in India. Like a pyramid structure in which one can see and understand everything at one's own level and below, while what is above is shrouded in darkness, I was familiar with the work of every dancer but had no insights into who their patrons were or how patronage functioned. In my early years in India there were occaisonally invitations to perform which were clearly based on being a foreigner and a curiosity. I felt that it was not a wise idea to take advantage of these invitations just for an opportunity to perform because if the level was poor (i.e., a fledgling student more than a polished performer), then that would be the end of performance for me. The novelty would be exploited for one program, everyone would say, "Aha, isn't that nice," and there would be no opportunity to establish a serious reputation. So I didn't perform for a couple of years except for one Fulbright function, as they were supporting me, and had extended and renewed my grant from nine months to two years. They had a right to expect me to demonstrate something even though I still felt it was premature to present a full recital. The program was held at India International Centre, a small and highly respected stage for dancers in Delhi.

An interesting sidelight to the stage of awareness of a student in transition to performer is that some people know who you are even though you have not met them. I discovered this years later, through reviews and even patronage, and I am still constantly amazed that people will say, "We know that you were . . ." or "We've been watching your progress for the past ten years," when I may not have met them or even heard their names until recently. One makes important impressions on others early in a career even as a student.

## Introducing a New Artist

New artists are generally as naive about patronage as they are about their dance form (if *not* from traditional artist family). One learns them together, if lucky; otherwise one may train for years only to then watch from the sidelines. Typically, dancers have someone behind them. Usually it is a father or husband, or someone with a lot of push and connections. One such example is that of a nice young dancer with good training, though not necessarily more exceptional than her peers. She had never particularly wanted to dance, but had an insistent parent. As her parent runs an arts institution, the best teacher available was arranged on the premises so that she had only to go downstairs for practice, and she turned out to be a lovely dancer. At the appropriate time, her parent hosted select cocktail parties and invited the critics and patrons. Favors granted over the years would now be collected. A European impresario, who had used the institution's facilities while in India, was now called upon to tour this girl abroad. She did well, as could at least half a dozen other young artists who would never get the opportunity because they did not have such a connection. Since that time she has danced in many festivals through her parent's patronage network without ever having to exert herself to arrange concerts personally. This young dancer came to the States for an extended stay and was most unhappy to find it impossible to get programs here, or at least on the level to which she was accustomed. She complained, "I can go to India for two weeks, earn enough for the ticket and more, without making any effort to get programs." She did not see that her smooth success in India was through her parent's patronage network. She was appalled at the minor programs she was offered in America through her own efforts. Yet it would be the same in India if she were without a support system.

A leading dance teacher has trained his eldest daughter with hopes for her career on the stage. Since program venue is very important, he planned her *arangetram*, a dancer's debut recital, at the largest theatre in Delhi, Kamani Auditorium, rather than at a more customary recital hall such as the India International Centre. He hoped to launch her in a big way, but whether or not he has the connections to generate the necessary patronage for a young artist remains to be seen. Ability and attractiveness are there and without question her training is excellent. Yet his wish for her to share some programs with other artists, during the year before her debut solo recital, never came to pass, possibly because he does not have leverage with patrons. He can train an artist, but he can not create the performance opportunities, whereas a patron-sponsor can just arrange concerts without difficulty.

### Performance Opportunities

There are many performance situations for dancers in India in addition to regular public concerts. Every organization under the sun has meetings or functions which, at least once a year, include a cultural performance. The choice of artist is often dependent on whether they want "Mrs. So and So's" daughter to perform. If "Mrs. So and So" on the selection committee has anything to say in the decision, the choice is clear. The result may be fine or excruciating, but the organization will be satisfied that the aim of holding a cultural event has been served. It may also have cost a more talented junior or senior artist a platform. Fledgling artists like "Mrs. So and So's" sixteen year old daughter need to perform; however it is asking a great deal of her to hold the audience's attention for a two hour solo presentation. Other opportunities such as *puja* celebrations or shared programs of peers or opening a concert of a better known dancer or musician, offer a chance to dance for perhaps ten to thirty minutes.

Performing specifically for tourists, either in hotels or theatres booked by travel agencies, may be a source of stage experience but carries no prestige. There are exceptions such as Bombay's Taj Mahal Hotel Theatre which is considered a reasonable performance venue. Otherwise, tourist shows are strictly something artists will do for income.

An excellent introduction to audiences and patrons is the increasing number of festivals specifically for young artists. Some are very prestigious and may help serve as springboards to a budding career.

**Logistics of a Performance**

What a dancer goes through to perform at a young artists' festival—that is, the logistics of performing apart from the actual practice and dancing—may be exemplified by my experience at the Sur Sringar Samsad's Kal-Ke-Kalakar Festival in 1977. I was invited to perform Manipuri through the recommendation of a Delhi critic familiar with my work. Funding was very low, but one was entitled to half-fare railway tickets if one visited all the appropriate offices for forms.

After I was invited, collecting the musicians took some time. My own Manipuri teacher was not willing to come with me to Bombay as he has a dance company which he did not wish to leave for four days. Thus it was necessary to take time to train new musicians (but that is another story). Accompanists are in such demand that dancers will plan their programs as much around the availability of musicians as any other factor. I had planned to share some accompanists with another Delhi dancer going to the festival and had delayed making train reservations only to find that she had decided not to attend without bothering to tell me. I immediately went to the Sangeet Natak Akademi for advice and forms for rail fare concession. There I discovered that there were absolutely no reservations available to Bombay for two months and that it would therefore be impossible for me to get to the festival. Eventually after fifteen trips to various offices, including that of the Minister of Railways, I was able to get bookings for myself and my group of musicians. My persistence paid off but it would have been unlikely for a dancer less determined to reach the festival.

On arrival in Bombay, I discovered that the accommodations

arranged for the musicians by the sponsors were wretched and unsuitable for my female vocalist and other musicians. So I took them with me to the large home on Puchkhanawala Road where I had been invited through Delhi friends and was fortunate to have a hostess willing to accommodate us all graciously.

I was surprised to find myself billed as "Sharon Lowen from New York" at the entrance to the theatre. When I protested, "I'm not from New York," they replied,"New York—it's America, New York, that's fine." I said, "It's Detroit." They said, "Nobody knows where Detroit is. New York is fine."

My dressing room turned out to be adjacent to the one lavatory in the entire theatre. This would be less significant if I had no costume changes. As it was I was performing Manipuri, a style which is comprised of five different traditions, and requires different costumes. I had seven costume changes to do within my one hour performance so I had to lay out the costumes very carefully in sequential order for quick changes. This meant literally guarding the door to prevent access to the bathroom over a pathway of my costumes. Somehow, a desperate gentlemen managed to sneak in and when he thought everything was quiet, he came out of the bathroom to my consternation.

Each festival evening began at six with two one-hour presentations followed by several half-hour music performances. Just at six o'clock, when I had carefully planned exactly one hour of setting up in order to be ready to go on stage at seven, I was informed that the six o'clock artist had not appeared and that I should go on immediately. An earlier warning to be ready, "just in case," would certainly have been appreciated. I explained, "I'm scheduled to go on at seven; I've timed it so that I'll be ready at seven." They said, "Fine, there's five thousand people sitting out there waiting. It's up to you." Obviously keeping the audience waiting for an hour does not enhance their receptivity and I managed to be ready in forty minutes. The performance itself went beautifully. Critics and audience were amazed to see a solo Manipuri dancer manage the logistics of the quick costume changes and techniques so well. It is just as well that they could not see me backstage as I struggled up stairs and through narrow doors sometimes wearing a traditional Manipuri Ras skirt, which is designed rather like a very large hat box or barrel

Events surrounding performances, such as receptions and other social occasions, can also serve to introduce a new artist into the arena of arts patronage. The evening following my Bombay Kal-Ke-Kalakar performance I was invited to the home of a much respected patron of the arts. Not so incidentally, he was later instrumental in getting my supposedly confirmed return railway reservations to Delhi with only four different office visits as I had his note as a top railways official.

His gathering included Mulk Raj Anand and his wife, who had reviewed my previous night's performance most favorably, the dancer Sanjukta Panigrahi and her husband vocalist Ragunath Panigrahi, Guru Kelucharan Mohapatra, Kathak dancer and teacher Kumudini Lakhia, critic Sunil Kothari and many others I did not know. As the evening progressed, many of the artists gave informal performances and I was requested to demonstrate some Manipuri dance. As I had no musicians present, Guru Kelucharan Mohapatra, the Odissi master, was kind enough to play *pakhawaj* to give a rhythm base to work with. (I had begun Odissi training with Guruji in 1975, but was not yet prepared to perform this style on stage after only two years of study.) Shri Ragunath Panigrahi was kind enough to sing a song from the Gita Govinda to which I could dance in Manipuri style. This was the first chance I had to discover the possibilities of improvising a song simply by following the lines without a set number of repetitions or fixed composition. The challenge was exciting and it was very satisfying to create this way while dancing, particularly in front of a group of supportive artists and *rasikas* (connoisseurs). The entire evening, coupled with the previous night's performance, helped my gradual process of gaining recognition as an Indian performing artist.

## Patronage and Performance Revisited

The logistics of arranging programs and how patronage functions, may be seen in two back-to-back concerts in Delhi and Calcutta during the spring of 1982 after a performance hiatus in India for me of over three years. I arrived in India in 1981 with the intention of spending approximately eight months studying and working on dance technique while carrying my baby internally, and then to arrange some performances soon after her birth, carrying her around externally. I attended an Odissi dance workshop in Calcutta in November with the baby due in a month and a half. I took this opportunity to agree to an old friend's oft repeated suggestion that I perform in Calcutta and asked him to go ahead and arrange it. Not a producer himself, he took me to his friend who was more directly involved in performance patronage.

We found his friend in the center of a perpetual open house, with many artists, primarily musicians, constantly coming and going, touching his feet and waiting for his blessings in the form of validation for their art through his patronage. I joined the circle, looking for all the world as if I had a soccer ball under my sari, and requested his support for a Calcutta program in two months. I explained that my Odissi guru was going abroad from mid-March through the end of the performance season, and I hoped to perform before that. We talked about the logistics of what to do and it was decided that it would be better to have an invitational program rather than a ticketed one as I was not yet known in Calcutta.

Choice of a theatre really revolved around the only two first-rate ones. We decided not to use the government theatre because one can always get bounced at the last moment if a troupe of visiting foreign dancers shows up on tour. This can be very inconvenient, to say the least, particularly if the dancer and musicians are coming from out of town. That left Kala Mandir, an auditorium owned by the Birla family. Although many think of it only as the best known, publicly available concert hall, Birlas do not quite look at it in that way. It is primarily their hall for in-house functions which is made available to other groups when free, usually week-day evenings. My program was directly sponsored by them which meant a prime weekend evening at Kala Mandir. There are approximately three cultural programs per month for their three invited music circle organizations. Such a sponsor has relatively unlimited funding and chooses artists on the basis of whom they want to present and project, rather than the artist's fees.

The pattern of connections leading to my first Calcutta performance is fairly typical of the network behind the fact of any program. While an undergraduate at the University of Michigan studying humanities, fine arts and Asian studies, I began studying Manipuri dance under Minati Roy who had been a well known dancer in Calcutta and Santiniketan, and was now a graduate student at Michigan. In time we became close friends and this friendship extended to her long term friends in India. It was one of these Calcutta friends of nine years who took me to his friend who contacted his friend in the Birla organization managing the Kala Mandir to recommend me for a concert. Since this is a typical pattern leading to a concert in India, rather than a Western model of an artist's booking agent contacting arts administrators and other arts producers through booking conferences and mailings, the performer who enters the game late, especially a foreigner, is obviously at a disadvantage or at least slowed down in getting support for performing.

The date in Calcutta was set in conjunction with a preceding Delhi concert. The sponsor wanted a press conference in Calcutta several days before the concert but unfortunately I could not arrive that early because I could not get my preceding Delhi program on my date of choice. The theatre that I wished to use in Delhi was apparently available only a limited number of days that month with the impression given that the other dates had already been booked. Yet another disciple, on learning that our guru would be in Delhi for my program and not wishing to lose the opportunity of having him accompany a program of her own, was instantly able to schedule a program in the same theatre on a date that I had been denied. I was at a level where I could get a well-sponsored program and the accompaniment of the master of Odissi, but not the "open sesame" to a preferred date at the theatre.

The programs were now scheduled and it was decided that I should do two styles, Manipuri and Odissi, which meant rehearsing and transporting two sets of musicians. For the Manipuri, I took two singers as I was not able to get one in Delhi with the range to sing both the uniquely Meitei emotional quality of the Lai Haroba as well as Geet Govinda. My Manipuri drummer, really a dancer from the song and drama division, could play adequately. The flutist was someone I had helped at the 1977 Bombay Kal-Ke-Kalakar. He had accompanied another artist from Delhi who could not get him a return ticket, in spite of the fact that he had done a lot to promote her previously. Now he will not give her the time of day and goes so far as to suggest that she is little heard of today because she lost the support of her musicians. I got him his ticket back to Delhi in 1977 and now I feel I have his good will and can count on him to be available if at all possible for my programs. When I asked the flutist if he was free on March 12th, he said, "I'm sorry I'm going to be in Calcutta on the 13th." I said, "Terrific, my program on the 12th is in Calcutta." He said, "Other dancers come in tears because they try to get me, and cannot get me." He's just never free. "You're just very lucky," he said. "You show up and the date you want I'm always free, somehow."

Because I had programs in Delhi and Calcutta two days apart, it was necessary to fly to Calcutta to be in time for my press conference. I did not feel that it was appropriate for my guru to take the train if I was flying. The other musicians could take the train, my husband could take the train, but not my teacher. So we flew to Calcutta with my two month old daughter while my husband was in charge of the musicians on the train so that they would feel cared for and important. Such logistics are crucial—how people are cared for, the fact that they are met, that they get meals on time and that everything is fine. They were all very pleased.

The musicians were very impressed with the Calcutta sponsor because they all thought they might get a music recording contract out of it. They were also very pleased with the audiences and reviews. In fact, when the same musicians played in Delhi, they commented that they had rarely seen so many dance gurus of different styles and other connoisseurs in one auditorium at the same time. In the months that went by after this performance, the Delhi based musicians would run into me and always say, "Anytime you have a program I will be happy to be available."

I believe this attitude reflected more than a natural desire to work. Some dancers do not treat their accompanists as fellow artists. Dancers who treat their musicians as incidental baggage to their personal glorification are asking for trouble, not to mention lackluster support and the eventual unavailability of first rate accompanists. Perhaps because I must often perform with recorded music abroad, I very much value musicians when I have them. They are all soloists in their own right who are joining the dance artist to create an ensemble. I am delighted to have introduced my accompanists in such a way that more than one younger accompanist has been offered solo performances directly from having appeared with me. This proves the reverse of the idea that accompanists will not be seriously considered as soloists.

## Performance Afterwaves

Though my teacher was leaving the country a few days after my Calcutta program, he was prevailed upon to do a performance for a prominent Calcutta patron the next day. He chose to include several local students to give them visibility and spare him the demands of offering a full solo evening. That morning he informed me that I must also appear as a featured artist. I danced the opening invocation, with the others joining in. Then I danced a duet with *sloka* (verse) followed by Kelubabu's marvelous *abhinaya* (expressive dance). It was a lovely program in a beautiful outdoor setting at an elegant home. It had earlier been the setting for a lavish dinner reception for participants in the 1977 Chhau Festival with the Chhau dancers and musicians served on palm leaves out back.

Another offshoot of the Calcutta performance was a television broadcast. I later learned that classical dance is generally shown only through national programming and an exception was made through the request of my sponsor. I had my teacher's permission to use pre-recorded music as he could not remain in town, however at arrival at the studio, despite assurances that they had a tape recorder, I discovered that they did not have what was needed. A quick call to a friend resolved the situation (fortunately the phones worked).

During the performance the television technicians did a very interesting thing. They turned off the monitor in the studio for a minute and I could no longer hear the music to which I was supposedly dancing. I never found out what prompted them to do this during a live broadcast nor whether the audience found me in rhythm during that minute though I was in step with the *tala* when the music returned.

Broadcast scheduling demanded that my televised dance not exceed twelve minutes. The taped music was fourteen minutes, which unfortunately meant cutting the composition at the beginning and/or end. The programs preceding mine were not as strict about their timing so mine actually started twenty-five minutes late. In the interim, my infant daughter became ravenously hungry which required partial disrobing to feed her. She finished in time to spare the Calcutta viewers from having to stare at a blank screen or some filler in lieu of the dance.

After cutting out the introductory music because of the time shortage, the camera showed scenery during the first section of the dance, and eventually moved to the performance somewhere in the second line of the song. This *ad hoc* approach to television production was reminiscent of my earlier experiences with television in Tijuana, Mexico, so I knew what to expect. Too often the camera, at least in my experiences with Delhi and Calcutta Doordarshan (TV), will focus on hands when intricate foot patterns are performed or in framing Manipuri, which has minimal facial expression, the cameraman will stick to the face throughout the dance. Afterwards the production crew congratulates themselves on their brilliant work without any feeling that there is room for improvement or interest in suggestions as to what might have been done better or the possible need for rehearsal.[1]

In spite of all the minor difficulties the broadcast in Calcutta was well received and reached a wide audience. At the airport ticket counter the next day I was recognized and the security did not frisk me as she also recognized me. A taste of being a V.I.P.!

What requires constant attention in this business of performing is the problem of keeping a balance between the art of the performance and the logistics of the performance. One problem for new artists is that once a program is actually scheduled they naively think they have the last week or two before the performance to rehearse and put the final touches on the art form to be presented. In fact one runs out of time because days are filled with necessary details like multiple trips to the costume tailor to wring your hands and beg him to finish the costumes, trying to contact musicians who are seldom reachable by telephone, travel arrangements and even distributing invitations to the program, customarily done in person. If one is not already well rehearsed, the last two weeks is too late and the performance will show it unless the gods are kind.

Yet all this seemingly peripheral effort is necessary. One may just want to dance and not be bothered with it all, but it is unrealistic to think that it is possible to stay in the studio and practice with all these other things magically taking care of themselves. Likewise, one cannot just stay home and expect audiences or patrons to open the door and exclaim, "Oh my god, here you are and you're wonderful. Let me make you a star!" It is difficult

[1] In Doordarshan recordings I have done since this paper was written, I see some improvement in the dance video work. These include some rehearsal in front of the camera, more concern with what to frame when, etc. Film and video of dance is a valued and developed specialty in the United States today. Indian television will want to refine its efforts in line with current work in the field.

to step forward and promote one's own performance; it is difficult to attend to all the myriad details of performing professionally. In fact, sometimes the years of study and training in the dance seem easier than finding one's way through the labyrinth of performance and patronage, particularly in another culture.

It is possible to say that I have the advantage of the novelty of being a foreign artist in India. However, this is a dubious advantage outweighed by the necessity of being seen in performance before people are willing to give up an inherent bias about who should dance. Fortunately Indian audiences are more able than western audiences to differentiate between the performance of a style and the dance itself, and so are more secure about their opinions of the quality of the performance.

In the long run, a career in the arts will succeed based on merit, hard work, and steadiness to the values imparted by the teacher. In the short run, one can hardly begin without some support system, which in India means parents, husband, or others who have economic and/or political influence and can provide financial backing. Sponsors and patrons are essential and the influence of early patronage in an artist's career will expand to wider patronage like any network as one proves one's ability. Of course, there are patrons with varied interests and motivations just as there is variety in artists. Whether the word used is "patron" or "sponsor", people in India tend to ask who one's patron is as a way of ascertaining where you stand. As Delhi is the seat of political patronage, many artists come to live there to be near the sources of government patronage. Those outside Delhi have more difficulty organizing tours abroad. Artists in Delhi may have more frequent tours out of the country, not to mention frequent programs at state and embassy functions and sometimes better chances at perks like government housing.

Maintaining a balance between the art of performance and the logistics of performance promotion requires diligence and walking a fine edge. Classical Indian dance is not entertainment, although it may be entertaining. Having evolved out of a spiritual consciousness in the temple context, the modern performance setting is more commonly the concert stage. Increasingly dancers face the risk of neglecting the rich metaphysical and spiritual import of the dance traditions as they compete for opportunities by catering to popular tastes for entertainment. This results in such things as excessive reliance on pyrotechnics, only performing the most accessible dances of the repertoire and abandoning those which demand more of the audience's sensibilities, more abbreviated concerts, and emphasis on the display of the dancer rather than the dance form.

Fortunately these tendencies are not characteristic of the entire dance scene and there are many artists who maintain a clear vision of aesthetics and values in the dance. As with artists, so too with patrons. While some private patrons value the arts primarily as an excellent method of raising their social status in line with their economic standing, there are many who are true connoisseurs and support the arts in the finer traditions of pre-modern India, to enhance the quality, meaning and beauty of life.

# INDEX

Note: Words like arts, patrons, patronage, and performers, which occur on almost every other page in the text, have been omitted from the index.


*Abhinaya, see* expression
Abu'l Fazl, 143, 187, 190-91
accompanists, 61, 229, 231, 233-34
actors, 11, 99, 113, 115, 124, 126, 130, 132
administrators, 93, 120, 129, 144, 148, 150, 164, 170, 233
aesthetics, 12, 31, 100, 103, 109, 111, 116, 124, 126, 130, 133-35, 139, 217, 220, 238
Ahirs, 56, 59
*Āin-i-Akbarī*, 143
Akbar, 143, 187, 190-91
*Akbar Nāmā*, 191
*Akhāṛās*, 63-65; *see also* guru-disciple tradition
*Akramana*, 202
*Ālhā* tradition, 4, 35n, 47-88
*Ālhā* meter, 60-62, 66-67, 70-73, 77, 79-81
*Ālhā* melodic structure, 66-69
All-India Radio, 162
Allowance (*parvārish*), 146, 158, 160
*Ālvārs* (Vaiṣṇava saints), 213
Alvin Ailey Modern Dance Company, 225
Amateurs, 52
Anand, Mulk Raj, 231
Anantha Murthy, U.R., 198
Anthropology, 10, 20, 31, 148-49
*Anveshana*, 203
apprenticeship, 7; *see also* guru-disciple tradition
*arangetram*, 228
*Arivu*, 207
Art collectors, 12
Artisan castes, 37, 43, 93-94, 137, 154
Artists, 3-8, 10-16, 19, 93-95, 102, 116, 119-23, 137, 144-48, 150-52, 155, 160, 162-63, 169-74, 208, 223, 226, 228, 231, 234-35
Arts administrators, *see* administrators
Arts management, *see* management
Ashiq Hussein Pakhawaji, 147
*Aṭṭam* (interpolation), 112-13, 115
Audiences, 1, 3, 5, 7, 12, 14-16, 32-35, 38, 42-45, 47-48, 53, 56-60, 76, 79-81, 86-87, 93, 96, 106, 110, 114-15, 122-32, 135-40, 196-99, 208-10, 216-21, 225, 227-28, 230, 234, 236, 238; *see also* elites, middle class, village
Aurangzeb, 218-19
Authors, 100, 110-11
Avadhi speakers, 59
Awards, 54, 195, 203-07, 211-12, 221
*Ayappa Caritam*, 127
Azim Bux, 158-62, 172
B.R. Pantalu Films, 200
*Baka Vadham*, 112-13
*Bālarāmabharatam*, 110-11

Balasaraswati, 19
Ballet, 226
Banaras, 58
Bangalore, 199-202, 204
Baniya, 164
Baroda State, 153
Baul singers, 192
Baz Bahadur (Raja of Malwa), 187
Benegal, Shyam, 196n, 209
Berland, Joseph, 4
Bhagavatar, Kanniah, 187
*Bhagtaniya*, 146; *see also tawā' if*
Bhairappa, S.L., 198
*Bhakti*, 24, 98, 191
Bharat Ram, 6n, 226
Bharata, 134-35
Bharata Natyam (dance), 186
Bhatkhande, V.N., 14, 185
*Bhāva* (mood), 26, 74-76, 103, 112-13, 131; *see also* emotions, expression
Bhojpuri, 55-56
*Bhuvan Shome*, 195
Bikaner, 150-151
Birlas, 6n, 226, 232-33
Birthright, 144, 157-59; *see also* inheritance
Blackburn, Stuart, 15-16, 125n
Bloch, Marc, 149
Block booking, 201
Board members, 93, 120
Bogatyrev, Petr, 47n
Bombay, 5, 202, 229-31
Bow song tradition, 16, 31-45
Box office earnings, 197, 199-200, 202, 209
Brahmins, 6n, 33-35, 134, 167-168, 182
  Bhats, 56
  Namboodiri, 96-97, 101-02, 109, 121
Braj, 79n, 82
British Arts Council, 8
Budgets, 151, 173, 199
Bundeli speakers, 64
Bundelkhand, 48-49, 51, 55, 58n, 59-61, 76
Bureaucratic-patrimonial code, 155
Buwa, Balkrishna, 182

C.H. Nagaraj Film Distributors, 201
*Cakyar* lineages, 105
Calcutta, 231-36
Capitalist enterprise, 196-97
Carnatic music, *see* music, Karṇatic
Carpenter caste, 36
Caste, 32-36, 45, 55-57, 96-99, 105, 107, 115, 134, 140, 167-68
Censorship 208-09
Center/periphery model, 94, 106, 119, 122-30, 132, 135-40
Chagan *Tawā'if*, 166-68
Charat Ram, 6n, 226
Chatterji, Basu, 195-96
Chauthmal Sarangia, 156-57
Chetty caste, 39
Chhau dance, 226
*Chomana Dudi*, 198
Choreography, 99, 132
Classical music, *see* music
Cochin, 109
Cohn, Bernard, 149n
Committee on Southern Asian Studies, 3, 11
Communist Party (Marxist), 196n
Competitions, 13, 21, 143, 189, 210
  *Alha*, 53-54, 57, 63, 79, 86
Complete *Rāmāyaṇa*, 127-28
Conceptual structures, 149-50
Concerts, 237-38
Connoisseurs, 3, 16, 48, 57, 108, 111-16, 118-19, 123-27, 129-30, 137, 139, 148, 168-69, 172, 175, 238
Contests, *see* competitions
Context, 131, 150, 181, 237; *see also* texts
Contracts, 15, 226, 234
Coorgi language, 204

Costumes and properties, 61, 120, 236
Court language, 155
Courts, princely, 2, 37, 143-76, 183, 213
Crooke, William, 49n
Craftspeople, *see* artisan castes
Critics, 3, 12, 114, 223, 229; *see also* press, reviews
Cultural performances, 1-4, 7-10, 12-15, 19-27, 123, 128, 140, 170, 228; *see also* programs
Cultural policy, 8-9, 14-15, 196, 201, 206
Cultural preservation, 176
Cultural zones, 9
Culture concept, 19-20
Culture theory, 20
Cutler, Norman, 11, 16

Dagar, Behram Khan, 144
Dance, 2, 132, 137, 225-38
  classical, 14, 25
  company, 130-31, 225-26, 229
  modern, 137
  music, 186-87; *see also* accompanists
  programs, 128-29, 136, 226
  solo, 225
  teacher, 186, 228; *see also* gurus
Dancers, 32, 130, 145, 150, 164-71, 188, 225-38
Dancing girls, 161, 165; *see also* *tawā'if, bhagtaniya*
*Dārogā* (*Guṇijankhānā*), 145, 150, 153-54, 159-61, 164-66
Department of Virtuosos, see *Guṇijankhānā*
*Devadasis*, 186
Devan, P.K., 132-37, 140
Devotees, 216
*Dharma*, 37-38
Dhrupad, 181, 183, 189
Dhundhari dialect, 151-52
Dikshitar, Baluswami, 187
Dikshitar, Muthuswami, 187
Direct patronage, 183-92, 221
Disciples, 225, 233; *see also* guru-disciple tradition
*Diwan-i-Ām*, 165
*Diwan-i-Khās*, 165
Donations, 34-36, 38, 58; *see also* gifts
Dramatization, 48, 55, 62, 65-76, 102
Drumming, *see Ālhā* meter
Durkheim, Emile, 21-22, 25

Elites, 54, 102, 105, 116, 135, 183-85
*Ellindalo Bandavaru*, 196n, 208
Emotions, 133-34; *see also bhāva*
Employer, 144, 147, 172
English language, 155-56
Entertainment, 55, 168-69, 173, 184, 187-88, 206-07, 209, 237
Epic narrative, 47-88
Eroticism, 135
Ethnocentrism, 1
Enthnotheory, 24
Ethnographer, 150
European Courts, 162
Expression (*abhinaya*), 61-62, 74-76, 108, 111-14, 123-24, 126, 235-36

Farber, Carole, 11
Fees, 6n, 33, 232
Festivals, 32-33, 38-44, 53, 86, 98, 122-23, 127, 145, 188, 215, 217-18, 221, 229-30
Fifth International Conference-Seminar of Tamil Studies (1981), 223
Film, 12, 14, 16, 213
  commercial, 195-96, 199, 201, 203, 207-09
  distribution, 16, 196, 199-200, 210, 221

exhibition, 196, 199, 201, 206, 210
feature, 196-97
financing/production, 196, 198-200, 203-204, 210, 221
Hindi, 199, 202
Kannada, 198, 204
industry, 195-212, 220-21
language, 204
New Wave, 16, 195-213, 221-22
regional, 202
studios, 204
Tamil, 198-99
Telegu, 198-99
theatres, 200-01, 208, 214
Finance records (Jaipur), 151
Financial backing, 237
Financial stringency, 146, 155, 173
Fixed-share basis, 200
Folk performances, 7-8, 11, 13, 14, 32-33
Foreign artists, 225-26, 232, 237
Forward selling, 206
French Ministry of Culture, 8
Fulbright function, 226-27
Funding, 229

*Gānebhajānewāllā*, 158
Gangeshvaranand, Swami, 63-64, 66-87
Gangore procession, 151, 165, 168-69
*Ganika*, 170n
Geertz, Clifford, 149
Gestures, 61, 75, 103, 127, 129, 140, 215; *see also* expression, *mudrās*
*Gharānā*,|171n, 185
Ghatak, Ritwik, 195
*Ghatashraddha*, 207
Gifts, 35-36, 44, 58, 99, 191, 215, 217
*Gita Govinda*, 103, 231
Gluckman, Max, 22
Gohar Jan Tawā'if, 164-66, 169
Gopi Asan, 110
Gopinath, Guru, 130-37,140
Gorakhpur, 58
Government patronage, 3, 7-8, 13-14, 54, 120, 205, 221, 226, 237
*Grahana*, 202
Gujarat, 3
Gujarat Milk Cooperative Society, 196n
*Guṇijankhānā*,|4, 143-76
*Guṇijans*, 145
Gurus, 64, 123, 127, 129, 182, 226, 233
Guru-disciple tradition, 55, 57, 60, 64-65, 104-05, 120-21, 164, 171, 215, 225; *see also paramparā, sampradāya*
Guru-*paramparai* (lineage of teachers), 215-16
*Gurukkula* system, 120-21
Gurukulam Kathakali Yogam, 133

Hamid Ali Khan, Nawab of Rampur, 185-86
Hargovind 'Vishva', 58n
*Harikatha*, 191
Harmonium-*wālā* 151
Haydar Ali, 108
Hein, Norvin, 2
Higgins, Jon, 2
Hindi language, 16, 49-50, 54n, 76-78, 155, 209-10
Hindi Prachar Samiti, 54n
Hindu musicians, *see* musicians
Hindustani language, 151-52, 155
Historians, 10
Homo Performans, 20
Honors, 148, 217, 221; *see also* awards
Hood, Mantle, 1
"House and land", 96-98, 100-01, 106, 109, 116, 119, 137
Household, royal, 163, 170-71, 173-74

departments (*Karkhānejāt*), 145, 147, 153, 160
service, 149, 153, 188
Huizinga, J., 20-21

Impresario, 226-27
India International Centre, 227-28
Indian Council for Cultural Relations, 6n
Indian People's Theatre Association, 14
Indian Tobacco Company, 6n
In their own terms, 24, 150
Indirect patronage, 184, 187-92, 219
Informal performances, 52, 56-57; *see also* private performances
Infrastructure for arts, 203, 206, 221, 226
Inheritance, 144-45, 147-48, 160, 162
Institutions
cultural, 54, 119-23, 125-27, 129, 139, 227
government, 6
Instrumental music, 183; *see also* accompanists
Intention, 16, 219
Interdisciplinary studies, 10
International tours, 129, 227, 237
Interpolations, *see aṭṭam*
investor risk, 204

Jaichand, King, 82
Jaipur, 2, 16, 143-76, 190
Jairazbhoy, Nazir, 11
*Jajmān* system, 119, 173
Jakobson, Roman, 47n
Jameson, Judith, 225
Japan, 196
Jason, Heda, 47
*Jatis*, 93, 98-99, 101, 105, 116
Jayadeva, 103
Jehangir, 190
Jodhpur, 190
*Jogī*s, 56
Jones, Betty, 99n

*Kaadu*, 198
*Kadu Kudure*, 207
Kal-ke-Kalakar Festival (1977), 229, 233
Kala Mandir, 232-33
Kalakshetra (Madras), 14
*Kaḷarippayaṭṭu*, 103
*Kalavantkarkhānā*, 153
*Kalāsam*, 114-15
*Kāma Sūtra*, 170n
Kamal Jan Tawā'if, 165
Kamani Auditorium, 228
Kanauj, 47n, 49, 51, 55, 58-63, 65, 72-73, 76
Kannada language, 196n, 199
Kaplingattu Namboodiri, 99n, 103-05
Karanth, B.V., 198
Karnad, Girish, 198, 202, 209
Karnataka, 195-213
Karnataka Film Development Corporation, 207
Kartika Tirunal (Maharaja of Travancore), 110-11
Kasaravalli, Girish, 198, 202
*Kathak* dance, 185
*Kathakaḷi* dance-drama, 16, 91-142
*Kathakaḷi* clubs, 122-23

Kaul, Mani, 196
Kerala, 91-142
Kerala Kalamandalam, 14, 113, 120-21, 125n, 126, 128, 130, 136
Kesavayya, 189-90
Kharela (U.P.), 64
Kharela performance, 66-87
*Khyāl*, 181, 183-85, 189, 192
*Khandavideko Mamsavideko*, 208
Konkani language, 204
Kothari, Komal, 7n
Kothari, Sunil, 231
Kottarakkara prince, 104

Kottayam prince, 95, 99n, 102-03, 111-13
*Koyil Oḷuku*, 214, 217
*kṛṣṇāttam*, 95, 98, 100, 103, 105n, 106
Ksatriya rulers, 95-97, 101
Kunju Kurup, Guru, 124
Kurundwad ruler, 182-83
*Kūṭiyāṭṭam*, 98, 103, 105-06

Lakhia, Kumudinī, 231
Lalit Kala Akademi, 15
Landowners, 57; *see also* "house and land"
Langa musicians, 7n
Language choice, 155
Lankesh, P., 198, 202, 205, 207-08
*Larāī* (battle; episode of *Ālhā*), 52, 58-59
Lecture-demonstration, 128-29
Lineages, royal, 96, 98-100, 105, 109, 115, 121-22, 156, 169-70, 226
Linguistic community, 174
Lobbying, 202, 204
Logistics, *see* performance logistics
Lowen, Sharon, 11, 171

*Mā-Bāp*, 159, 162
MacCannell, Dean, 95n
Madho Singh II, Maharaja of Jaipur, 144, 147-48, 156-58, 161, 167, 170, 176
Madras, 7, 23, 197
Madras Music Academy, 14, 19
Madras Presidency, 109
Madurai, 223
Madurakavi, 2, 15-16
*Mahābhārata*, 95, 128
Maharajas, 40, 96, 100, 146-47, 154; *see also* lineages, Rajputs, specific rulers
Mahoba, 47n, 49, 51-53, 58-59, 65, 82, 85
Malabar District, 109
Malayalam language, 103
Man Singh II, Maharaja of Jaipur, 161, 170
Management, arts, 5, 6n, 11-12, 16, 120, 127, 135, 140, 226
Mandra Brothers, 200
Manganiyar musicians, 7n
*Manipravālam* literature, 100, 120
Manipuri dance, 226, 229-30, 232-33, 236
*Manthan*, 196n
*Mardānā*, 145, 188
Margi Kathakali Yogam, 125n
Market structure, 195-212
Markets, 4, 11, 16, 116, 118, 122, 136, 139, 220-22
Marriages, *see* wedding perform-ances
Marriott, McKim, 24
Martial arts, 99; *see also kaḷarippayaṭṭu*
Masters, *see* gurus
Mathura, 2
Media, 11, 14, 25, 123; *see also* press
*Melās* (fairs), 53, 64
Menon, K.P.S., 123-24
Menon, Nanu, 102
Merchants, 13
Merit, 4, 144, 148, 171-72, 175
"Meta-patrons", 172
Methods, 157-58; *see also* performance logistics, petitions
Meyerhoff, Barbara, 22
Middle class, 53-54, 63-64, 76
Mithila, 55, 59
"Model" patron, 139, 222-23
Modernization, 8, 14-15, 25, 118-19, 125, 128-29, 132-33, 135, 139, 176, 223
Mohanlal, 156-57
Mohapatra, Padmashri Guru Kelucharan, 225, 231, 233-35
Monopolies, 201-02, 210
Monsoon season, 52
Mood, *see bhāva*
Moore, Sally, 22

Motivations, 16, 183, 187-88, 191-92, 213; *see also* performance logistics
*Mudiyettu*, 103
*Mudrās*, 104, 106, 125n, 131, 134; *see also* gestures
Mughal court, 143, 155, 188, 191-92, 199n, 213-14, 218, 220-21
Mughal rulers, 183-85, 187
Muhammad Shah, 184-85, 189
*Murukan*, 35-37
Music, 181-92
  conferences, 166
  Hindustani, 181, 183-85;
  ensemble (*mēlam*), 43n
  instruments, 60-61, 190
  Karnatic, 2, 186-87
  vocal, 181, 183, 189
  *see also Khyāl*
Musicians, 144-45, 150, 164-65, 169, 171, 181-92, 218-21, 233-336
  court, 186, 191
  Hindu, 183
  Muslim, 155, 164, 183
Musicologists, 10
Muslim artists, 55-56, 146
*Muttu Ondu Muttu*, 207
Mysore, 204

*Naandi*, 199
Nagendra Rao, R., 205
*Nala Caritam*, 100-11
Namboodiri Brahmins, *see* Brahmins
National Endowment for the Arts/for the Humanities, 8
Nationalists, 54
*Naṭs* (acrobats), 56
*Nātyśāstra*, 126
*Naubat Khānā*, 150-51, 190, 218-19, 222
Navashakti Films, 196n
Nawab of Rampur, 185
Nayakkar caste, 40
*Nammālvār*, 214-217
*Nāyanmārs* (Saiva saints), 213
Nayars, 33, 95-102, 109, 118
Nehru Yubak Kendra, 54n
Networks, 98, 226, 228, 232-33
New Wave cinema, *see* film
New Delhi, 5, 49, 72, 228, 231, 233-34, 237
New York, 230
Notation, 185

Odissi dance, 225-26, 231-333
Oral tradition, 32, 45, 48, 113-14, 151
Organizations, cultural, 162, 232; *see also* institutions
Organizers, 12, 54
Oudh, 185; *see also* Avadhi speakers

P.S.V. Natyasangham (Kottakkal), 127-28
Padding, 202
Paintings, 181, 188, 219
Pakistan, 4
*Pallavi*, 205
Paluskar, Vishnu Digambar, 182-83
Panigrahi, Ragunath, 231
Panigrahi, Sanjukta, 231
Panikkar, Velattu Cattu, 99n, 102-03
Panikkar, Ittiri, 99n, 103-05
Pantulu, B.R., 205
*Paramparā* (lineage tradition), 171, 174, 225; *see also* guru-disciple tradition, inheritance
Parent, 149, 173; *see also Mā-Bāp*
Parnnal, King, 85
Participant-observation, 2
*Pātarkhānā*, 150-51
Pathans, 60, 87
Patrimonial-bureaucratic functions, 170
Patronage System, 33-35, 38, 41-45, 119, 171
Peirce, Charles S., 15, 23-24
Pendakur, Manjunath, 11, 16, 213, 218, 221
Performance

conventions, 93n, 103, 123-24, 126, 132
determinants, 92n, 103, 118, 124
frames, 93n, 103
group, 33-34, 60-61, 64-65
logistics, 225, 229-34, 236
model, 16, 213-23
paradigmatic, 215
score, 111, 113, 134
season, 55
techniques, 92n, 103, 111-12, 118, 124
text, 92n, 96, 103, 110-12, 114, 125n, 128; *see also* text
theory, 9-10, 15, 20, 25
tradition, 92-94, 101, 103, 105, 107, 112, 115-118, 133, 136-37, 147-49, 152-53, 156, 158, 163, 171-74; *see also* *paramparā*, tradition
Persian language, 151-52, 155
Petitions, 4, 143-76
Philanthropy, 10
Pingal, 79n
Play, 21
Poets, 38
Political patronage, 54
Popularization, 186; *see also* public
Post (*asāmī*), 144, 146-48, 157-61, 171
*Prahlada Caritam*, 115
Prasad, V.R.K., 203
Pratap Singh, Sir, 161n
Precedent, 161
Press, 196, 203, 207, 233-34
"Preventive censure", 16, 47-48, 86-87
Princely courts, *see* courts, princely
Princes, 2, 3, 13-14, 16; *see also* maharajas
Prithviraj, King, 49, 59, 73
*Prithviraj raso*, 60n, 82n
Private performances, 189, 231, 234-35
Privileges of artists, 151, 153
Prizes, *see* awards
Processions, 172
Professionals, 53, 55-56
Profit, 200
Programs, 227-28, 231, 236
invitational, 5, 226, 232, 236
ticketed, 5, 15, 232
Prostitutes, 166-68
Protector, 144, 159
Public, 2, 7-8, 11-14, 16, 122-23, 126, 128, 170, 172-75, 203, 208-10, 221-23
audiences, 57
concerts, 228
event, 169
morality, 166-68
performances, 53
women, 168
*Putani Agents*, 207
Puttana, S.R., 205
Qalandar, 4
*Qawwālī*, 181, 192

R.N.R. Pictures, 200
Radcliffe-Brown, A.R., 21
Radha-Krishna *bhajanas*, 7, 23-24
Raghavan, V., 14
Ragini Devi, 130-31
Raina, Raghunath, 195
Raj Kapoor, 202
Raj Kumar, 201-208
Rajasthan, 3
Rajasthan State Archives, 150-51
Rajputs, 49, 56, 59, 61, 155, 164
Baghel, 58
Banaphar, 49, 85
Chandela, 52
Chauhan, 49, 72
Rajshree Pictures, 200, 202
Ram Chand, Raja of Pannah, 190-91
Ram Singh II, Maharaja of Jaipur, 144, 147-48, 171
Rama Reddy, Pattabhi, 198
*Rāmanāṭṭam*, 95, 97-98, 100-03, 108

*Rāmāyaṇa*, 95, 103
Ramlila, 2
Rampur State, 185
Ramunni Menon Asan, Pattiyakkantoti, 112-13, 115, 118
Ranga, T.S., 202
*Rasa*, 26, 74-76, 86, 102, 109, 111, 123-24, 126, 129, 134, 166
*Rasika*, 96, 102, 108, 140, 231; *see also* connoisseurs
Ray, Satyajit, 195
Records, archival, 148-52
Redfield, Robert, 20, 23-24
Refinement, 108, 110-12, 114-16, 118, 139, 171, 173-74
Reforms, 170-72, 174, 176; *see also* modernization
Regional culture, 196, 202
Religion, 13, 21, 184, 188, 191-92, 219
Religious performances, 172
Religious processions, 168-69; *see also* Teej, Gangore
Reviews, 234; *see also* critics
Rights of artists, 147, 151-53, 156-57, 162, 175
*Rishyashrunga*, 203
Ritual, 12, 15, 21-22, 24-25, 32, 102, 217-18
Ritual arts, 97, 100, 109, 135
Ritual context, 216
Role sets, 93, 95, 123
Roles, patron, 41, 95-124, 139-40, 153-54, 181-92, 221; *see also* *rasika*
Roy, Minati, 232
Rukmini Devi (Arundale), 14
*Rundīkarkhānā*, 163, 169

Sacrifice (*yagna*), 6
Sahaswan *gharānā*, 185
Sahitya Akademi, 15
Samanthans, *see* Nayars
Sambamoorthy, P., 189
*Sampradāya*, 104-08, 111-18, 121, 123, 125, 137-39
*Samskara*, 198-99
Sangeet Natak Akademi, 6n, 15, 229
Sanskrit, 100-01, 103, 110-11, 120
Santiniketan, 14, 232
*Sara Akash*, 195-96
Sarabhoji, Maharaja of Tanjore, 189
*Savithri*, 202
Schomer, Karine, 15-16, 35n
See India Foundation, 132-33
Selection committee, 228
Semiotics, 23
Sen, Mrinal, 195
Seni *gharānā*, 185
Service, 43, 101, 119, 147, 173-74, 216-17, 219-21
  castes, 1 ,2
  household, 144-45
Sexual acts, 170
Shah Jahan, 190
Shankar, Rajendra, 6n
*Shankaraguru*, 208
Share (*paṅku*) system, 33-34
*Shishya*, *see* guru-disciple tradition
Shivaram, 136
Shivram Singh (Kharela), 64-65, 79; *see also* Kharela performance
Singer, Milton, 1, 3, 7, 10-11, 15, 19-27
Sign systems, 15, 23, 150, 175
Sileh Khana (Armory), 154
Singers, 41-45, 148, 150
Śiva, 35, 38
Socio-cultural system, 148-49
South Asia Language and Area Center (Chicago), 3
Specialization, 121
Speech community, 164
Sponsors, 6n, 63, 93, 121-22, 125-26, 135, 139, 225-28, 230, 232, 235, 237
*Śṛṅgara rasa*, 111; *see also rasa*
Staal, Frits, 24-25
Stage, 53, 126, 227-29, 237

State Band (Jaipur), 151
Subsidy, 118, 198, 203-07, 221-23
State Council (*Mahākma-Khās*), 151, 154, 159, 164-65
Status, 15, 45, 98, 152-53, 156, 164, 166, 169, 173-74, 181-84, 188-91, 216, 218-20, 226, 238
Students, 119-21, 137
Subbalakshmi, 19
Subramonia Iyer, S. Vankita, 186
Support, 7-8, 11-13, 15-16, 34, 38, 44, 93, 97, 99, 101, 120, 137, 139, 173, 222, 237
Sur Sringar Samsad, 229
Swati Tirunal, Maharaja of Travancore, 186-87, 191
Syama Sastri, 187, 189-90

*Tablā*, 3
Tagore, Rabindranath, 4
Raj Mahal Hotel Theatre, 229
*Tāla*, 131; *see also* *ālhā* meter
Tamil language, 15, 36
Tamilnadu, 31-45, 213-23
Tanjore court, 189-91
Tansen, 190-91, 218
Tatas, 6n, 226
*Tawā'if*, 145-46, 168-70
Teachers, 120-21, 237; *see also* gurus
Teej procession, 151, 165, 168-69
Television, 235-36
Temples, 2, 13, 32-33, 35, 39-43, 96-98, 120, 122-23, 127, 145, 168, 170, 172, 192, 216, 237
Texts, 13, 15, 25, 82, 84, 104, 106, 110-11, 120, 133-34, 149, 214-15
    and context, 16, 31-45, 125n
Texture, 48, 62, 76-86
Theatre, 126-28, 133, 200, 229-30, 232-33; *see also* film, theatres
Theatre-state, 9
*Thumrī*, 181, 185
Tippu Sultan, 108
Tirunelveli, 36
*Tiruvāymoli*, 215-17
Tourists, 133, 137, 190, 229
Trade union patronage, 54
Tradition, 2, 7, 9-10, 23, 55, 91
    Social organization of, 152-53
    *see also* guru-disciple tradition
Training, *see* transmission of tradition
Transcendentalism, 24
Translators, 10, 126
Transmission of tradition, 104, 119, 121, 137, 144-45, 147-48, 156-62, 172, 174; *see also* guru-disciple tradition
Travancore, 109-10, 125n, 130, 135
Tulu language, 204
Turner, Victor, 20-23
Tyagaraja, 187
Tylor, Edward, 19-20

Udal (a.k.a. Rudal), 49, 58, 65, 80-82, 84-86
Uday Shankar India Culture Centre, 14
United States, 196, 227-28
University of California at Los Angeles, 1
University of Chicago, 11
University of Michigan, 232
Untouchables, 33-37; *see also* caste
Urdu language, 76-77, 155-56, 158
Ur-performance, 215-16
Urs, Kemparaj, 207
*Uski Roti*, 196
*Ustād* (master), 159, 171, 182
Uttam Singh (Kharela), 64-65

Vadivelu, 186-87
Vallathol, 14, 94, 120
*Vamsya Vruksha*, 198
Variyar, Unnayi, 110
Vazir Sultan Tobacco Company, 6n
Verma, Martanda, 109-10
Vedic rites, 6, 25

Village, 32, 35, 40, 53
  audiences, 57, 64-65, 76
*Vīra rasa*, 99, 109; *see also rasa*
Virtuosos, 163, 169
Viṣṇu, 214-17, 220
Viswa Kala Kendra, 130

Wade, Bonnie, 11, 16, 213, 218
Wajid Ali Shah (Oudh), 185
Waris Shah, Haji, 53
Warner, Lloyd, 21-22, 171
Wedding performances, 53, 55, 58, 145, 169n, 180
Western patronage models, 120, 170, 233
Wesleyan University, 1
Women artists, 169-70; *see also tawā'if*
World view, 23, 176

Yankee City, 22

Zarrilli, Phillip, 16
*Zenānā*, 145, 147, 165, 168-69